INTRODUCTION

An Apple a Day by Andrea Boeshaar
Brian Coridan is a burned-out medical doctor. Talia Fountain is a health food store owner who hopes to have a boom in business by adding to her wares sugar-free, homemade apple pies, but Brian is taking offense with some of her products' claims to health. Could Brian come to realize that what he's hungered for is the exact thing Talia has to offer?

Sweet as Apple Pie by Kristin Billerbeck
Construction foreman Adam Harper enjoys the simple things in life while Kayli Johnson yearns to make a name for herself among the wealthy and famous, creating fantastic desserts. Will Kayli continue her European training, or will she turn in her apron to create Adam's favorite pie?

Apple Annie by Joyce Livingston
Brad Reed, frequent patron of the Apple Valley Farm Restaurant, is a confirmed bachelor and everyone's favorite customer. He has loved Apple Annie from the start, but he's sure there can never be a serious relationship between them. After all, why would a woman like Annie saddle herself with a man like him?

Apple Pie in Your Eye by Gail Sattler
Rick Meyers has loved Lynette Charleston, the pastor's daughter, from his youth, but she doesn't date people from her father's congregation. When church obligations force them together, will he be able to show her that, together, they can make a congregation of their own?

AS AMERICAN AS APPLE PIE

Four Contemporary Romance Novellas
Served with a Slice of Americana

Kristin Billerbeck
Andrea Boeshaar
Joyce Livingston
Gail Sattler

BARBOUR BOOKS
An Imprint of Barbour Publishing, Inc.

An Apple a Day ©2002 by Andrea Boeshaar
Sweet as Apple Pie ©2002 by Kristin Billerbeck
Apple Annie ©2002 by Joyce Livingston
Apple Pie in Your Eye ©2002 by Gail Sattler

Cover photo: ©PhotoDisc, Inc.

ISBN 1-58660-505-4

All Scripture quotations, unless otherwise noted, are taken from the King James Version of the Bible.

Published by Barbour Books, an imprint of Barbour Publishing, Inc., P.O. Box 719, Uhrichsville, Ohio 44683, www.barbourbooks.com

ecpa Member of the
Evangelical Christian
Publishers Association

Printed in the United States of America.
5 4 3 2 1

AS AMERICAN AS APPLE PIE

AN APPLE A DAY

by Andrea Boeshaar

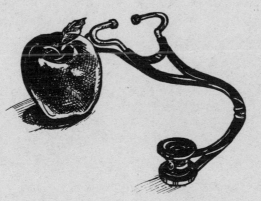

Dedication

To my aunt, Lisa Johnson, with love. . .
Thanks for all your encouragement!

Chapter 1

D
r. Brian Coridan turned the key in his palm. It felt cold, despite the torrid heat in this last week of June. He looked up then at the leafy-green canopy, fashioned from the trees that hung over the narrow dirt driveway. Slivers of sunshine made their way through the natural arch and peppered the ground with light.

He glanced at the rustic-looking cabin and beyond it to the silvery lake, gleaming beneath the sun. Breathing in the clear northern Wisconsin air, Brian decided his buddy Seth had been right; this sabbatical from the clinic was exactly what he needed. Up here in the North Woods, by a calming lake, he could fish as often as he liked, collect his thoughts and pray about what he should do regarding his medical career.

He grunted as the latter topic came to mind. His practice at the Family Medical Clinic had grown old and distasteful. What had begun as a deep desire to help people had become, instead, big business, and people were not a significant part of it. Sure, he had his patients, but he couldn't spend much time with each one. According to the clinic's administrator, Brian was allotted seven minutes—tops—to perform an evaluation. Then it was write out a prescription and send the patients on their way.

In Brian's eyes, medicine was all about money now, and he felt burned out trying to keep up his imposed status quo. Worse, he feared the day when, in his haste, he would make an incorrect diagnosis, inadvertently causing a patient's death. He had to get out before that happened.

But was that what God wanted? Brian had spent tens of thousands of dollars putting himself through medical school. God had seen him through every step of the way, even providing some of the funding through grants and scholarships. Why would He want him to quit now? It made no sense.

And that's why Brian had come here—to seek God's guidance for his future. It seemed he'd found a paradise in which to do his soul-searching too. Just thinking about being at beautiful Blossom Lake for the summer caused him to relax.

Turning to his SUV, Brian gathered his belongings and headed for the cabin. He let himself in and found the log structure contained one large room, divided into a living room and a kitchen area. Off to the side were two small bedrooms. One room had bunk beds, so Brian chose the other room and its double bed.

He set down his suitcase and opened the windows to let out the musty air. Seth told him he hadn't used the cabin much this year. After a few more trips to his vehicle, Brian had brought in everything.

He stood in the middle of the cabin, arms akimbo, and sighed. Well, here he was. What should he do first? Swim in the lake? He noticed the white refrigerator in the small kitchen area. On second thought he'd better go to town and buy some groceries.

He climbed into his SUV and drove back onto the highway in search of the nearest food store.

"I dropped off the rest of the apple pies at the Foodliner."

Talia Fountain looked up from the shelf she'd been stocking and smiled at her mother.

"It sure was good of Jim Graves to agree to sell our day-old apple pies at his grocery store. Of course," Marlene Fountain added with a wink, "they are the best apple pies in the world, if I do say so myself."

"Of course," Talia agreed, smiling broadly.

Her mother baked the pies fresh each morning—all natural with no preservatives or chemicals. The apple pies were sought after in the small town of Blossom Lake. Tourists from every state in the union vacationed in this town—and looked forward to Marlene Fountain's pies, sold exclusively at Talia's health food store, the Fountain of Life, and now at Jim's Foodliner.

"I think you made a wise decision, letting Jim sell our day-old pies," Mrs. Fountain continued. "It might persuade some of his customers to stop in your store for their vitamins and herbal supplements."

"That was my thinking exactly."

Talia stood and stretched the kink from her lower back. She had been dusting and arranging the lower shelf for the last forty-five minutes. The task seemed unending, and more so depending on the volume of customers. She rejoiced that the number had been increasing. Talia had been in business for only a year, and she'd almost had to close, what with the slow winter that had passed. But business had picked up after the Memorial Day weekend—an answer to her prayers.

She glanced around her store at the walls lined with shelves. Her father had built each unit to fit the old walls, since the building in which the Fountain of Life resided was over 130 years old.

Talia smiled. She loved this old place. Sometimes she imagined what the walls would say if they could talk. She imagined the history they'd experienced over the last century. From horses and buggies to high-speed sports cars, they'd seen it all—if they could truly see, which of course they couldn't.

"Talia, are you daydreaming?"

She snapped from her musings and grinned at her mother who was chuckling.

"Well, what else do you want me to do?" the older woman asked.

Talia studied her mother for a moment where she stood near the checkout counter, clad in navy-blue walking shorts and a red-white-and-blue striped T-shirt. Her blond hair hung loosely to her slender shoulders, and her peaches-and-cream complexion spoke of good eating habits, sunshine, fresh air, and daily exercise. At sixty-three years old, Marlene Fountain didn't look a day over fifty. She was, in fact, the one who had influenced Talia to pursue a career as a dietitian, now turned health-food store entrepreneur.

"A shipment of vitamins came in this morning," Talia said in reply to her mother's inquiry. "Want to unload boxes?"

"Sure."

Mrs. Fountain walked to the back of the store, and Talia smiled after her. She felt so fortunate to have a close relationship to her mother.

Thank You, God, that my mother is my friend—and an employee who doesn't expect a paycheck.

She realized, not for the first time, that she would have been discouraged the past year if it hadn't been for her mother's support and her father's financial advice. She'd been blessed with Christian parents who wanted her to succeed financially as well as her business to glorify the Lord. *And I pray it does, Lord Jesus.*

Talia resumed her duties. Minutes later, the shop door opened, its brass bell signaling a customer's entrance. She glanced over her shoulder in time to see Dirk Butterfield strut in, wearing an expensive-looking gray suit and coordinating silk tie.

Talia frowned. The man was all pomp and circumstance. He was an official on the town board and a friend of the owner of a national drugstore chain and, as such, wanted the Fountain of Life to go out of business. If he had his way, this whole historic corner of shops, one of which Talia rented, would be torn down and, in its place, a large drugstore and convenience center erected. A town hall meeting was scheduled for September on the very subject, but Talia felt confident that she and the other shop owners would prevail. Dirk Butterfield wasn't going to rob her of her business—that was for sure. She'd fight with everything in her. But the fact that he had entered her store now was not a good sign.

She stood, forcing a smile. "Good afternoon, Mr. Butterfield," she said with feigned politeness.

"Good afternoon," he replied, glancing around her store. "Not many customers today, eh?"

"You missed the rush."

He gave her a condescending grin. "My wife asked me to pick up some concoction here that she says is guaranteed to relieve allergy symptoms."

The man wanted to spend money at her store? Surely not. Maybe this was a trick. Talia tried to shrug off her suspicions. After all, she was a Christian. She could, at least, be nice and give him the information he requested. Perhaps she could show off her knowledge of herbal remedies in the process.

She walked to the far end of the store. "This allergy-relief tea might be what your wife needs." Talia handed him a box.

"What is in it?" he asked, turning it over and studying the label.

"Ginger and licorice root, Eucalyptus and orange peel—the ingredients are listed on the package."

"Hmm." He furrowed his auburn brows. "And you guarantee this product will take away my wife's sneezing and watery eyes?"

Talia put her hands on her hips. "I make the same guarantees the doctors make." She tilted her head. "Have you ever heard physicians guarantee their medical cures, invasive or otherwise? They don't. They can't. And neither can I. All I can say is to try the herbal remedy and see if it helps. It's been known to help millions of others."

He handed her the box of tea. "Don't you have something in pill form? That's more convenient."

"Sure." Talia replaced the tea on the shelf and walked to the middle of the store. "Your wife can try this," she said, handing him four white plastic bottles with a blue and white label. "I recommend a combination of alfalfa, vitamin C, garlic, and zinc."

"All of that?" The man pulled his chin back sharply. "Why, I could buy an antihistamine/decongestant at the pharmacy for ninety-nine cents."

So that's what this game is all about. He means to ridicule my wares and me.

She returned the bottles to the shelf and smiled coolly. "Yes, you can purchase whatever you'd like. The choice is yours. Now if you'll excuse me, I have some work to finish up."

"By all means. I'll just browse."

Talia wished he would leave. Couldn't he find someone else to pester?

She went back to stocking and arranging. Minutes later she heard the bell on the door and saw Butterfield's retreating form. She sighed with relief.

Brian let the apple pie melt in his mouth. This was the best! He hadn't had apple pie in what seemed like a lifetime. He'd had to buy one, no, two, when he saw them on sale at the Foodliner. Jesus said man could not live by bread alone, but Brian suspected man would do all right for a long time on these apple pies.

He took another bite. Cinnamon and tart apple flooded his senses. He looked at the printed wrapper covering the rest of the pie. "No chemicals or preservatives," it touted. "All natural ingredients." That didn't impress him much, but the fact that they were homemade did. The woman at the checkout said someone named Mrs. Fountain baked them fresh every day at her daughter's health food store down the street.

Brian chuckled inwardly. Health food stores were nonsensical in his opinion, although he couldn't discount the fact that herbal inventions seemed to help some of his patients. But he figured they were more a psychological aid than a physiological one. The idea of natural medicines was growing in popularity around the United States, though. Still Brian found no scientific proof to support the medicinal value of vitamins and herbs so, as far as he was concerned, they possessed no medicinal value.

He finished the first slice of pie and cut another one, enjoying every bite. His mother had worked at a career when

Brian was a boy and had never acquired culinary skills by any stretch of the imagination. Brian's father worked equally hard, so the son had grown up on quick meals that had sustained him into his adult life, especially after April died. Funny how a hollowness filled him whenever he thought of her, even after ten years.

Brian walked through the living room and onto the screen porch. Gazing down the hill, past the forest to the sparkling lake, he recalled his short but intense marriage. Just three months after they'd taken their vows, April was diagnosed with ovarian cancer. Ten months later she was dead. But through the awful trial by fire, God had shown Brian he was to pursue a career in medicine. So at the age of twenty-five, he'd enrolled in medical school. Now, however, he felt confused. He felt like the proverbial doubting wave upon the sea, being tossed to and fro.

"Lord Jesus, what do I do?" he muttered.

With his gaze still resting on the serene lake below, he thought of a line his father often used. "When the going gets tough, the tough go fishing."

Brian grinned. Sounded like a good idea to him.

He set his plate back in the sink and hunted for his fishing gear. Then he made his way down to the peaceful lake.

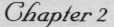

Chapter 2

T hat rat stole four bottles of my best vitamins and herbs along with a box of herbal tea!" Talia exclaimed the next morning as she and her mother restocked shelves.

"Oh, Talia, Dirk Butterfield would never do something like that! He's an upstanding member of our community."

"He's a thief!" Talia declared.

"You can't prove it," Mrs. Fountain warned, "so you can't make your accusations public. It'll only make you look bad."

"And don't think that highfalutin' Mr. Butterfield doesn't know that either." Talia let out a breath of frustration. "If he ever comes in here again, I'll watch him like a hawk."

"I guess that's all you can do for now," her mother replied. "Oh, Talia, you don't really think Mr. Butterfield stole things from your store, do you?"

"Of course, I do. He had to be the one."

"Oh, dear." A worried look creased Mrs. Fountain's blond brows.

"Well, we can't spend our lives fretting about it. I'll have to be smarter in the future where that man is concerned."

The bell on the door jingled, and Talia turned to see a man with dark-blond hair enter. He wore blue jeans and a forest-green polo shirt that accentuated his hazel eyes. He had an attractive face, Talia decided, one that reminded her of Matt Damon. She'd seen the actor's photos spread over the front of the local cinema.

"Good morning," he said, a twinkle in his eyes. "I'm looking for the lady who makes those scrumptious apple pies."

"That would be my mother." Talia smiled and turned to her. "Marlene Fountain."

"A pleasure to meet you. I'm Brian Coridan," he said stepping forward and offering his hand.

Mrs. Fountain grasped it, wearing a friendly smile.

"I've enjoyed your pies." A flush spread over his face. "I ate one for dinner last night and finished the other one at breakfast."

"Well, they are small. But I'm glad you liked them," she said, looking thoroughly pleased.

Brian turned to Talia. Taking his proffered hand, she introduced herself.

"So," he said, as his gaze wandered about the store, "you're the owner of this place."

"Yes, she is," Mrs. Fountain said proudly. "And if your diet consists of only apple pies, you might be interested in purchasing some multivitamins."

Brian laughed. "I'm a physician and don't take much stock in vitamins. Thanks anyway. But I will buy another apple pie."

"Coming right up. I have several pies on the cooling rack right now."

Talia watched her mother walk into the back of the shop where the kitchen was located. Then she turned back to the doctor. "Where are you from?"

The man intrigued her, but she didn't know why. Since tourists flocked to Blossom Lake, Talia had met people from various parts of the country, but none had piqued her interest as this man suddenly had. Perhaps it was because he didn't fit her typecasting of doctors, whom she considered to be arrogant, vain, indifferent creatures. In contrast Brian Coridan had a very caring face and warm, sensitive eyes that were looking back at her with similar curiosity.

"I'm originally from Virginia," he said, "but I was accepted to med school in Milwaukee and ended up going into practice in the same vicinity."

"I see." Talia felt herself flush at his open appraisal. Did he find her plain, the way most men seemed to? Would he think her hair was a mousy-colored tangle of curls or that her eyes were an ordinary brown? Would he conclude that she had a so-so figure? Nothing special here. And did he think she was another health-food freak, or would he respect her views on natural remedies versus prescription and over-the-counter drugs? Judging from his statement about multivitamins, it wouldn't seem so.

"And you?" he asked. "Do you hail from around here?"

She nodded. "I was born and raised in a town south of here. It's so tiny it isn't even on the map." She smiled. "Then my parents retired here in Blossom Lake, and after college I decided to join them—so here I am."

Brian appeared to have to force himself to remove his gaze from her face, causing Talia to feel awkward. Turning, he then walked several feet away and began inspecting the free literature on the black wire spinner rack near the doorway. "How'd you get into all this New Age, health food stuff?"

"Actually"—Talia stepped toward him—"I don't consider the concept of natural wellness to be New Age at all. It's old age, really, and much of what is on the market today in the way of herbal remedies dates back to biblical times."

"Lots of people died in biblical times, Miss Fountain, because physicians didn't have the resources known to them today."

"True, but so much of medicine today is profit and gain and putting money into the pockets of executives at insurance and drug companies. It's not, in my opinion, about the welfare of patients."

Brian gave the rack another spin. "I might agree with you there." He paused before adding, "It is 'Miss,' isn't it?"

"What?" Talia's eyes widened.

He turned toward her. "When you introduced yourself, I assumed you're a 'Miss' Fountain and not a 'Mrs.'"

She almost laughed aloud. "You assumed correctly, Dr. Coridan."

Talia thought he looked pleased but then discounted it as her overactive imagination.

Her mother reentered the shop at that moment, carrying an apple pie covered in a brown paper sack. "Here you are," she said and quoted him the price.

Brian pulled his wallet out and paid for the freshly baked dessert. "Thanks very much." He nodded toward Talia. "Nice meeting you—and you too, Mrs. Fountain."

"The pleasure was ours. Stop in again," the older woman said.

Watching Dr. Coridan's retreating form, Talia found herself hoping he would do just that!

Brian walked slowly down the street, wondering why his heart beat in the most unusual way. Was he suffering a myocardial infarction, known as a heart attack to the general public? Why did his knees feel so weak? It couldn't have anything to do with that pretty owner of the health food store.

Or could it?

For the past ten years Brian had kept himself out of most social circles, except for church functions. He never wanted to be in a position where he would meet single women. He had no intentions of replacing his deceased wife, April. He was convinced she was the only woman he could ever love. He'd attended medical school with plenty of unattached females, and he worked around them at the clinic, but he had never felt particularly attracted to any of them. Why did he suddenly feel like a clumsy sixteen-year-old again? Was Talia Fountain the cause of it?

Maybe it was the summer heat.

Of course, that was it.

Shifting the paper-encased pie to his other hand, Brian shook off his thoughts of Talia and continued his trek toward Blossom Lake's city hall—the next stop on his list. A neighbor had spotted him out on the water last night and suggested that Brian obtain a fishing license for the summer. Wouldn't be much fun to get a ticket, the neighbor said, and he then informed Brian that the lakes up here were heavily patrolled. Being a city boy at heart, he hadn't any idea, but he was one to do things the right way. So this morning, since he was in town and city hall was within walking distance, this was as good a time as any to take care of any fishing legalities.

Entering the red brick building, Brian immediately noticed a smartly dressed man leaning on the counter, talking to the receptionist. On second thought he decided "flirting" was a better word. The man's auburn head tilted ever so slightly as he droned on about the expensive sports car he'd recently purchased. The petite blond in a red dress on the other side of the desk didn't look a day older than twenty-one.

"Oh, Dirk," she crooned on an excited note, "you'll have to take me for a ride."

"You got it, Babe."

The man suddenly spotted Brian and straightened. He looked guilty, like a naughty child. Regardless, he nodded a curt hello.

Brian returned the gesture.

"Oh!" the receptionist exclaimed, looking startled. "I didn't see you there, Sir. What can I do for you?"

Brian stepped forward. "I'd like to buy a fishing license."

"Sure, I can help you with that." She reached under the counter and pulled out a form. "Just fill out this section," she said, sliding it and an ink pen toward him.

Setting his apple pie on the counter, Brian wrote out his name, address, and phone number.

"So I see you found our local health food store," the man beside him said. "The Fountains are the only people I know who package their pies in brown paper bags."

Brian looked up from the form, and the man extended his right hand.

"Dirk Butterfield."

"Brian Coridan," he replied, shaking his hand.

"On vacation?" the man asked. "Or are you mixing business with a little pleasure?"

"Vacation," Brian answered.

"Hmm—well, if you like it up here, we still have land for sale." He grinned, displaying large, white, even teeth. "I run the biggest real estate firm in the county. Let me give you my business card."

Brian glanced at the card before slipping it into the pocket of his jeans. "Thanks."

"Anytime." Dirk leaned his elbow on the counter. "Now let me give you some advice, if I might. Stay out of that health food place. The lady who owns it is a wacko, and the concoctions she sells are nothing but pulverized lawnmower shavings sold in capsule form."

Brian couldn't help but smile about the lawnmower shavings. "Well, Miss Fountain didn't seem wacky to me, and her mother's apple pies are delicious."

"I'll agree with you on the latter," Dirk said.

"I used to buy my vitamins at the Fountain of Life," the blond behind the counter said. "But then Dirk—uh, Mr. Butterfield—made me realize how much money I was wasting. I mean, they sell the same thing at the drugstore and for less!"

Brian gave the young lady a patient smile and looked at Dirk in time to see his patronizing grin.

"Judy has the gift of gab," Dirk remarked, turning to Brian. "She's got the perfect job. Gabbing all day long."

Brian expected the young woman to be insulted by the remark. He himself was, at best, uncomfortable. But she surprised him by laughing it off. Then she quoted him the price for the fishing license.

After paying the fee, Brian excused himself. He didn't have a good feeling about Dirk Butterfield and felt sorry for Judy if she was falling for him. He had also seen a gold wedding ring on the man's left hand. If he was indeed married, his behavior toward Judy was inappropriate. Brian had a high regard for marriage vows, and it irked him when he saw people treading on the sanctity of that special union.

It's none of my business, Brian thought as he reached his SUV. *I'm here on vacation, and I refuse to get involved in anyone's personal affairs—especially if her name is Talia Fountain.*

Unlocking the door, he climbed in, set his pie on the floor of the passenger side, and headed for the solitude of his cabin.

Chapter 3

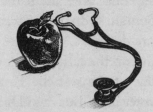

O n Sunday morning Brian dressed in navy casual pants
and a light-blue shirt. Knotting his tie he wondered
again if Talia Fountain was a Christian—and why he
couldn't stop thinking about her. Yesterday, while fishing, the
memory of her sparkling brown eyes flittered across his mind.
The gentle ripples in the lake reminded him of Talia's wavy
hair, and he found himself imagining how soft it would feel to
his fingertips. She had crept into his thoughts far too often in
the past twenty-four hours. It troubled him too, because his
uncharacteristic preoccupation with her was overshadowing
memories of his deceased wife.

"You've only met her once, you idiot," Brian told his reflection. "That hardly constitutes your odd behavior for the
past two days." He squared his shoulders. "Now get your head
together, Coridan, or you'll be late for church."

Brian grabbed his Bible and left the cabin for Calvary's
Cross Christian Church. He'd found the name in the phone
book the night before and, since it wasn't too far away, decided
to visit there.

As he drove down the gravely road to the highway, Brian
couldn't help smiling at the morning sunshine streaming through

the treetops. He breathed deeply through the open window, filling his lungs with fresh air. Northern Wisconsin on this glorious summer morning, with its tall pines and crystal-clear lakes, seemed like a taste of heaven. With happiness welling in his heart, Brian whistled along with the number playing on the Christian radio station, "Joyful, Joyful, We Adore Thee."

He reached the country chapel and noticed the building's blue-painted wooden siding and white-trimmed windows. Its ivory-colored steeple reached high into the sky as puffy clouds floated gracefully past. What a great day to be alive, he thought, stepping up to the front door and entering the tiny foyer.

Then his foot faltered. He could suddenly hear his heart throbbing. There before him stood Talia Fountain, handing out bulletins. Wearing a long, printed skirt and short-sleeve, green sweater, she was even lovelier than he remembered.

Don't hyperventilate, he told himself, suddenly feeling like a clumsy moron instead of a seasoned physician.

Talia saw him, smiled, and Brian noticed the dimple in her left cheek.

"Well, Dr. Coridan, how nice to see you again."

The fact she remembered his name impressed Brian. He accepted the bulletin and nodded cordially, his mouth too dry for any intelligent reply.

"Sit anywhere in the sanctuary," Talia said. "We're very informal here. No assigned seats or anything." She chuckled at the jest.

"Thanks," he managed to say. Forcing his legs to carry him forward into the church, he encountered Judy, the girl who had sold him the fishing license at city hall.

"Good morning," he said politely.

"Oh, hi," she replied. "Catch any fish yet?"

"Nothing to speak of."

"Well, keep trying," she advised. "My brother caught a two-foot salmon last weekend."

Brian narrowed his eyes. "That's not one of those infamous fish stories, is it?"

"Fish story?" Judy blinked. "Well, it is about a fish—"

Brian grinned. "Never mind. Have a good day."

"Sure." She smiled in return. "You too."

Making his way up the center aisle, Brian tried to dispel all the dumb blond jokes suddenly running through his head. Poor Judy seemed to fit each one.

Lord, forgive me, he prayed. *My entire family is blond—and not one is dumb.*

He sat down at the end of a pew and opened the bulletin. He noticed an announcement for volunteers to help grill hamburgers and hotdogs at the annual Fourth of July picnic.

Brian wondered if Talia would be there. Would she insist upon eating veggie-burgers?

Stop thinking about her, you nut! What in the world was wrong with him? Maybe he ought to ask Talia if she could suggest some herb that would put him out of his misery.

Brian shook his head, grinning inwardly.

"Oh, look, Frank, there's that man I told you about. The one who's been living off my apple pies."

Brian snapped from his musings in time to see Marlene Fountain making herself comfortable in the pew in front of him.

"Nice to see you," she said. "Talia told us you were here."

"She did?" Why did he suddenly feel encouraged?

"This is my husband, Frank," the older woman continued.

"Good meeting you, Doc," Mr. Fountain said. His voice, so deep and loud, was like a natural bullhorn.

"A pleasure to meet you too." Shaking the man's large hand, Brian thought that with his woolly gray hair Frank Fountain looked like a mad scientist—or one of his favorite professors in medical school.

"Nice day, isn't it?" the man boomed.

"Sure is."

The organist began to play, and Mr. Fountain settled in beside his wife. Moments later Talia joined her parents.

Now how am I supposed to concentrate on the sermon, Lord, if she's sitting in front of me? Brian sighed, remembering that a fruit of the Spirit was self-control.

The hymn ended on a long note, and the organ stopped. The pastor walked to the pulpit and welcomed his congregation.

"And now for our announcements." The balding reverend nodded at Frank Fountain.

Talia's father stood and, not needing a microphone, belted out one announcement after the other, occasionally glancing at the bulletin in his hand.

"And we need volunteers to barbecue at our picnic in two days. Who's man enough for the job?"

Brian chuckled under his breath. If that didn't get a few hands raised—

"Hey, Doc, what about you?"

The blood drained from Brian's face. "Me?" he mouthed.

"Can you flip burgers?"

He shrugged. Sure, he knew how to cook on a grill, but he had no idea who these people were.

"May I volunteer, Dad?" Talia said, her hand in the air. "I might be a female, but I can flip burgers as well as any man."

Brian smiled at her words, but her father didn't appear to like the idea.

"I don't know, Tal—"

"I'll volunteer if she does," Brian heard himself say. Had those words really departed through his lips? Was he daft?

"You're on, Doc." The older man smiled. "You too, Tal. I'll man the third grill." He looked over his shoulder at the pastor. "Guess that'll do it."

"Well, amen!" the pastor replied, looking pleased.

Mr. Fountain took his seat while Talia turned and smiled at Brian.

He smiled in return.

What am I doing? I came up here for peace and solitude, not to go crazy over some woman and grill at her church picnic!

"Turn in your Bibles to Isaiah chapter 55," the pastor said. "Our text this morning is verses eight and nine. 'For my thoughts are not your thoughts, neither are your ways my ways, saith the Lord. For as the heavens are higher than the earth, so are my ways higher than your ways, and my thoughts than your thoughts.' " The minister smiled warmly. "Let's pray."

Bowing his head, Brian suddenly felt doomed.

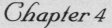

Chapter 4

After the service Talia made her way toward Pastor Leland. He was standing in the lobby doorway, bidding his parishioners a good day. She could see Dr. Coridan's blond head and broad shoulders two people ahead of her. Talia hoped she'd get a chance to talk with him before he left, although she couldn't imagine what she'd say.

She felt both flattered and confused by the conditions of his volunteering to flip burgers on the Fourth. "I'll volunteer if she does," he'd said. What did he mean? Probably nothing, she told herself. But she recalled the way his eyes seemed to caress her every feature when they'd first met. She tried to discount the memory, but it wouldn't go away.

"Well, good morning, Talia," Pastor Leland said, a grin spreading over his tanned face. "How's business?"

"Very well, thank you."

"That's an answer to prayer."

Talia smiled. "It certainly is!"

After shaking the older man's hand, Talia walked into the foyer. She noticed Judy McEnvoy standing to the side, waiting for the rest of her family.

"Hi, Judy."

The young woman nodded curtly but didn't seem to want to talk, so Talia walked on to the rest room. She paused for a moment to scrutinize her reflection in front of the mirror. Her curly hair sprang out in every direction, thanks to the summer humidity. Perhaps she should have braided it—well, too late now.

Out in the hallway she passed Judy again, and this time the girl averted her gaze. . . The strained relationship with Judy troubled Talia. . . Judy had been in her Bible study in the spring. The other participants had told Talia the lessons had blessed them, but Judy must have been offended somehow. If that were so, Talia wished Judy would talk to her or someone else about it.

Talia left the building and walked through the parking lot. She saw her parents standing beside their car, talking with Dr. Coridan. She quickened her step. Perhaps she'd get to talk to him after all.

Brian saw her coming and smiled a greeting. He thought Talia looked like a breath of fresh air, if such a thing could be captured in the visual sense. She had a natural, healthy glow in her complexion, and her brown eyes sparkled as she returned his smile.

"Say, Doc, did you hear anything I said?"

Brian tore his gaze from Talia, feeling embarrassed. "Oh—sorry. What were you saying?"

Frank Fountain glanced at his daughter then back at Brian. "Just wondering if you'd like to join us for brunch this morning, since you were asking about restaurants in the area."

"Sure. Thanks for the offer." Brian hoped Talia was going.

"Every Sunday we go to Blossom's Boathouse for an all-you-can-eat brunch," Mrs. Fountain added. "But they only serve 'til one o'clock, so we'd better get moving."

"I'll follow you there," Brian said.

He glanced at Talia, and she smiled at him. Was she glad he'd decided to come along for brunch?

On the way to the restaurant, Brian fought with his emotions. He considered himself to be a practical man, principled and skilled. He rarely gave in to his feelings, knowing the medical field had no room for sentiment. He would be crying every day over his patients if he allowed himself such a luxury, and they would be calling him at home after hours and on the weekends if they discovered how much he cared.

And maybe that was his problem: He cared.

Brian slowed at an intersection and followed Mr. Fountain in a left turn then a sharp right into the restaurant's parking lot. It looked crowded, and he might have been deterred if he hadn't agreed to join the Fountains for brunch. For that matter, Brian told himself, he wouldn't have agreed to come at all if he didn't think he'd have a chance to know Talia better.

"No harm in that—right?" he muttered. Besides, maybe he wouldn't like her, what with her being such a health food freak. He turned off the engine and climbed out of his SUV, thinking that their health care philosophies were as different as carrot sticks and chocolate bars.

Making his way through the parking lot, he tried to convince himself of that, but when he found Talia waiting at the restaurant door for him, all reason took flight.

"Mom and Dad are being seated," she told him. "We have reservations, and it looks as if we'll eat on the back deck. I hope you don't mind eating outside."

"No, that's fine."

Talia reached for the handle on the glass door. "Well, come

on then," she said and waved him inside.

Where are my manners? I should have opened the door for her.

"Miss Fountain." He took her elbow lightly as they stepped into the lobby.

She turned toward him. "Call me Talia. May I call you Brian?"

He nodded. He wanted to tell her he hadn't been on a date in almost twelve years and that he felt awkward. Would she understand?

"Don't be nervous around my parents and me," Talia said, as if guessing his thoughts. "I know it can be uncomfortable meeting new people. I mean, here you are in Blossom Lake, not knowing a soul in town." Her warm smile melted Brian's insecurities. "We're everyday country folks who don't put on airs. What you see is what you get with us." She laughed and led him to the back of the restaurant and then onto the outer deck that was lined with tables. "That might turn you off, being from the city—and being a physician too. I'm sure you're used to fancier things and more sophisticated people."

"On the contrary. I'm not turned off in the least."

Talia grinned as they reached her parents, and Brian saw a spark of amusement in her eyes. She obviously wasn't such a backward country girl that she didn't pick up on his attraction. Well, at least she wasn't "turned off."

Brian held the chair for Talia and then sat down next to her at the large, square table.

"What kind of doctor are you?" Mr. Fountain asked as the waitress set two carafes of coffee on the table. One was labeled decaf, and the other, regular.

"I'm a family practice physician, and I work in a multi-specialty clinic."

"Oh, good. I need some free advice," the older man said.

"Dad," Talia gave him a warning look.

"Well, docs are expensive," he retorted, "and my insurance doesn't pay much."

Brian smiled at the man's candor. "What kind of problem are you having, Mr. Fountain?"

He raised his arms and tilted his head back. "Doctor, Doctor, it hurts when I do this."

"Don't bite, Brian," Talia murmured, a twinkle in her eyes. "My dad is the king of obnoxious jokes."

Brian grinned. "My advice, Mr. Fountain, is—don't do that."

"Oh, you two aren't any fun at all," he said, righting himself in the chair.

Mrs. Fountain glanced at her husband. "Pour me some coffee, Dear."

Brian thought the older man looked like a little boy whose prank hadn't been appreciated.

Talia's mother then turned to Brian. "Are you visiting family up here?"

Brian reached for the carafe and filled his own cup. "No, I'm renting a friend's cabin for the summer."

Mr. Fountain let out a long whistle. "That's a lot of vacation time, isn't it? What about your patients?"

"They're in good hands. The other family physicians are absorbing my caseload. I might lose a few patients to other doctors, but I really needed the time away." He sipped his steaming brew. "I guess you could say I'm taking a sabbatical from the medical field."

"You don't like being a doctor?" Talia asked.

"Yes, I do. That's not it. It's not doctoring that bothers me. It's the politics that goes with the profession."

Mr. Fountain looked at the younger man. "Tell me a job that doesn't have politics. Wherever you find self-serving people, you'll find politics."

"You're right about that," Brian agreed.

"Even Talia, being self-employed, can't avoid politics. Why, that weasel Dirk Butterfield would love to turn the whole town against her so he can—"

"Shh, Dad. That's enough." Talia touched her father's arm gently. "I'm sure Brian doesn't want to hear about Blossom Lake's own little soap opera."

"Guess you're right," her dad admitted. "Sorry, Doc."

"That's all right."

"But after a couple of weeks in your cabin alone," Mrs. Fountain said, "you might want to hear what's going on. Then we'll tell you."

"But get the scoop from us first," Talia's father advised.

Talia shook her head at her parents. "You guys—"

The waitress appeared and took their order. Then they all went back inside the restaurant for the buffet. Brian noticed that the tables belonged to a collection of old, wooden country kitchen sets, probably dating back to the early 1900s. None had been refinished, as far as he could tell, giving them more charm. Fishing nets and anchors and other boating gear adorned the walls. He was surprised to see a full-size rowboat on display, its hull fastened to one large wall in the main dining room.

"Interesting place," Brian remarked, standing behind Talia at the buffet.

"This building used to be an old warehouse."

"I assumed as much."

"What gave it away, the lofty ceiling or the scarred wooden floors?"

"Both, I guess." Brian smiled.

He watched as Talia selected several pieces of fresh fruit. "I love historical places, so I enjoy coming here." She put a bagel on her plate and then scooped out some scrambled eggs. "In the late 1800s a logging camp used to be north of here. The men would put the wood on flatbed railroad cars and haul it down here."

"I thought loggers used rivers to move wood."

Talia paused. "I'm not sure. What I just told you is what I read in some of the historical documents concerning the area."

Brian helped himself to the eggs. Out of the corner of his eye, he saw Talia take two sausage links.

"Don't eat the bacon," she whispered.

"Why not?" he whispered back.

"It has nitrites in it."

"All meat has nitrites in it."

"No, only processed meat, like bologna and hot dogs. But the sausage is fresh. I asked the cook."

"Nitrites don't hurt you. The FDA wouldn't allow the preservative on the market if it was harmful."

Talia stared at him. "You trust the government with your health? I don't."

"I'll take my chances," he said, picking up two pieces of bacon and setting them on his plate. "I'd rather eat preservatives than bad meat and die of food poisoning."

"The choice is yours, of course."

Brian smiled inwardly. The health food nut in her was coming out, and he didn't like it. They'd just had a very polite debate, but as soon as they got to know each other better, they'd most likely be arguing one philosophy against another. In his opinion they weren't suited at all.

Heaping fried potatoes onto his plate, Brian sighed with relief. Maybe after brunch he could return to his cabin and push Talia Fountain from his thoughts forever.

Chapter 5

L istening to Brian share a bit of his background, Talia felt sad when she heard he was a widower. He seemed too young to lose his wife to cancer, although Talia knew death didn't respect age. According to Brian, he and his wife had been married only a short time before she died. He said she was a believer, so there was comfort in that. Furthermore, God had used her death to lead him into the medical field where he could help others.

It was too bad, she decided at last, that he didn't believe nitrites were carcinogens. How could he think he helped his patients if he didn't warn them about the food they ate? Talia bristled thinking about how uninformed most medical doctors were these days.

"Well, Doc, it was a pleasure meetin' you," Mr. Fountain said when they reached the parking lot.

"Same here."

Talia watched the two men shake hands.

"Oh, and about the Fourth," her father added, "just meet us at the park. You can't miss it. It's right off the highway, across from the grocery store."

"I've seen it," Brian replied. "And I'll be there."

He nodded a farewell to Mrs. Fountain and then to Talia, who felt a little disappointed at the impersonal good-bye. She'd thought for certain Brian was interested in her. Wasn't he going to ask her out—or at least ask for her phone number?

Maybe I imagined his interest, she thought, climbing into the backseat as her parents slid into their respective places in the front.

"I just might marry you off yet," her father said, glancing at Talia through the rearview mirror.

"What do you mean?"

"That doctor has eyes for you—that's what I mean."

Talia was silent. So her father had the same impression. Perhaps she hadn't imagined Brian's interest after all.

"I thought the same thing, Tal," her mother said, "from the minute Dr. Coridan walked in the store."

"Well, he might have been interested at first. But I don't think he is anymore."

"Why do you say that, Honey?" Her mother turned to look at her.

"For one thing our beliefs about health care lie at opposite ends of the spectrum. For another"—Talia leaned forward—"we barely know this guy, Dad. Don't you think it's a wee bit early to start thinking about a wedding?"

"Now, Tal, I'm just being open-minded. Isn't that what you and your sisters have wanted all these years? An open-minded father?"

Talia shook her head. "That was when we were teenagers and wanted the car. It's too late for open-mindedness now." She laughed. "We have our own cars."

"I can't win," her father muttered.

Talia laughed at her father's favorite line. He'd used it for the past twenty-five years, maintaining it wasn't easy living in a household full of females. As the youngest of three daughters, Talia figured she'd caused him the most grief. Her sisters had finished high school, married, and borne children. They led decent and quiet lives, owned homes and lived for their kids' next soccer game. Nothing wrong with that—in fact, Talia often wished she had a similar lifestyle. Unfortunately Mr. Right hadn't come along and swept her off her feet.

Talia's father often said she asked for too much. "Real men don't 'sweep,'" he would say. "You need to start thinking practical."

Practical. Nothing about Talia's nature was "practical." She was a dreamer, and the more people urged her into sensibility, the more she longed to see her dreams realized.

Her first dream had come true when she opened the Fountain of Life.

Her second dream seemed much less attainable. She wanted a man who would sweep her off her feet and share in her entrepreneurial aspirations. She didn't consider herself a raving beauty, however; so she figured Mr. Right would have to have cataracts or, better yet, stars in his eyes. Love would indeed have to be blind.

And Dr. Brian Coridan wasn't that. Handsome, sophisticated, accustomed to city life—what would he possibly see in a tall, large-frame, country bumpkin like her?

If he'd had the slightest bit of interest, she felt sure he'd come to his senses today.

"Glad you made it, Doc!"

Brian walked toward Frank Fountain and grinned. "I'm a

man of my word."

"So I see."

"Hope I'm not too late."

"Nope. That third grill over there is waiting on you. Coals are nice and hot."

"Great."

Brian looked over at Talia who was wearing a long skirt printed in red, white, and blue and a navy T-shirt. She was concentrating on the food she was cooking over smoky flames and didn't even glance at him. He didn't know why he felt disappointed.

"Grab yourself a plate of meat and slap it on the grill," Mr. Fountain told him.

Brian retrieved the raw hamburgers and hot dogs from the picnic table. The red-and-white checked cloth was barely visible under the bowls of potato salad, the baked bean casseroles, the fruit pies, and several pans of chocolate brownies.

"Sure is a lot of food over there," Brian remarked as he returned to the grill.

"Yep, and there'll be more once we've cooked up these dogs and burgers. Folks will be expecting to eat at noon—sharp."

Brian didn't waste another moment and set to turning the meat. Every now and then he glanced in Talia's direction but never caught her attention. She seemed absorbed in her duties at the grill. He knew it shouldn't bother him since they had nothing in common, and yet he felt compelled to win her affections.

Must be pride, he decided. Or the thrill of the chase. Being an outdoorsman, he could understand the psychology behind his motives.

If that was really it.

But of course it was. What else could he be feeling?

Finally, the meat was grilled to perfection. The pastor prayed, and two lines formed on either side of the picnic tables. Brian hurried to the rest room in the pavilion to wash up before eating. After a quick lunch, he planned to leave. As he entered the octagon-shaped building, he almost collided head-on with Talia who was on her way out.

"Whoa! Where's the fire, Dr. Coridan?" she asked with a laugh.

"Sorry about that," he said, smiling sheepishly. "I guess I was trying so hard to avoid the rocks and gopher holes that I didn't watch where I was going."

"No harm done," Talia replied with a friendly smile.

Suddenly her gaze darkened, and the smile left her face. Brian followed her line of vision and saw a shiny yellow convertible. The passenger door opened, and Judy McEnvoy stepped out. But the driver, Dirk Butterfield, stayed in the car.

The scene didn't look good, not even from Brian's perspective, and he was a newcomer to Blossom Lake. Judy seemed like a nice, church-going young lady. Why would she get involved with a married man?

Brian turned back to Talia. "I think the soap opera is unfolding before my eyes."

Talia looked at him as if to gauge his reaction.

"I'm assuming Dirk is married—to someone other than Judy. Am I right?"

Talia nodded.

Brian glanced over his shoulder in time to see the sports car speed away and Judy head for the picnic area.

"Is she a Christian?" Brian couldn't help asking.

"Yes."

"Is he?"

"No—well, not that I know of. I suppose he could be."

Brian wondered why he cared. He was in Blossom Lake on vacation, not on an investigation.

"Well, I'll keep both of them in prayer," he said lamely, although he meant it.

"Me too," Talia said, staring across the park's vast lawn. Then she glanced at Brian and grinned. "Do you play volleyball?"

"Not in about fifteen years."

She laughed. "You'll have to join us after lunch. We aren't pros, but we have a good time at the game."

"Maybe I'll take you up on the offer."

She nodded, smiled, then left the pavilion.

Brian watched her walk away in her long skirt and platform sandals. He wondered if she were going to play volleyball dressed like that or change into something more sensible.

He decided he'd better stay and find out.

Chapter 6

Brian watched Talia kick off her sandals and walk onto the sand toward the volleyball court. So she planned to play in that outfit, eh? Brian found it both strange and intriguing. The other participants, an even number of women and men, wore blue jeans, as he did, or shorts.

"Aren't you afraid you'll hurt yourself, playing in a long skirt like that?" Brian called over to Talia where she stood a few feet away.

She shrugged. "Well, it isn't as if I'll be running bases. All I have to do is stand here and hit the ball."

Brian chuckled.

"Talia always wears a skirt," a petite woman on the other side of the net informed him. "She's an odd duck."

"Oh, be quiet, you old married lady," Talia retorted.

The other woman laughed and glanced at the man next to her.

Smiling, Talia turned to Brian. "That's one of my best friends, Joellen Patterson. Well, no, it's Sullivan now. Joellen and Todd, the guy beside her, got married six months ago. It was a beautiful Christmas wedding."

Brian nodded politely at the reply. He wanted to ask Talia

why she'd never married. The answer seemed obvious, though—the Lord hadn't brought the right man for her.

And I'm sure not the right one, Brian thought, stepping back and taking his place in the last row. At least that much was obvious. She was a health food nut, and even her girlfriend called her an "odd duck."

"Hey, Greg!" Talia yelled, her hands cupping her mouth. "Are we going to stand here all day, or are you going to serve that ball?"

The dark-haired man on the other side of the net looked at her. "I'll serve—but only if you don't send it back. How's that?"

The ball came flying over the net. The man next to Brian volleyed it, and a woman beside Talia bumped it back over to the other side where it hit the ground.

"Yea!" Talia cheered, her hands in the air. Then she swayed her hips from left to right. "Ha, ha, Greg. You're going to lose this game."

Brian laughed and shook his head at her teasing.

"Bet you an apple pie we don't," Greg said, wearing a mischievous grin.

"You're on."

The sun beat down on the players as they volleyed, bumped, and spiked the ball back and forth. At one point Talia's baiting made everyone laugh. She was obviously trying to distract Greg, who appeared to be a professional volleyball player. Brian heard someone comment about Greg's winning "his last tournament." But Talia's jokes appeared to be keeping the man humble. After one heroic save she shouted, "Whoo-hoo! That was great! But this isn't the Olympics, Greg. It's just the Fourth of July."

Everyone burst into laughter, and Greg seemed to take the game less seriously after that.

After awhile, the sparkling blue lake, only a few feet away, began to invite Brian into its cool depths. Drenched in perspiration, he wondered if anyone would miss him if he stole away for a swim.

Just then a young lady on the opposite team suddenly doused Greg with a bucket of water. The game stopped, and the other players hooted with laughter.

"That's for giving me such a hard time for missing the ball a few minutes ago," she said indignantly.

Even Greg laughed.

"Water fight!" someone yelled.

Brian grinned, heading for the lake with the others. He would get his swim after all.

In one moment, he saw Talia walking toward the water with everyone else, but in the next, she was sitting down on the sand, holding her left ankle.

"You okay, Tal?" her friend Joellen asked, coming up behind her. "That was a pretty nasty spill you took."

"I must have stepped in somebody's archaeological dig," she said facetiously, "and now I've twisted my ankle."

Brian crossed the sand to where Talia sat. "May I have a look at your ankle?"

"I think it's fine," Talia replied, wincing at the obvious pain. "I feel so dumb. I'm such a klutz."

"No use in berating yourself. Accidents happen."

Brian knelt in front of her and cupped her heel in his hand, gently inspecting her ankle. Already it had swelled, and a nasty bruise was forming.

"It's probably just a bad sprain, but I think you need an X-ray to be sure," he said, setting her foot on the sand with care.

"But that means I'll have to go to the hospital!"

Brian nodded.

"But it's the Fourth of July."

He gave her a sympathetic grin.

"Want me to get your dad, Tal?" Joellen asked.

She nodded, and her friend dashed to the picnic area.

"Let me help you to your feet," Brian said.

Talia took his hand and tried to stand. But as soon as she put weight on her ankle, a sharp cry escaped her lips. The next thing she knew, Brian had scooped her up in his strong arms and was carrying her toward her parents' car.

Lying on the hospital bed, Talia couldn't believe what had happened to her.

Lord, why did You allow this to happen to me?

She recalled the book of Job and how God had taken that faithful servant of His through a deep valley of pain and suffering and how, in the end, Job had come forth as gold.

A broken ankle isn't anything compared to what Job went through, she told herself.

Talia took a deep breath and willed her anxiety away as she waited for the emergency physician to return. The man had told her the X ray showed a broken bone. He said he would call the orthopedic specialist and find out the next step. Apparently surgery wasn't out of the question.

Talia felt scared. She'd never had surgery and enjoyed good health—up 'til now. Also, for the past five years she had taken extra precautions not to put anything artificial into her body. Glancing up at the IV threaded into her right arm, she wondered what chemicals entered her system in the form of pain medication.

"So how's the patient doing?"

Talia looked at the curtained doorway as Brian Coridan walked in. He'd followed her parents' vehicle to the hospital.

She smiled at him. "I'm okay. A little scared, though." She felt tears prickle the backs of her eyes. "On second thought, I'm a lot scared."

"Of what?" Brian stood beside her bed, leaning his tanned forearms on the guardrail, and looked down at her.

"I'm afraid of having surgery." Talia sniffed. "Not only am I a klutz, but I guess I'm a big baby too."

"Well, it doesn't look as if surgery is in your future so you can relax."

"Really?"

"That's right." Brian nodded and smiled at her. "I was with your parents when the ER doctor showed us the X rays. Oh, by the way, your mom and dad said you should call their cell phone when you're finished here. They went back to the picnic to clean up."

"Okay."

"I told them I'm happy to give you a lift home and save them a trip back out here."

"That's nice of you." Talia was touched by the man's benevolence and remembered how effortlessly he had swooped her up into his arms. "But I hate for your holiday to be ruined on my account."

"Don't worry about it." He straightened and then stepped over to the padded green chair next to the bed. "Of course, I will expect to be compensated for my time."

Talia turned her head and noted the teasing gleam in Brian's hazel eyes. "Oh? What do you want? A year's supply of my mother's apple pies?"

"Oh, I hadn't thought about that one." He looked upward, as if to be contemplating the idea. "Here I was thinking of dinner and a movie or something."

Talia managed a smile. So Dr. Coridan was interested in her after all. Well, she was interested in him too. But could he accept her with her philosophy on medicine and all her quirks? Could she accept him with his?

"I don't go to movies," she blurted out. "But I don't look down on others who do. It's just a personal conviction with me."

"Like always wearing a skirt?"

Talia nodded. "Most people think I'm weird—even some of my Christian friends. But God spoke to me about my clothes, movies, and music when I was in college." Her smile deepened. "But we could go to dinner and then to an outdoor concert. A small symphony plays in the park every other Saturday night."

"Sure, that sounds nice," Brian said, looking back at her in a curious way.

Talia wondered about the strange light in his eyes. Maybe he wouldn't want to go out with her now that he knew her personal beliefs. But while she wasn't sure what he was thinking, she was glad he'd accepted them without criticism.

A moment later the ER physician entered the room, a smile on his face. "I spoke with the orthopedic specialist and faxed him the radiologist's report. It doesn't look as if you'll need surgery."

Talia looked at Brian, feeling a bit awed. His diagnosis had been correct.

As if guessing her thoughts, he smiled at her.

"We'll put a cast on your ankle and get you out of here," the doctor continued.

"Hallelujah!" she exclaimed.

The doctor's words sounded better than music to her ears right now. Suddenly Talia's world seemed right again.

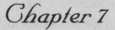

Chapter 7

Two days later Talia sat in a recliner her father had brought over to the store. Her ankle was elevated, and an ice pack lay across the cast to keep the swelling down. The pain was nearly intolerable, and Talia wondered why her herbal remedies weren't doing their job.

"Why don't you take one of those pain pills the doctor prescribed?" her mother suggested.

"Because I don't want any chemicals in my body," she replied tersely. "Who knows what the lasting effects might be?"

Mrs. Fountain put her hands on her hips. "Did you ever think that maybe God allowed man to make those pain pills for such a time as this?"

Talia was silent. The truth of the matter was, she thought she would feel like a hypocrite relying on pain medication instead of on God and His organic creations to ease her pain.

"Mom, would you mind slicing up a power protein bar and then put the pieces on a plate?" she asked, deliberately changing the subject. "When customers come in, I'll continue being the greeter with the broken ankle, but I can also offer them a taste of the power bars. Maybe we'll generate some sales."

"Certainly, Dear," her mother said. "I wouldn't mind in the

50

least." She selected a power protein bar from a box and walked to the kitchen area.

Talia lay back in the recliner and shut her eyes against the overwhelming pain in her ankle. A moment later she heard the bell on the door signal a customer's arrival. Opening her eyes, she saw Brian Coridan entering the shop. He held a bouquet of blue wildflowers.

Talia forced a smile. "Hi."

"Hi, yourself." He crossed over to the recliner. "Nice setup." He glanced at the chair then presented her with the flowers.

Even with her ankle throbbing, Talia was touched by his gesture. "Thanks."

"I thought you'd appreciate them," he said, a twinkle in his eyes. "They're organic. Right from the hill behind the cabin I'm renting. I picked them before I came here."

Talia wasn't in the mood for his teasing, so she ignored it. "You're very thoughtful, Brian. Thanks."

He narrowed his gaze. "Ankle bothering you?"

Talia moaned and nodded. "How could you tell?"

"You don't seem like your spunky self—not that I expected you to be with your injury."

"You're right. 'Spunky' doesn't describe me now at all. 'Crabby' might be a better word."

"Uh-oh, maybe I'd better leave."

Talia grinned. "You're in no danger."

Her mother reappeared with the slices of protein bars and set the plate on a table beside Talia's chair. "Well, hello, Dr. Coridan. Nice to see you again."

"It's good to see you too."

"Care to try a protein bar? We're giving away sample bites."

He shrugged. "Sure," he said and reached for one.

"My poor mother has been good enough to put up with me the past few days," Talia said.

"Jewels in my crown—that's for sure." Mrs. Fountain's expression grew serious. "But her discomfort could be avoided if she'd only take her pain pills."

Brian's eyes widened. "You're not taking your medication? Are you nuts?"

"I suppose I am, but I thought we had already established that fact," Talia retorted. She shifted in the recliner, trying to get comfortable. It seemed a hopeless cause. The throbbing in her ankle caused her whole body to hurt.

Brian shook his head at her. "Take your pain meds, Talia. Don't be silly."

She gritted her teeth, stifling a caustic reply.

"She's afraid they might do some permanent damage," her mother said.

"Our bodies are in perfect balance," Talia added. "Synthetic pain medication is liable to throw my whole system off for months—maybe even years."

Brian shrugged. "Well, then, you will have to put up with the pain."

Talia felt like crying. She knew what he said was true, but she hadn't wanted to hear it.

"Personally," he continued, "I'd take the pain medication and then worry about my body's balance after my ankle healed."

"Spoken like a true physician." Talia saw the tautness around his mouth and the hurt look in his eyes and regretted her biting remark.

"I guess I'll be leaving. I hope you feel better." He turned to go.

"Dr. Coridan, can I interest you in an apple pie?" Mrs.

Fountain asked. "It's on the house since you've done so much to help us."

"I think I'll pass for today." His smile was cool and polite. "I'm still full from the Fourth."

"All right then. Have a nice afternoon."

"You do the same."

After glancing in Talia's direction, he left the store.

Mrs. Fountain clucked her tongue. "Where are your manners, Talia Jean Fountain? Of all the things to say—and after he'd brought you flowers."

Tears spilled from her eyes. She hadn't meant to offend Brian. But perhaps a relationship between the two of them wasn't meant to be anyway. They seemed worlds apart.

Gazing at the wildflowers she still held, Talia decided she felt just as blue.

That woman is the craziest, Brian thought as he walked back to his SUV. Main Street in Blossom Lake was bustling this afternoon, so he'd had to park a few blocks away from Talia's store. All the way he fumed. *No wonder she isn't married. She probably runs off every eligible guy she meets—including me!*

Brian admitted to himself that his pride had been wounded. When he'd left the cabin earlier, he felt like moving the friendship to another level. But Talia had squelched those ideas. Now he wouldn't date that woman with any seriousness if someone paid him!

Except she does have a broken ankle, he reminded himself. Even so, she'd feel a whole lot better if she'd take some pain medication.

"Well, well, we meet again."

Brian shook himself from his musings and discovered Dirk Butterfield standing on the sidewalk in front of him. He nodded at the man.

"Judy tells me you're a doctor and you play a decent game of volleyball."

"Yes, I'm a doctor, but that volleyball thing is just a nasty rumor," Brian joked.

Dirk's brows pulled together in a frown. "Say, how's the little health-food store owner? I understand she hurt her ankle."

"She broke it."

"Really? Well, that can't be good for business."

"I think her mother helps her out."

"Ah, yes, of course."

Brian suddenly noticed they were standing outside Dirk's storefront office. The sign overhead read Butterfield Realty.

"So what does a respected medical doctor like you think of the herbal concoctions Miss Fountain sells in her store?" Dirk crossed his arms and tilted his head.

"I think they're quackery at its finest," Brian said, unable to keep the edge out of his voice.

"I take it you're not a believer in vitamins and herbs?"

"Well, I'm sure they serve some small purpose, but not to the extent that—Miss Fountain takes it."

"I agree. Say, would you like to step into my office for a glass of iced tea? It's freshly brewed, courtesy of my secretary."

"Thanks, but—"

"Really, Doctor, I can make it worth your while. You see, we're having a town hall meeting in September, and one of the topics on the agenda is whether to demolish that corner building. It holds those three useless shops—the ice cream parlor, Miss Fountain's health food store, and that despicable resale shop. I think you can be of some help to me since I'm in favor of the demolition."

Brian shook his head. "Mr. Butterfield, I'm here on vacation. I don't want to get involved in Blossom Lake's politics." *Or its soap operas,* he added silently.

"I can understand that." He pulled out his billfold, extracted some bills, and slapped them into Brian's palm. "Give it some thought. An hour of your time is all I ask, and as you can see, I'm willing to pay for it."

With that, Butterfield turned and entered his office.

Brian stood staring after him and then glanced at the money in his hand. He counted it—a thousand bucks! No one had ever tried to bribe him or "buy his time." Sure, his patients paid for his time, but this was different. It seemed criminal.

Brian glanced at the passersby, hoping no one had seen the transaction. He knew he couldn't keep the money. Taking hold of the brass knob, he opened the door and stepped into the realty office, intending to return the thousand dollars.

"Listen, Tal—I know what I saw."

"Dad, you can't be right."

"Well, given the way you spoke to Dr. Coridan," Mrs. Fountain said, "it might be true."

Talia turned her head and stared at her mother. "If he's consorting with the enemy to spite me, then he's a vindictive person, and I don't want anything to do with him."

"He seemed like such a nice man." Mrs. Fountain looked at her husband. "Are you sure you saw him take money from Dirk Butterfield?"

"Sure as the sun sets in the west. After he took the money,

I saw him go inside Butterfield's office."

Talia's heart sank. "I hope Brian knows he's doing business with the devil himself."

"Of course, he doesn't know that," her mother said. "Let's ask him over for supper tonight and enlighten him. Then you can tell him how sorry you are, Talia, for acting like such a smart aleck."

"I don't owe that man an apology!" She raised her chin. "He's so full of himself that he can't take a joke." It wasn't completely true; she knew she'd been unkind. Still, the fact that Brian might somehow be involved with Dirk Butterfield made Talia nervous. After all, what did she know about Dr. Brian Coridan anyway?

"I suppose I could walk up the street and see if the doc is around," her father offered.

"Yes, do that," Mrs. Fountain agreed.

Talia groaned. "No, let it be. Besides, I'm not up for dinner guests."

"But if the doc is a Christian man—and I think he is— then we have a responsibility to warn him about Butterfield."

"Brian knows what he's like," Talia said. "He saw him drop off Judy at the picnic on the Fourth, and he asked some blunt questions—which I answered."

Her parents didn't seem to be listening.

"Hurry, Frank!—See if you can catch up to Dr. Coridan."

Mr. Fountain left the shop, and Talia looked at her mother. "Maybe I'm going to need a pain pill after all." *I can't think of a bigger pain right now than Brian Coridan*, she added to herself.

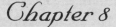

Chapter 8

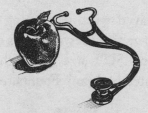

Brian returned the money and hurried to his vehicle. He couldn't believe the man wanted medical information so he could topple Talia's business. Well, he wasn't about to get involved in dirty politics, and he refused to share any of his knowledge, much to Butterfield's annoyance. *This town seems more like a soap opera. Who needs TV?*

Pulling open the door of his SUV, he felt a tug on his shirt sleeve.

"Say, Doc, before you go I'd like a word with you."

Brian whirled around to find Frank Fountain standing beside him, with a solemn expression on his face. "If it's about Talia," he said sharply, "she has to follow up with her own physician—not with me."

Mr. Fountain's eyes widened in surprise, and Brian instantly regretted his harsh words.

"Talia's been hurting for the past four days," her father explained.

"She chose not to take her pain pills, so she can't complain—and you can't feel sorry for her. Neither can I."

An odd look crossed the older man's face. "Excuse me, Doc—I thought you were a Christian man. I guess I expected you to act like one. My apologies."

"Don't throw my faith in my face," Brian said to Mr. Fountain's retreating back. "I'm a Christian, all right. I'm just not a gullible one."

Mr. Fountain waved without turning around, and Brian watched him walk down the sidewalk to his daughter's store. The doctor climbed into his SUV and started the engine. He wasn't about to be manipulated by Frank Fountain—or anyone else.

"Feeling better, Honey?"

Talia was settled on the sofa in the family room and looked up at her mother. "I hate to admit it, but the pain medication worked."

"That's good."

"No, it isn't. It means I've lived a lie for years." Talia's throat felt tight with her pent-up emotions. "I believed that natural products, vitamins and herbs, did the exact same thing prescription drugs did. I was wrong. My business is a sham." She wiped a tear away.

"Nonsense, Talia. Think of how many people you and your store have helped. Remember that woman who came in complaining of migraines?"

"Kathy Krueger."

"Yes, that's the one!" Mrs. Fountain snapped her fingers. "You suggested she take at least twelve hundred milligrams of calcium magnesium a day, and what do you know? She followed your advice and hasn't had a headache since. And what about that poor older woman with the chronic insomnia? You sold her a bottle of melatonin, and she's been sleeping like a log every night since."

Talia shrugged. The testimonies were true. "But I couldn't help myself. I looked through a dozen textbooks on nutritional helps and healing and didn't find a remedy that worked."

Her mother sighed. "Perhaps there's a point where God and science meet. That is, God allows the scientists and pharmaceutical companies to discover what He has known since the beginning of time."

"But it isn't natural," Talia argued. "It's man-made."

Her father was sitting in his favorite chair by the fireplace, reading the newspaper. The paper rustled as he laid it in his lap. "This house isn't 'natural' either, Tal. It wasn't standing here in the woods, and I happened to find it. No, it took a lot of hard work to build. Cost me money to buy it."

"But that's different."

"How so, Dear?" Mrs. Fountain asked, sitting down on the edge of the sofa, careful to avoid Talia's propped-up ankle.

"This house was built with natural things. Like wood and stone."

"I beg to differ. Brick is man-made, as far as I know," her dad said, "and what about the insulation and roof, not to mention the electricity and plumbing? Those pipes didn't just magically appear one day."

"All right, all right," Talia said impatiently. "Point taken."

Her father grinned and picked up the paper. For several moments only the buzz of the cicadas outside could be heard through the open patio doors.

Talia thought about what her parents had said. Maybe today's medical science and the art of nutritional healing could join forces for the good of mankind.

The question in Talia's mind was. . .how?

July melted into August in hot, humid heat that only a swim in the lake could cure. Several feet from shore, Brian floated on an inner tube, his eyes closed, listening to the sounds around him. The twittering birds. The wind rustling trees whose limbs bowed in reverence over the peaceful lake. The roar of a motorboat off in the distance. A child's laughter coming from somewhere across the water. These certainly weren't city noises, and Brian wished his time in Blossom Lake weren't running out. But his sabbatical was nearing its final days.

And I haven't made a decision yet.

He thought he'd have figured out what to do by now. Worse than that was he couldn't seem to hear God's voice anymore, speaking to his heart. When he opened his Bible, the words stared back at him, devoid of their usual depth and meaning. And, against his will, a vision of a brown-eyed young woman with wavy hair flittered across his mind at the most inconvenient times.

Like now.

Brian sighed, feeling too lazy to fight off thoughts of Talia Fountain. He hadn't seen her in weeks. He'd avoided going into town, even attending other churches in the area, despite his preference for her church. He had to admit he missed seeing her, whether she was handing out bulletins or playing volleyball. He wondered how her ankle was healing, and then he realized he hadn't prayed for her a single time.

Lord, I guess in trying not to think about her, I neglected to pray for her too. But if I pray for her, I have to think about her.

Brian moaned, sensing that if he allowed Talia room in his thoughts, she would slowly find her way into his heart.

Best not to think about her.

Brian paddled his inner tube toward the shore. He felt like a drowning man, and yet he saw no present danger. Instead, the sinking feeling that God wanted him to pursue a relationship with the little health food nut scared him. He sensed he would have no peace, though, until he obeyed and followed what he thought were the promptings of God's Spirit.

Reaching the sandy shoreline, Brian recalled Jesus in the Garden of Gethsemane, praying "not My will but Thine." He realized God wasn't asking him to bear the sins of the world and die a cruel death. He was asking him for his life.

It's always tough to give up control. He trudged uphill to the cabin, the inner tube tucked under his arm. *And if I've been resisting You, Father, I'm truly sorry. I'm confused—and scared. I don't know what to do with my life or my relationships. I need You and Your guidance. I'm willing to listen now.*

Brian reached for the doorknob to the cabin and suddenly felt he was where God wanted him to be—surrendered and depending on his heavenly Father.

Talia used a cane to limp across the foyer of the church and then encountered Judy McEnvoy near the ladies' rest room. She noticed her puffy eyes and red nose. Either she had an awful summer cold, or she'd been crying.

"Good morning." Talia expected to be snubbed.

"Morning." Judy lowered her chin and gazed at the carpet.

Talia felt encouraged. "Are you feeling all right? You look as if you might have a sinus thing going on."

"Allergies."

"Ah." It made sense. This was hay-fever season in northern

Wisconsin, and several of Talia's customers had come in with allergy-related complaints.

"The allergy tablets from the drugstore make me so tired. I feel almost worse."

"I'm sure. Well, you know where I am and what I sell," Talia said. "Stop by the store sometime, and I'll try to help you."

Judy raised her head and gave Talia a bland smile. "Thanks."

Talia stepped closer, leaning on the cane, and peered into the younger woman's face. "Have you been crying?"

Tears suddenly filled Judy's eyes, and she nodded hesitantly. "What's wrong?"

Judy shook her head. "Nothing. I don't want to talk about it."

"All right. But I'm here for you if you change your mind, okay?" Talia suddenly sensed that Judy's tears had something to do with Dirk Butterfield. It was, perhaps, a lofty assumption, but Talia thought she should address it. "Just for the record, you can't say anything that will shock me. I didn't become a Christian until my sophomore year in college and—well, let's just say I'm not as naïve as some people might think."

Judy nodded weakly but remained silent.

Talia waited a moment and then hobbled into the sanctuary. Her parents had taken their usual pew in front, but she didn't feel like limping all the way up there to join them, especially since the service would begin at any moment.

A movement to her right caught her eye, and at first Talia thought it might be Judy. Instead she turned to find Brian Coridan standing a few feet away.

Talia didn't know what to say when their gazes met. She supposed a simple "hello" would be a good start.

"Hi, Brian."

"Good morning," he said. The smile on his face appeared

more wary than warm and friendly.

Talia looked away and then decided to speak directly. "I've been praying you'd come back to church."

When he didn't reply, she glanced at him again.

"Guess it worked," he said at last, his smile broadening. "How's the ankle?"

"Pretty good. I had this walking cast put on two days ago, so I'm more mobile." She grinned. "If you think I was a klutz before, you should have seen me on the crutches. My father was sure I'd break my neck."

Brian laughed softly.

Just then Mr. Sanders, an usher, approached them. "Two seats right here in the back row," he said, pointing to the space.

Talia didn't care for the last pew since it was hard to hear the pastor, but she wasn't in any position to be choosy. She nodded to the usher and slipped into the pew, and Brian followed. The first hymn was announced. When the congregation stood to sing, one more person squeezed into the last pew, claiming a seat on Brian's other side.

It was Judy McEnvoy.

Chapter 9

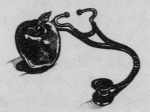

Talia felt as though she were walking on clouds—even with a limp. After the service Judy asked to speak with her and told her the whole sordid story. Dirk Butterfield had strung Judy along, making her believe he would leave his wife and children for her. Then, a few days earlier, he announced he was bored with their relationship. Talia felt Judy's hurt and humiliation. She even shed a few tears of her own. But she also helped Judy see that her pain was a result of sin. Judy acknowledged her part, confessed it, and received God's forgiveness. And God took the guilt and shame from her, as far as the East is from the West, because of His Son's death on the cross for her. Talia knew it would be hard for Judy to forgive herself, so she promised to be available to her if Judy needed her.

I'm so glad the Lord would use me to help Judy this way, Talia told herself as she stepped onto the sun-baked parking lot. She saw her parents inside their car, with the engine running and windows closed, signaling the use of the air-conditioning.

"Sorry, I made you wait so long," Talia said, sitting down in the backseat, then lifting her foot into the car.

"I'm going to assume it was for a good cause," her father said, "since we missed our reservation time at the Boathouse."

"Oh, Dad, I apologize, but your assumptions are right. I can't say much more, unfortunately."

Her father backed the car out and drove toward home. Meanwhile, Talia thought about the morning's events and felt a twinge of remorse at not being able to talk to Brian after the service. Judy had claimed her time immediately, and Talia never even got to say good-bye.

Well, Lord, I prayed You would bring Brian back to church, and You did. Now I'm asking You to bring him into the store—and sometime soon.

Brian wondered if he was being too forward by showing up at Talia's house uninvited. He knew where she lived because he'd driven her home from the hospital on the Fourth of July. But what if the Fountains had company this afternoon? It was Sunday, after all, and for some folks that meant family day. He didn't want to impose.

Thinking about the "what ifs," Brian nearly turned his vehicle around, but he finally decided to take his chances. He wanted to see Talia, though in retrospect he didn't know why. The last two times they'd been together, their opposing philosophies on health care got in the way.

Would it be the same today?

Talia had finished lunch and was making herself comfortable on the couch with the Sunday newspaper when she heard a car pulling up to the house.

"Dr. Coridan's here," her mother announced from the front hallway.

"Really?"

Talia limped to the door and saw Brian climbing out of his SUV. She turned to her mother. "Do I look okay?"

Mrs. Fountain smiled. "You look adorable."

"Now hold it," her father said, coming around the corner. "I don't know if I want this guy in my house. He was rude the last time I saw him."

"Maybe he came to apologize," Talia said.

"Maybe." Her father's frown deepened. "What about his involvement with Butterfield?"

"Let's ask him about it."

"Your daughter has an answer for everything, Dear," Mrs. Fountain told her husband.

"Oh, so now she's my daughter, eh?" He smiled at his wife.

"Behave, you two." Talia could hear Brian's steps on the front porch.

She opened the door without waiting for his knock. "Hi, Brian, this is a surprise."

"I hope I'm not intruding."

"Not at all. Come in."

"How about a piece of pie and a cup of coffee?" Mrs. Fountain offered.

"Sounds good," Brian said with a faint smile. He extended his hand to Mr. Fountain who, after a moment's hesitation, took it in a polite shake.

"I'm—sorry for the way we parted the last time," Brian said.

The older man nodded. "I am too—especially since I'd only wanted to invite you to dinner."

"I'm truly sorry."

"My dad also wanted to warn you about getting involved with Dirk Butterfield," Talia blurted out. "He saw the two of you talking earlier that day."

Brian seemed momentarily pensive, but then smiled. "Ah, yes, I remember. The truth is, we did more than talk that afternoon. Butterfield tried to pay me for a crash course in medicine. Apparently he wanted to use any information he gleaned against you, Talia, and your store at some upcoming town hall meeting."

"I don't doubt it, that toad."

"Leave the poor toads out of it," Brian quipped. "Rattlesnake might be a more deserving title for Mr. Butterfield."

Talia laughed. "Well, he doesn't stand a chance against the other two store owners and me. The man who operates the ice cream parlor printed flyers, and we're handing them out to our customers. We're expecting a good turnout for our side at the town hall meeting."

"So why are we standing at the door like this?" Mr. Fountain said. "Let's sit down and talk."

They walked into the living room, which Talia's father often referred to as "the sissy room." It was decorated in soft pinks, blues, and greens that complemented the floral printed fabric on the couch and matching settee. Talia sat down on the sofa, propping up her foot, and Brian took a seat near her. Mr. Fountain drew up one of the blue wingback armchairs.

"Just so you know, I didn't give Butterfield any information," Brian said, "and I didn't take his money. But I suspect he'll find someone else who will. You might want to be prepared at that meeting, Talia."

"I'm prepared," she replied, "but the issue isn't my business or the others'. It's whether the historic building we're renting is demolished or refurbished."

"True. From what I gather, though, Butterfield will try to

prove its worthlessness as well as cite the insignificance of the shops renting the old building. Why keep any of it? That'll be the question he poses to the community."

"Great."

Brian smiled at Talia's sarcasm as Mrs. Fountain carried in a tray with apple pie and freshly brewed coffee.

"Thanks," Brian said when she handed him a plate.

"You're more than welcome. Frank, will you pray?"

"Isn't dessert covered under the prayer we said at lunchtime?" he asked with a twinkle in his eyes.

His wife gave him an annoyed look.

"Okay, yes, I'll pray.

They all bowed their heads.

"Dearest Lord Jesus, we thank You for this pie and ask that You bless the hands that made it. In Your name, amen."

"Amen!" came the unanimous decree.

Talia watched as Brian took a bite of his pie.

"This is the best pie I've ever eaten," he said.

"The secret is the apples," Mrs. Fountain told him. "They need to be nice and tart, and I'll have bushels of them in another month or so. We've got a small orchard behind the house."

"Mom makes and freezes the filling," Talia said, "so she can bake apple pies all winter—and they're as pure and fresh as they come."

"I guess so," Brian agreed.

"And you know the old cliché, 'An apple a day keeps the doctor away—' "

Talia could have bit off her tongue. What a dumb thing to say! She glanced at Brian. "I didn't mean you," she said apologetically.

"That's okay. I didn't take it personally."

"Mom, that's what I've been doing wrong!" Talia said suddenly.

"What's that, Dear?"

"I've been eating an apple a day. Guess I'd better stop if I want Dr. Coridan to keep coming around."

Everyone laughed, easing any lingering tension.

Later, after the Sunday evening service, Talia and Brian took a stroll down the gravel road, which ran parallel to the Fountains' home. The sun looked like a giant orange fireball as it sank behind the tall pines.

"I'm glad you stopped over this afternoon," Talia said, holding onto the crook of his arm as she limped along beside him. "Think you can make a habit of it?"

Brian laughed. "You don't mince words, do you?"

"I try not to. I mean, what's the point?"

His smile widened.

"So when do you leave Blossom Lake and return to your practice?"

"Labor Day."

"Less than a month away."

"I know it, and I feel no closer to discovering God's will for my life than I did when I came here."

They walked on at a slow pace for Talia's sake while she listened to Brian's frustrations. She had the impression that he cared too much as a physician to compete in the impersonal medical world. He wanted to help people get well, not make money off their infirmities. Practicing medicine was more to him than a job; it was his livelihood, and it gave him a sense of purpose. Medicine to Brian was like ministry to a preacher.

"Sorry," he said at last. "I shouldn't have unloaded all that on you."

"Hey, not a problem. In fact, I'm glad you confided in me. I'll pray for you regarding your decision. It can't be an easy one."

"It isn't," Brian agreed. "But I suppose the simplest way out would be to do nothing and accept my present circumstances."

"You don't seem like the kind of man who'd be happy doing that."

"I'd be miserable."

They returned to the Fountains' home and sat down on the front porch steps. By now Talia's ankle was throbbing.

"I think I overdid it."

"Some doctor I am," Brian said. "I didn't give a single thought to your ankle."

"You and me both." Talia laughed and stood up again. "Excuse me for a moment. I need to take a pain pill, and the bottle's in the house."

Talia took a step up, and Brian placed his hand over his heart, feigning cardiac arrest.

"Knock it off, will you?" she said. "You're as bad as my father."

"You succumbed to pain pills?"

"I had to. It was either that or lose my mind to the pain. But you know what I've concluded?"

"What?" he asked, a hint of a smile playing on his lips.

"I've concluded that God calls us to a balance. Too much of anything isn't good—except I still believe people should take their health into their own hands instead of relying on doctors for everything."

"I agree."

"But medical doctors have a purpose too. I learned that

firsthand on the Fourth of July."

His smile broadened. "Maybe there's a middle ground here after all."

Talia nodded and then hobbled up the rest of the stairs. "Yes, maybe there is."

Chapter 10

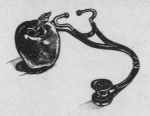

Talia heard the bell on the door announcing a customer. She glanced up from the invoices she had totaled at the checkout counter and saw Judy McEnvoy entering the store.

Judy smiled and headed straight toward her. "That licorice root tea really helped my congestion. I slept all night without coughing."

"I'm glad to hear it!"

"I also came in to tell you that I've been spreading the word around town about how terrific your store is. I feel as if I might have damaged its reputation when I was under the influence of Dirk Butterfield."

"Don't worry about it, Judy. The main thing is that it's over and your relationship with the Lord has been renewed."

"You're very understanding." Judy pushed the loose strands of blond hair out of her eyes. "I don't know if I would be so nice if I were you."

Talia laughed softly. "Yes, you would. Forgiveness is what our faith is all about."

"True."

Talia set her paperwork aside. "Want a glass of iced tea?

It's sun tea, and I brewed it this morning."

"Sure."

Judy followed her to the kitchen area.

"My friend Sarah said she saw you and Brian at the park last Saturday night. She said it looked as if you were having a cozy picnic while the symphony played."

Talia smiled as she poured two glasses of iced tea. She and Brian had seen each other every day for the past few weeks. They had talked and become better acquainted with each other during moonlight strolls and outdoor symphonies or just sitting on her front porch after dinner. Last Saturday night had been no exception, and if they looked "cozy" it was only because they felt so comfortable in each other's company.

"Brian's a terrific guy," Talia murmured.

"Uh-oh." Judy frowned. "I think I see stars in your eyes."

"I'm sure you do." Talia handed Judy a glass and laughed at her astonished expression.

"This sounds serious."

Talia's voice grew quieter. "It is—on my part anyway."

"It isn't on his?" Judy took a sip of the tea.

"I'm not sure. He's rather guarded about his feelings. Keeps a lot of them to himself—unless I pry them out of him." Talia smiled again. "He's one of those deep-thinkers."

Judy set her glass on the table and focused her attention on her friend.

"But the biggest hindrance in our relationship is that Brian has a medical practice in Waukesha, which is about three hundred miles from Blossom Lake. He doesn't believe in that old cliché about absence making the heart grow fonder either. I found out that much from him—and I have to agree."

"That's too bad."

"No kidding."

"Well, why can't Brian move his practice up here?"

"I'm hoping he'll consider it."

Judy picked up her glass of tea again. "Why don't you move closer to him?"

"I thought of that too. But my parents are aging, and I wouldn't feel right about moving so far away. Besides, I'm not sure how serious Brian is about me—us. That's one subject I don't want to force."

"You're wise not to, that's for sure."

Talia sighed. "Brian has to make the first move, and he isn't one to make a quick decision." She took a long swallow of her tea. "Sometimes it looks hopeless, since he's supposed to leave next week. But I'm determined to rest in knowing that nothing is impossible for God."

"That's good. It'll be neat to see how the Lord works everything out."

"It sure will," Talia murmured as she set down her glass.

Brian finished reading the last chapter in the book on nutritional healing, then set it down. He couldn't find medical fault in the author's argument, and he clearly saw how a combination of diet and osteopathy could improve a person's health. Perhaps those were the two elements missing from his medical practice.

He walked into the kitchen area and pulled a bottle of filtered water from the refrigerator. After taking a long drink he returned to the living room and sat down again.

Some weeks ago Talia had said, "God calls us to a balance," and he believed it.

He also believed he loved Talia Fountain. She was good for

him, countering his introspective moods with her outgoing, fun personality. But his feelings for her complicated matters in the way he had feared. Now, instead of one decision, Brian had to make two.

And next week was Labor Day. He was supposed to return to the clinic on Tuesday. He wondered what the clinic administrator would think about adding a health food store to the ever-growing facility. If it made money, he knew the man would be all for it.

But would Talia? She seemed bent on defending that historic building she loved so much. Did she love it more than him? Did she even love him at all?

Lord, I really care for her. But what am I to do?

He walked out onto the porch and then down to the pier that jutted out into the lake. In the past couple of months, he'd done a lot of thinking on the pier or out in the small motorboat.

As he reached the edge of the dock and started to sit down, he heard a car door slam at the top of the bluff.

"Brian?"

He smiled, recognizing the voice. "I'm down here, Talia— by the lake."

She made her way down the dirt path.

He walked out to meet her. "Be careful. I don't want you to injure—"

Before he could get the whole sentence out, Talia stumbled over a tree root. He ran to break her fall, catching her around the waist just in time.

"—your other ankle," he finished, smiling down at her.

"I'm such a klutz."

"But you're a very pretty klutz."

75

Talia shook her head and pushed several light brown tendrils off her forehead. "Have you had your eyes checked lately?"

He laughed, but inwardly he wished she wouldn't be so self-deprecating. In his opinion Talia Fountain was a lovely woman —inside and out. He'd come to admire her personal convictions and even agree with many of them. Now he wanted to marry her before someone else noticed this rare gem.

"You wouldn't believe what happened today!" she said. "I couldn't wait to tell you so I rushed over here."

"What?"

"Well, I suppose in one sense it could be considered bad news, but I don't think so."

Brian gave her his undivided attention.

"Dirk Butterfield strutted into my store this afternoon and announced he'd just purchased the building in which my store is located. He said a town hall meeting was no longer needed and, now that he owned the property, he planned to develop it."

"I thought the town of Blossom Lake owned the building."

"Dirk Butterfield has friends in high places," Talia said with a note of disgust in her voice. "But you know what? I don't care. While he was telling me about how he planned to demolish the historical building, I kept thinking of what the Bible says in Second Peter—about the day of the Lord coming like a thief in the night."

" 'In the which the heavens shall pass away with a great noise, and the elements shall melt with a fervent heat,' " Brian quoted; " 'the earth also and the works that are therein shall be burned up.' "

Talia nodded. "You see? It doesn't matter. Buildings will

come and go, but my faith, my beliefs—they're imbedded in my soul, and Dirk Butterfield or any other rattlesnake can't take them away."

Brian stroked her cheek with the back of his hand. "You are a wise woman, Tal."

A mischievous gleam sparkled in her brown eyes. "That's because I took my ginkgo biloba today. It's ideal for mental alertness."

Brian laughed. She made him laugh, she touched his heart, she occupied his thoughts—what more could a man want?

"Will you marry me?" he asked, slipping his arms around her waist and pulling her close.

"Whoa! Where did that come from?"

"My heart."

The surprise on Talia's face vanished, and in its place came a look of tenderness. "Oh, Brian—"

"Hey, Talia, what's going on down there?"

Her eyes widened, and then she grimaced. "Did I forget to mention that my father drove me here and was waiting for me in the car?"

"Um, yeah, I think you might have forgotten that little detail."

"Oops. So much for mental alterness."

"How long does it take to tell the doc one simple thing?" her father called out, his deep voice carrying across the lake like a foghorn.

"Hang on, Dad—Brian's proposing to me!" Talia shouted back. She returned her gaze to Brian's. "Sorry about that. Now where were we?"

"I believe I already proposed," he said. "I'm just waiting for an answer."

"Are you sure you know what you're getting into?" she countered.

"That wasn't the question. The question was, will you marry me?"

"But I haven't met your family yet."

"You will," he promised, wondering at her hesitation. "And they'll love you because—because I do."

"Oh, Brian, that's what I wanted to hear. I love you too," she said in a voice that was just above a whisper. Then she smiled through her tears. "Yes, I'll marry you. You're the first man to sweep me off my feet—literally."

"So how long does it take to say yes?" Mr. Fountain shouted down the hill. "For pity's sake, it's dinnertime!"

Talia groaned and rolled her eyes.

Brian laughed. "Come on—let's not keep your dad waiting a minute longer."

He helped her up the winding path until they met her father standing by the car.

"Well?" he asked impatiently.

Talia grinned. "I'm going to marry him."

Mr. Fountain nodded his approval, and Brian silently thanked the Lord. To Brian, his future father-in-law's support of the union was confirmation of the Lord's blessing.

"What about your medical practice, Doc?"

"It's still there. And it can stay there. I have something else in mind."

Talia turned to face him. "Like what?"

"Like a medical practice that teaches patients how to care for themselves instead of relying solely on doctors and the prescriptions they write. I'm thinking of a practice that promotes the art of nutritional healing as well as medical science."

"Oh, Brian! That's wonderful! It's always been my dream to share a business with"—she swallowed, a misty look in her eyes—"my husband."

He smiled, took her hand, and squeezed it gently.

"You thinking of opening this practice in Blossom Lake?" Mr. Fountain asked abruptly.

Brian nodded. "I love it up here."

"Okay—so when's the wedding?" The older man stepped into the car and closed the door.

"Soon," Brian said, his gaze fastening on Talia. "I don't want a long engagement."

"Me either." Then a curious light entered her shining, brown eyes. "What about a Christmas wedding? I've always wanted one, and I felt so envious of my friend Joellen last year."

"Sounds fine." Brian opened the door for his new fiancée.

"You'd better come along to dinner too, Doc," Mr. Fountain said, starting the engine. "My wife will want to discuss wedding plans."

"Yes, Brian, please come for dinner tonight."

"I'd love to." He smiled into Talia's eyes, but he couldn't help teasing her. "And to think it all began with your mother's marvelous apple pies."

Dear Reader;
I obtained this recipe at a ladies' retreat that I at-
tended. It was held at beautiful Camp Joy in Whitewater,
Wisconsin.

Andrea Boeshaar

Marlene's Marvelous Apple Pie

PAT-IN-PAN CRUST

1 ½ cups unbleached flour	½ cup canola oil
2 tsp sugar	2 tbsp whole milk
1 tsp salt	

Combine first 3 ingredients. Add oil and milk. Blend well and pat into a 9-inch pie pan. Flute edges. Fill with apple filling (see below).

APPLE FILLING

6 cups peeled and sliced apples	⅔ tsp nutmeg
½ cup sugar	½ tsp salt
3 tbsp tapioca	½ tsp fresh
⅔ tsp cinnamon	lemon juice

Mix all ingredients but the apples. Once blended, add apple slices to mixture. Pour into pie shell and top with streusel (see next page).

STREUSEL TOPPING

½ cup unbleached flour   ½ tsp cinnamon
¼ cup oatmeal   ½ cup butter
½ cup packed brown sugar

Combine all ingredients until mixture is crumbly. Sprinkle over fruit filling. Bake at 425° for 40–45 minutes or until bubbly. Cover pie with tin foil for the last 10 minutes if the top browns too much.

ANDREA BOESHAAR

Andrea was born and raised in Milwaukee, Wisconsin. Married for nearly twenty-five years, she and her husband Daniel have three adult sons. Andrea has been writing ever since she was a child. Writing is something she loves to share, as well as help others develop. Andrea has written twelve **Heartsong Presents** titles of inspirational romance and for the past few years has been voted one of Heartsong's top ten favorite authors.

As far as her writing success is concerned, Andrea gives the glory to the Lord Jesus. Her writing, she feels, is a gift from God in that He has provided an "outlet" for her imagination. Andrea wants her writing to be an evangelistic tool, but she also hopes that it edifies and encourages other Christians in their daily walk with Him.

SWEET AS APPLE PIE

by Kristin Billerbeck

"Be kindly affectioned one to another with brotherly love; in honour preferring one another."

ROMANS 12:10

Chapter 1

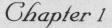

"Watching the door isn't going to make him appear." Kayli Johnson laughed, but she didn't tear her gaze from the bakery storefront. "Maybe not, but I don't want to miss him. I'm going to smile at him today, and maybe he'll come in." Kayli's stomach churned at the very thought of such uncharacteristic boldness.

"In my day men came calling properly. There was none of this spying out the window business." The stout older woman wiped the glass countertop with vigor. Kayli feared being a dirty appliance in Mrs. Heiden's path.

She plopped a fist to her hip. "You never had a crush on anyone? Come on, Mrs. Heiden. There was never anyone who set your heart aflame?"

"Never."

"Then how did you meet Mr. Heiden?"

"He was just lucky, I suppose."

Kayli let out a short laugh. "I suppose he was at that." Rearranging the apricot Danish into a more elegant design, she spoke again dreamily. "But this man, Mrs. Heiden"—she erupted into a long sigh—"he is unlike anyone I've ever seen around here. I can't explain it. I want to know who he is and ask him all sorts of questions. Maybe we're soul mates." She immediately regretted adding the final bit.

"Rubbish! Maybe you spend too much time watching old romantic movies. A girl your age should get out more, not day-dream constantly."

"I was born a hundred years too late." Kayli shrugged. "Going out doesn't interest me much. I would have been per-fectly content to pad around my sitting room and wait for suit-ors to call."

"You were born at the right time, Kayli. May I remind you a woman wouldn't have owned a business like this? If she did, a man would be fronting it."

"So what do you suggest, Mrs. Heiden? Should I accost this man on the street and introduce myself?"

"I suggest you get your dreamy eyes off that window and worry about your chocolate molds. They are nearly ready. Love will come calling when it's time."

Kayli gasped. "There he is!" Her heart thumped against her chest, and she closed her eyes. "Please come in—please come in," she repeated to herself.

Before opening her eyes she heard the jingle of the store bell. Shaking, she blinked several times. He stood before her, in all his masculine splendor.

Light brown hair shorn close to his head, and incredible clear green eyes, like the finished edge of glass. She heard her-self exhale. His set jaw exuded confidence, and his towering height, probably about six-three, rendered Kayli speechless. Sin-cerity was in his eyes, and a warmth emanated from him. Some-thing told her immediately he would be a good father. She chastised herself for mentally sharing children with a man she hadn't yet spoken to. What was wrong with her?

"Hello?"

He waved his hand in front of her dazed eyes, and she nearly collapsed from embarrassment. Where was her voice? She swore she'd talk to him, and now nothing came from her mouth except gurgling noises.

"Good morning." Mrs. Heiden finally rescued Kayli. "What can we get you?"

"Coffee."

Kayli had to say something. "How about a cappuccino? It's on the house today." She forced the words so they sounded completely unnatural, as if they'd been thrown and she were the puppet fronting the conversation.

"Cappuccino?"

"Italian espresso with steamed milk. I make the best in Palo Alto."

His eyes narrowed. "Is this how you get customers hooked on three-dollar coffees instead of the regular stuff?"

"You'll try it." Mrs. Heiden ordered. "You can order the plain stuff anywhere. This is a European bakery. Kayli is trained as a renowned pastry chef. You'll not drink standard fare with her delicacies."

"This is a European bakery?" He looked confused for a moment, then flustered, and focused on the backward words on the window.

"Yes, why?" Mrs. Heiden inquired. "Didn't you read it on the glass?"

He shook his head. "Never mind. It's not important." He looked back toward the window for a second. "I didn't realize a European bakery was already here."

"What do you mean 'already'?" Mrs. Heiden asked.

"Nothing. I'll try one of those cappuccinos." His clear eyes gazed directly at Kayli. She froze in the moment, and her stomach fluttered. *Does he know what I'm thinking? Does my face give it away?*

"Single? Tall?" Kayli stammered.

"Yes, I am." The stranger held open his hands. They were strong hands, if a bit rough-hewn. "Is that a requirement for the free coffee?"

Kayli blinked rapidly. "No, I meant do you want a single cappuccino or a double? A standard cup or a tall? You know, small or large?" Mortification settled over her as she rambled endlessly.

"Ah, so this is how you do it. You get people so confused about ordering a cup of java that we leave totally confused and satisfied we've gotten our three dollars' worth because we figured something out." His eye held a sparkle, and Kayli noticed he winked at Mrs. Heiden.

"No, I only meant to offer you a free cup since I see you walk by each day." She bit her lip.

"You're very observant."

"You're hard to miss." Kayli wiped her hands nervously on her apron. "Being so tall and all." She turned on the espresso steamer, thankful it drowned out her ridiculous babbling.

"I'm building the restaurant up the street!" he yelled over the machine. "I did the owner's house, and now he asked me to work on the restaurant. It's almost finished, and then I can head home. To a place where the coffee comes only leaded or unleaded."

"Home?" Kayli stopped the machine.

"Montana, blue sky as far as the eye can see." He waved his large hand in the air. "And the closest neighbor has an udder."

Kayli heard Mrs. Heiden laugh, and she shot the elder

woman a grimace. "Why would you want to move away from all this?"

He looked out the shop windows again. Several impeccably dressed business people passed, a few foreign cars stopped at the light, and a woman strode by, looking as though she belonged on a soap opera rather than walking down a city street. "What part do you think I'll miss?" He crossed his arms across his wide chest.

"For one thing I imagine not many people want luxury homes or restaurants there. What will you do?" Kayli wiped the extra foam from the outside of the cup.

"Whistle Dixie if I have to. Maybe I'll raise llamas."

Kayli handed him his coffee; her heart slowed. He was a cowboy let loose on the city streets. He wasn't her soul mate at all but a gorgeous impostor. Kayli sniffed. "If that's your true calling, I wish you luck."

"Mmm," he said after his first sip. "This is incredible coffee. I've never tasted anything like it. I'm beginning to think the three dollars might be justified. Maybe the Europeans know something." He winked again.

"Do you want anything else?"

He looked into the glass counters, his eyes brightening. "Do you have any apple pie?"

"Apple pie?" Kayli was almost offended. "This is a European bakery."

"So you said."

"I have tiramisu that will melt in your mouth and make you forget you ever ate such a trite dessert like apple pie."

"I have no idea what tiramisu is. Apple pie is American. What kind of American are you? Running a European bakery?"

"A European-trained pastry chef." She squared her shoulders.

"And a patriotic American. Tiramisu is a delightful Italian dessert made with marscapone cheese and lady fingers soaked in espresso. The word means 'to lift you up,' and it does just that."

"So pastry chefs can't make apple pie?" He shook his head. "What a waste of talent. My mother," he groaned, "could make an apple pie crust that would disintegrate in your mouth. You never tasted anything like it."

"I can make a piecrust that would do the same thing. I just choose not to." She crossed her arms. "There's not a lot of money in apple pie around here. I have to make a living."

He seemed unimpressed. "You know, it's easy to say you can make an apple pie like my mother's, but why should I believe you? You might be like those gourmet chefs who can't microwave a hotdog."

"I studied pastry for years. I think I could take on your mother's crust." Kayli shook her head. An apple pie. . .really!

"Do you?" His eyebrow lowered. "I'd like to see you try."

"You come back Friday afternoon. I'll have an apple pie that will knock your socks off."

"I'll believe it when I taste it."

"And you'll pay for it this time."

He laughed. "I think I already have. But I'll see you Friday. You'll have my pie ready." The jingle of the bell annoyed her.

"How dare he!"

Kayli picked up her chocolate molds with force, and a few of them collapsed under the pressure. Mrs. Heiden took the tray from Kayli before any further damage was done. Her assistant's bent frame shook with laughter, and Kayli felt incensed.

"Just what is so funny?"

"Kayli, my dear. I can't help but giggle at the notion that your soul mate, as you so romantically put it, lives next door to cows. Have you even seen a cow?"

Kayli stood tall. "I have. We went to a working dairy when I studied milk chocolate in Switzerland."

"I certainly hope there's another soul mate out there for you because that one sounds distinctly like Annie Oakley's soul mate. His America is far different from yours."

"I'll grant you that. An apple pie! Honestly, I think he's looking for a diner on Route 66, not Les Saisons Bakery."

"So will you make this apple pie?"

"You bet I will, and it will leave him wondering how he ever stomached his mother's."

"You're cruel, Kayli, and far too competitive. You'll never get a husband that way."

Kayli grinned. "Maybe not, but I didn't study for six years to make apple pie either. I can't believe I ever found that man attractive. Perhaps I should have kept believing in my dreams and let him keep walking by."

Adam Harper exited the fancy bakery with a heavy heart. Mike Williams never told him a European bakery already existed on University Avenue. Adam might not have noticed if he hadn't seen the beautiful owner. That forced him into acknowledgement, made her real, and guilt weighed heavily on him. A ruthless businessman, Mike Williams would undercut this elegant little bakery until it couldn't afford to operate; then he'd raise his prices and force rents up in the neighborhood. The owner's big brown eyes resonated in Adam's memory. He would remember them always and what he'd done to remove some of their sparkle.

Adam sighed. Taking money from a man with no morals,

he supposed, made him just as bad. He brought out the wrinkled picture of his Montana property. Was it worth it? He looked back to the tiny bakery, thinking about those wide, innocent eyes gazing back at him.

"You ought to be ashamed of yourself, Adam," he muttered. You're as bad as them and worse. You know better. The faster he was out of California, the better. Before he gave up everything he believed in.

"Hey, you checking out the competition?" Mike Williams met him on the sidewalk, nodding toward Adam's coffee cup.

"You didn't tell me there was any competition."

"All you had to do was pay attention, Adam. You walk by the shop every day." Mike waggled his eyebrows. "Did you get a load of that pretty little owner?" He motioned an hourglass in the air. "I'd like to get her on my payroll."

In Montana, Adam would have hauled off and socked the guy, but here in California he just clenched his teeth, quietly enduring the immorality. *Only a few more months, and I'll be out of here.*

"She seems like the kind of woman who wouldn't give you the time of day. Too sweet."

"Until she finds out about my mansion." Mike winked. "Women are more open to me then."

"Not this one, Mike. I think she's beyond your standard money-grabber."

"All women have their price—some are more expensive than others."

Adam's eyes narrowed. "If you believe that, you're more pathetic than I thought. What does your wife think of this opinion?"

"Careful, Boy. This job ain't over yet. You got a plumber

that hasn't shown up and a problem with the inspection on the stoves. I suggest you get to it. Swallow that sissy coffee and get a move on."

Adam clenched his lips between his teeth to avoid replying. In less than three months, he'd take his payment from Mike Williams and be long gone. He held to that with fervor. It felt like all he had right now.

Chapter 2

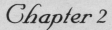

Friday came quickly, and Kayli manipulated the dough in her hands then rolled it out into a flat circle. She cut a perfect circle, tossing the scraps aside for later. She held up a pippin apple, crowned to perfection. "I really hate to dash your mother's title, but, alas, my pride has been wounded."

"Are you talking to yourself again?" Mrs. Heiden entered the back room. "My stars! You look like the wicked queen with that apple in your hands."

"I was talking to my former soul mate. I'm feeling sorry for his mother. Soon my pie will show her pie for what it is. A pale comparison." Kayli felt the corner of her mouth turn, and she tossed the apple playfully.

"You are a prideful thing—do you know that? And you know what they say about pride." Mrs. Heiden grinned. "It goes before the fall."

Kayli grimaced. "Mrs. Heiden, really. Do you honestly think some backwoods Montana mom could hold a candle to my baking expertise? I was born with gifted taste buds."

Her eyebrow raised. "And tiny hips. Life isn't fair, and, yes, I do think his mother's pie could outrank yours. Taste is subjective." Mrs. Heiden removed her red apron and hung it on a wall hook. "More important, I think it hardly matters. You should be doing something constructive to assist your social life, not baking pies for a man moving out of town. To get away from the likes of you, no less, and move back to the cows."

"Now you're being ornery. He is not moving to get away from me. He doesn't even know me."

"He knows all about your princess ways. They're not hard to see. What is that on the piecrust?" Mrs. Heiden bent over Kayli's pastry.

Kayli used her pastry brush to "glue" the decoration to the top of the shell. "It's a cow. See?"

"You put a cow on the piecrust." Mrs. Heiden shook her head. "You know, in some places, they would lock the likes of you away."

"I thought it was cute. A going-away present, you might say, to remind him of home and his America."

"Your friend Robert is here, and it's nearly time to close. I'll see you in the morning. I don't want to be seen here late in case they haul you off."

" 'Bye, Mrs. Heiden. Thank you for your help today. I'm going to bake this, and it will be ready when our cowboy comes. Fresh and warm, just like his mama makes, only way better." Kayli shrugged.

Mrs. Heiden clicked her tongue. "Get a life, as you young people say."

Kayli laughed and slid the pie into the oven. Then she emerged to the front counter. "Hi, Robert. How are you?"

"I'm good. Listen—a few of us are doing dinner tonight. A barbecue at my house—you interested?" Robert pressed his glasses to his face with an index finger. He crinkled his always-sniffling nose and smiled.

Kayli checked her watch. "I'm waiting for a customer pick-up. What time?"

"Not until six, but that isn't all I came to tell you." Robert pulled her around the counter by her elbow and sat her down at one of the two tables in the bakery. "You know that big restaurant going up down the street." He looked around the store, ensuring no one was about. "I could lose my job for this, so you didn't hear it from me."

"Well, tell me, Robert. I didn't know you had this mysterious side."

Robert grimaced, in his annoyed bureaucratic way. "I did the paperwork for it downtown. It's not just a restaurant. It's a European bakery during the day. They plan to sell out of a shop up front."

Kayli hunched over. She felt the blood drain from her face. Shaking her head, she finally looked up. "It's a restaurant, open for dinner—right? It has nothing to do with me."

"Right, a restaurant. But during the day they bake bread and desserts for the restaurant. They're going to open a bakery café."

Kayli shook her head. "No, Robert. The builder was here. He would have said something." Her hands trembled. "I can't go back to the hotels again. I've worked too hard for this. But if my business is split in half, what will I do?"

"I don't know, Kayli, but I thought you should know. I heard the Royal Court is looking for a pastry chef."

Kayli's head swayed violently. "No, never again! I'd rather be a dishwasher than work in a fancy hotel again. The hours are stifling, and the rewards are null. Half my desserts ended up in the hotel cafeteria, stale and unappreciated. No, I can't do that."

"Mike Williams is building this restaurant. He plays to win. I'm not trying to scare you, but I want you to be realistic. We in the city have seen him take out a lot of mom-and-pop shops."

Kayli's heart sank. Robert supported her in nearly every endeavor. He'd even loaned her a small bit of money to get started. If he thought her chances were slim, they were probably impossible. "I don't mean to shoot the messenger, Robert, but I need time to assimilate this information."

"Join us for the barbecue—you'll feel better." His brown eyes widened, and she smiled at his sweetest grin. Robert, as fine and decent a man as there ever was, and yet Kayli felt nothing when she stared into his eyes. Why was that? "Kayli?"

"I'm sorry, Robert. I'm still digesting what you've told me. I don't think so on dinner. I wouldn't be good company anyway. But wait a minute—let me get you a tiramisu to serve." Kayli went behind the counter and retrieved her signature dessert. She boxed it in an elegant gold box and placed a sticker on it. "Here, Robert—enjoy it with my compliments."

He reached for the box, grasping her hand as he did so. "I'd rather have you there," he whispered. "The dessert isn't nearly as sweet."

Kayli pulled her hand away. "Thank you, Robert, but I've got to be proactive. If I plan to beat Mike Williams at his own game, I'd better think of a plan. I wouldn't be able to concentrate on small talk."

"Maybe Mr. Williams is looking for a pastry chef."

"I like having my own business. Besides, if I can't handle a little competition, I'm not really that good—right?"

Robert brushed her face with the back of his hand. "You are awesome. Don't you forget it. I'll see you at church this weekend."

Kayli forced a smile. "Sure. Have fun tonight."

"Not nearly as much without you." He winked and turned.

Kayli sat for a long time with her chin in her hands. Wasn't this always the way? She rejoiced in having her own business, just finished bragging about it, and it might be snatched out of her very hands. Sometimes she didn't understand God. Hadn't she paid her dues? Wasn't this justification for all she'd missed in life? Kayli laughed out loud. This time she'd wrestle with God. She was sick of having to grin and bear it, and her business wouldn't go without a fight.

"You look heavy into thought. Is this a bad time?" The tall cowboy made his way into the shop. The bell announcing him didn't do him justice. She thought he should have his own special sound, maybe a bullhorn calling attention to his entrance. Though she doubted he had any trouble getting attention. Her eyes narrowed, thinking of all the information this man had kept to himself. That he had the nerve to walk into her shop.

"I've only just heard what you're building. Won't Mike Williams have your head for consorting with the enemy?" Kayli tried to sit tall, but her shoulders slumped again, and she felt the beginning of tears. She wiped away an escaped tear and looked away. "I'll get your pie, and then I'd appreciate it if you'd just let Mike's bakery serve your penchant for pie."

"No, wait." He grabbed her hand, and she turned to look up into his tropical green eyes. Her troubles seemed momentarily forgotten. What was it about this man? Why did she feel she'd known him for years? "I didn't know there was competition in town. Not until you handed me the cappuccino the other day. I wouldn't have done this knowingly."

"I should make you pay for the coffee now." Kayli sniffled. "So you think I'm about to go out of business too."

"I didn't say that," he whispered in a hoarse voice, and she felt herself swallow. Her hand was still in his. Such familiarity with a stranger was unknown to her, but she didn't pull away. Anger mingled with interest.

"How could you do this? Build something for that monster and harm a small business. My small business."

"I didn't know. Honestly I didn't. I'm not what you'd call an observant man. I passed by here every day and never bothered to notice."

She blinked away fresh tears. His guilt only confirmed her worst suspicions. Mike Williams would put her business under; it was only a matter of time. "When will the bakery open?"

"Three months."

"I'll get your pie." She turned to the back, but his hand squeezed hers. Suddenly she smelled something burning. "The pie!" She ran toward the back and opened the oven to see smoke. She fanned the fumes away, donning her oven mitts and coughing in the midst of gray clouds. She pulled out a blackened pie. It looked worse than it smelled.

The builder walked up behind her. "Is that a little cow on the pie?"

She nearly kissed him, so beautiful was his gesture to ignore the blackened pastry and focus on her handmade cow. She nodded.

"It's a lovely cow. Reminds me of home. Thank you." He took twenty dollars from his wallet. "You sure know how to impress a guy."

"You don't think I'm actually going to make you pay for this, do you?"

"I appreciate the effort. I imagine this hasn't been your best day, and I wouldn't do anything to make it worse. You take the money and buy essentials for another pie. I'm still dying to know if it beats my mom's."

Her tears started to roll again. Since when had she been so emotional? She shook her head, sniffing every few seconds. "I really can make an apple pie."

He laughed. "I know you can. In fact, I'm certain there's no end to all the things you can do. Have dinner with me. I want to let you know how sorry I am."

"Tonight?"

"Now. We'll go somewhere that Mike Williams doesn't own. You'll get to know me. I'll get to know you, and we'll share our contempt for everything Williams. Please. I could use a friend here."

"Shouldn't I know your name?" Kayli realized she didn't even know this stranger. She only felt as though she did. His regular jaunts past the storefront provided a familiarity with him that didn't extend into reality.

"Adam. Adam Harper."

"I'm Kayli Johnson."

"We'll leave my business card here on the counter, Kayli. That way, if you have any fears of walking up the street with me, someone will know how to find us. My cell phone number is on there. I don't think your assistant would think too much of your taking off with a stranger. She doesn't look like the type of woman I want to mess with."

She smiled. "Believe me—she's not. Let me turn off this oven and clean up a bit." Kayli left the door unlocked. No sense in turning away business today. She'd need customers more than ever if competition loomed.

She brushed away the remaining flour from her work table and tried to forget that the man she'd admired from afar stood in her shop, waiting to take her to dinner. She checked her reflection in a tiny compact and sighed. She looked worn and pale, covered by a light dusting of flour. Kayli shook out her long dark tresses and applied a bright red lipstick and a little blush. She puckered up, matting the lipstick, and drew in a deep breath.

The bell at the door jingled, and Kayli emerged to Robert's questioning glance. He looked toward Adam and back at Kayli, and Kayli felt her eyes drift shut. She opened them to Robert's sad brown eyes. "I thought you might be hungry for something. I got you a little soup up the street. I'll just leave it here." He placed a white bag on the counter and immediately left.

Kayli felt Adam's glare and avoided looking in his direction. "A friend from church," she finally said.

"A good one obviously." Adam searched the room.

"It's not what you think. He's having a group over for dinner and asked me to join them. I didn't feel like being in a group tonight, and I still don't. But I'd like to get to know you, Adam Harper, if you're still willing."

Adam brushed his chambray shirt. "Something tells me by the look in that man's eye, you're trouble, Kayli Johnson."

"You're probably right."

"You'll break my heart, won't you?" His gentle green eyes narrowed. He had mirth in his gaze, but also a sobering severity.

"Not over dinner, I won't."

"Fair enough."

Adam took her arm, and they entered the busy sidewalk together. She feared looking into those clear eyes again, but she felt his large presence even without gazing toward him. Adam Harper would not be easily forgotten, and she had little doubt that it would be her heart broken in two. Still, his invitation proved as powerful as any web. She was drawn to him and hoped an evening in reality would put aside this ridiculous crush on a myth.

Chapter 3

U niversity Avenue bustled with the wealthy of Palo Alto's elite, next to the backdrop of sweatshirted Stanford students on bicycles. Kayli's stomach churned from being on the arm of this man she had idolized for so long. He was real and, for the moment, unaware that Kayli Johnson was not his type. Neither glamorous nor into cows, Kayli tried to forget this man would bring about her ruin in business. Indirectly anyway.

"Do you know how long I worked to get my own business?" Kayli heard her voice speak. It wasn't like her to accept the invitation of a stranger, much less one with whom she obviously shared so little in common.

Adam turned and focused on her. His crystal green eyes narrowed, and she felt their weight. "I didn't know, Kayli. You had to realize that if you were doing something well in Palo Alto, someone might come in and try to do it better. All you have to do is look at the countless expensive retailers here to realize that. The shopping compares with New York. You're not that naïve."

Kayli frowned. "I think I was."

"Did you come out with me to bust my chops all night?" He stopped suddenly on the street, and Kayli gulped.

"Well, no."

"Come on—we're going in here." Adam opened the door to a quiet, Italian restaurant. The setting felt romantic, and Kayli felt a bit of her anger dissipate under the soft lighting and gentle music. They were seated at a quiet table in the corner by the window. The waiter handed them menus and set a wine list on the table. "Do you drink?"

Kayli shook her head.

"You can take this away." Adam handed the waiter the leather-bound drink menu.

The waiter sniffed and removed the wine list and the glasses with an angry clink.

Kayli opened the menu, and her eyes widened. She didn't partake of restaurants very often, and this one was certainly above her price range. "So what does a cowboy think about paying twenty-seven dollars for a steak?"

Adam grimaced. "Don't get me started. The same thing I think about paying three dollars for a cup of coffee—that's what I think. Is there anything that justifies these California prices?"

"The weather tax. That's what we call it. You get sunshine about three hundred and fifty days a year. No snow to shovel, and the ocean a rock skip away. So we call the prices the weather tax."

"Well, it's disgusting."

"Have you tried to pay the rent here? There's a reason we charge those prices, Adam. Someone charges us. Though I must admit the price of a steak makes me wonder if the cows live in a fancy hotel suite until their demise. Still, the rent is quite overbearing for most."

"Yes, my two thousand a month is buying me a lovely little one bedroom up the street, built in the forties. I'm praying we don't have an earthquake before I get out."

Kayli laughed. "Welcome to California, huh?"

"It's not exactly the most welcoming state. But judging by all the people here, there must be something people want."

"Have you walked Stanford's serene campus? Or taken a hike in the mighty redwoods? Have you felt the ocean waves lap at your bare feet? Have you stood on the floor of Yosemite Valley? God's creation is so apparent in California." Kayli laughed. "I sound like a praise song, but some things are worth their price."

He looked away from her and focused on his menu before lifting his gaze back to hers. "You're a Christian." It sounded more like an accusation than a question.

"I am," Kayli answered. "How did you know?"

"I saw the fish sign on your window. That's what pulled me in your shop that day. Almost like it was a sign."

Kayli looked away. Yes, she was a Christian, but little good that seemed to do her. While heathens like Mike Williams built bigger tributes to themselves, little Christians like Kayli struggled to make ends meet. Where was God in all this? And why was she facing her old life and those vicious questions again?

"I haven't been a Christian very long, and this is not the first time I've questioned my faith." Kayli shot a hand toward her mouth. Had she really uttered her fears?

Adam laughed, and Kayli bristled. "Life ain't fair—that's for sure. God never promised us it would be. When I get back to Montana, my faith will be restored. Clean air, blue skies, and honest people. It's easy to get lost in all the hustle-bustle here. You hold on. It won't always be this way."

"Easy for you to say. I'm glad it's perfectly acceptable for you to come here, take our money, build a monster restaurant, and go home with no guilt whatsoever. Is that His plan for your life? You can take people down as long as they aren't from your home state?" Kayli hated the sound of her voice. It sounded edgy and bitter.

Adam dropped his head, blinking quickly. His expression sent a pang of guilt through Kayli, and she instantly regretted her words and her tone. "Montana is no picnic, Kayli. There are no free rides. We all have our own crosses to bear. I'm sure you wouldn't want mine, and I wouldn't want yours."

Kayli opened her mouth to speak but closed it upon seeing the severity in Adam's eye. She breathed deeply before speaking.

"I envy your escaping your troubles—that's all."

"Montana is no escape. Responsibilities can be painful no matter where you're placed."

Kayli swallowed hard. Something about the grievousness of his expression told her something more went on in Montana, but she feared the answer. "I'm sorry. I plan to win this war with Mr. Mike Williams, Adam. You tell your boss that."

"No, I don't think I will. I'll let you prove it to him. He doesn't need the added challenge. It's better he looks at you as a fly to be swatted away."

"You don't think I can take him, do you? You think his bakery will do me in within a month?"

"Kayli, I've built enough for Mike Williams to know he is not a man I'd mess with. Do I respect him as a person? Not on your life. Do I respect his mind for business? Absolutely, and I wouldn't toy with him like a kitten's ball of yarn. You'll only hang yourself."

"Speak of the devil." Kayli nodded toward the door where Mike Williams had just come in. She noticed Adam shift uncomfortably. "Do you want to leave?"

Adam shook his head and crossed his arms, as though bracing for Mike's approach.

"Well, if it isn't my builder with Miss Johnson." He whistled, and the waiters looked angrily their way before noticing it was Mr. Williams and consequently ignored the breech in peace.

"Do I know you?" Kayli asked.

"Mike Williams." He held out a hand, which Kayli ignored. "I'm building the new restaurant and bakery up the street. Hasn't my trusty contractor spilled the beans yet?"

"No, actually, he hadn't, but your reputation precedes you regardless." Kayli narrowed her eyes, staring into Mike's cold gray ones. "I hope you're prepared with that bakery, Mr. Williams. I was trained at all the finest hotels in Switzerland. You'll have a hard time competing with me."

"I don't plan to compete. I plan to hire you, Miss Johnson. I can pay you twice what you must be earning in that little sweatshop of yours." He opened a palm pilot, studying the calendar before placing it in front of her and pointing to the date. "One year from today, Miss Johnson, and you'll be begging me for a job."

"I sincerely doubt that." Kayli forced her gaze from the PDA.

Adam cleared his throat. "This is a date, Mr. Williams. You know—a guy-girl thing. Do you mind? I'm not on the clock."

Mike laughed. "Okay, okay. I know when I'm not wanted."

Doubtful, thought Kayli.

"Just so you know, Miss Johnson—I don't take any offense at your refusal. I know that down the road things will look different. I'm a businessman. I don't let my personal feelings get in the way. Enjoy your dinner." Mike pulled at his sleeve and disappeared from the restaurant.

"Charming, ain't he?" Adam smirked.

Kayli tossed a hand. "It's not worth thinking about. Let's order." She looked up at him. His eyes were filled with pity. She felt her stomach turn. "I will win," Kayli said again, but this time her voice quavered.

"When I'm gone to Montana, you'll have to write and let me know how it goes."

"Why are you so eager to get back?" Kayli bit her lip.

"Someone waits for me in Montana. I must go back, and I must go with money. I have no more options than you do, Kayli. I hoped I'd see a friendly face when I saw your fish sign in the window. I hope I was right."

Kayli straightened. "I'm not at the mercy of Mike Williams, and neither are you."

"Oh, but you are." Adam's firm jaw hardened. "You're like a calf being dragged to the branding iron. You don't realize it yet. Excuse my pessimism, but I'm beginning to wonder if I'll ever cut loose."

"Well, I'm sure whoever waits for you back in Montana will wait a little longer." *I would,* Kayli wanted to add.

"I have to go to a dinner next Saturday night. Mike is celebrating the grand opening of his luxurious home. Would you care to come?"

"Will this affect whoever waits in Montana?"

"Not in the least, unfortunately. Come with me. You can infiltrate the enemy's camp." Adam laughed.

Kayli was about to answer when the waiter returned. He rambled off specials in some barely discernible English and waited for the two of them to order. Kayli ordered a modest ravioli dish, while Adam opted for rigatoni. Neither ordered an appetizer.

"How did you come to work for Mike Williams?"

"His wife was an old girlfriend of mine during high school. She's from Montana. She knew I was struggling in Montana and called to help."

Kayli heard herself sigh aloud. "You're still friends?"

"What better way to show me how much wealth and how successfully she married? Can you think of a more elaborate plan to disregard an ex than to offer him a job working for your husband?" Adam sat back in his chair.

"Surely you didn't have to take it."

"Oh, but I did, and Andrea knew it." Adam's eyes flickered, and Kayli pondered his conversation. So free with some pieces of information, so private about others. He seemed a man rooted in turmoil, and yet she felt even more attracted to him. As complex as he seemed, there appeared a simplicity, a line so true that she couldn't run. But she knew she probably should have.

"I'll go with you next week, if you're not embarrassed to have me in front of Andrea. I imagine she's quite glamorous."

"She's that and more. But I won't say anything else. I'll let you decide for yourself, and you could show up in a sack and be perfectly beautiful."

Kayli ignored the comment. "Are you over her?"

"I'm that and more." Adam grinned. "Somehow I suddenly have the heart for three-dollar coffees and French pastry." He winked.

"I thought you were an apple-pie man."

"I'll wait for my mother's."

"No, you don't. You promised you'd give me another shot. Next Friday evening you come in after work. I'll make you an apple pie you won't soon forget."

"I think I'll have a hard time forgetting you anyway, Kayli. With or without a pie." He smoothed the tablecloth before him, avoiding her gaze. Whatever secrets Adam Harper held close to his heart, Kayli longed to discover them. Even if it cost her, and it surely would.

Chapter 4

Kayli set about her apple pie with renewed fervor. She nibbled on her bottom lip as she focused on getting the consistency of the dough right. She covered her marble roller with flour and smoothed the pastry to a thin sheath. Mrs. Heiden's sigh interrupted the careful operation. Kayli placed a fist on her hip. "What?"

Mrs. Heiden put her head down, shaking it while wiping down the countertops. "What was this big plan you had to steal all the business from the new restaurant? Free samples, advertising, promotion? It's been a week."

"I'm working on it." Kayli pointed to her head. "But first I have to finish this pie."

"I think you've finally gone crazy, Missy. In a few short months, a monster bakery is opening, and yet you're competing with an unknown house frau from Montana."

"I am not competing. I'm only trying to prove myself as a baker."

"To whom? This is the equivalent of a dog marking his territory. Nothing more." Mrs. Heiden's sour expression erupted.

Kayli giggled aloud. "You're right, Mrs. Heiden. I am avoiding the inevitable. Let me top this pie and slip it in the oven. I'll get started on the ad blitz."

Mrs. Heiden looked over the pie, her eyebrows raised. "What, no cow?"

Kayli crinkled her nose. "A bit over the top, didn't you think?" Actually Kayli thought the cow was cute, but she didn't have time for such frivolity. The pie's taste would speak for itself this time.

"As if you ever listened to what I think. Seventy-two years of living I've done—you don't think I learned something?"

Kayli embraced Mrs. Heiden loosely. "I think you've learned a lot, probably more than you'll ever teach my hard head."

"You can say that again." Mrs. Heiden rearranged the remaining pastries from the morning, allowing the display to appear fuller and fresher. "I've spent ten years alone now. And I liked being married better. I want the same for you, Princess. You'll work yourself to the bone on this bakery and have nothing to show for it in the end. You only think you've received what you want by quitting the hotel, but this business will never satisfy. I know you, Kayli. You want it all. Ask God for it."

That was as close as Mrs. Heiden would ever come to true warmth. It brought a lump to Kayli's throat. The elder woman set about helping a customer until he ordered a cappuccino, and then she complained about the newfangled machinery that only young people could operate.

Kayli prayed silently that she would learn to concentrate on the things that mattered. Competing with an unknown baker in a far-off state seemed much easier than planning for the possible demise of her business. Kayli determined she must seek God more about His plans.

She wished to be married. Someday. But not to just anyone. Not to the first man who courted her properly, as Mrs. Heiden would suggest, but someone who sent her heart ablaze. Someone God ordained as her life partner. Kayli wanted to start with fireworks and explosions and work into faithful and loving. Was that too much to ask?

The front bell rang, and Kayli looked up to see Adam's towering frame. His smile set her heart pounding, and she took an audible breath. This is how she wanted to feel when she looked at her husband. His clear green eyes spoke to her, saying things his mouth might never utter. Whatever secrets Adam held close to his heart, his eyes didn't lie. Honest and shining, the emotion in his eyes connected with her. He didn't speak, and neither did Kayli. She took it all in, allowing this moment, this silent union, to continue. He'd been in for several cappuccinos during the week, and they barely spoke but said volumes.

"I hope you are not here for your pie yet," Mrs. Heiden barked.

"No." Adam shook his head. "Actually I came for the coffee. The normal stuff."

"Good. I can get that." Mrs. Heiden took a paper cup while Adam stared at Kayli. She didn't realize how much she was looking forward to Saturday night until she saw him again. Her instincts told her this was the man for her while her head told her otherwise, for how could he be if he was leaving town? Kayli had a thriving business. At least she did for now. Adam Harper had come to California to make his money and leave. He couldn't be the one, no matter how much wishful thinking Kayli might do.

"Tomorrow night still okay with you?"

Kayli nodded. "I'm looking forward to it. I bought a new dress," she blurted out.

"Mike's house is grand. I'll enjoy showing you my handiwork there. He spared no expense, and it was a contractor's dream to have free rein."

"So Mike isn't all bad."

Adam shook his head. "He's made his money in this corporate culture. He wants every town across America to look the same." Adam shrugged. "A lot of people agree with him. I happen to like towns with individual personality. I like the little mom-and-pop shops, not the same menu everywhere. It comes down to having options, which people are quickly eliminating with the box-store culture." Adam frowned.

Kayli searched Adam's eyes, willing the butterflies in her stomach away. "I'm glad. I bet it's the same with houses for you. It's like building a tract house over a custom home, I imagine."

"Now you understand."

"Your pie is baking. About another hour I'd say." Kayli lifted out a small mansion she'd created of chocolate. "This is for another millionaire celebrating his new home." She longed to turn the conversation to something she didn't have to stumble over.

"No shortage of egos in this town." Adam clicked his tongue. "Your work is beautiful though. I'd never thought I'd meet my equal in building, but your chocolate creations put me to shame." He laughed. "Shall I pick you up here tomorrow night?"

"No, I'll start doing something if I wait here. I'll probably end up with flour on my gown, so why don't you come by the house?" Kayli wrote her address on a scrap of paper.

"Here's my card again, in case you lost it." Adam reached into his pocket. She grasped it tightly, brushing his hand in the process. A current ran through her arm, and she saw the same question in his eyes that she heard swirling in her own head. Perhaps this attraction was too powerful. He took the cup of coffee and placed the money in Mrs. Heiden's hands. "I'll see you at the end of the day for my mouth-watering pie."

Kayli nodded, watching as he strode toward the door.

"That is not good," Mrs. Heiden said. "No good can come of that. You two have too much fire. Robert is a nice steady man. You need to find one like him. Adam is too dangerous for you."

"Adam's a Christian, Mrs. Heiden."

"He's dangerous. Too good-looking. You find a nice, homely man, Kayli. They make good husbands."

Kayli laughed. "I don't want a lap dog. I want a husband. What if I don't have a choice?"

"You always have a choice, Kayli. You go and have a nice evening tomorrow with Mr. Fire. Then you find someone worth having for a lifetime."

"Is someone worth having if you don't want him?"

Mrs. Heiden tossed a hand. "You young people! You're too spoiled for your own good. In my day we didn't expect so much."

Robert ambled in, and Kayli felt guilty, as if he might have sensed the conversation. His squared glasses complemented his innocuous face. *Loving a man like Robert would be easy,* Kayli thought. *He'd love you back—you'd get married—end of story. Why must I always take the hard route?*

Robert scratched his beard. "You look guilty."

Kayli brushed the flour from her apron. "Why should I?"

He cleared his throat, and Mrs. Heiden stepped into the back room. "I have a date on Saturday."

Robert had a date? Relief flooded Kayli. Robert must finally understand that friendship was all the two of them would ever share. She hoped so; he was far too sweet to hurt.

"That's wonderful, Robert."

"She has a brother. Thought you might be interested in joining us. It might not be so uncomfortable. It's been a long time since I went on a date. I know if you went along, I'd be my charming self."

Kayli groaned. "Oh, Robert, I'm sorry, but I have plans. I've been invited to Mike Williams's new house with the contractor. Can you believe I finally have something to do on Saturday night?"

"The cowboy?"

She nodded.

"Well, this guy is an engineer. He's a solid Christian and taller than you. What more do you need? Surely not some backwoods builder who has nothing in common with you. Cancel your date—it'll go nowhere. Come out with me. I'm a good judge of character for you."

Kayli laughed. "Your engineer sounds great. This isn't really a date on Saturday. I'm going to see the work he's done on the house and maybe get to know Mike Williams more. Maybe if I just talk with Mr. Williams, we can come to some type of agreement on the bakery. He can't want to divide the business either." Kayli wished she could believe the words, but saying them aloud almost made things worse. Robert seemed to realize it immediately.

"I think you're beyond optimistic if you think you can reason with him. He has a reputation in the city, but I understand your need to try. Maybe we could reschedule. The engineer sounded very interested in meeting you."

"Yes, that would be good. Adam will be returning to Montana in about two and a half months. Maybe we could do it then."

"You're not going to put your social life on hold?"

"No, of course I'm not. I thought I'd like to be with him while he's here. It's lonely in the city. Hard to get to know people. I thought I might invite him to the singles' group at church. Does this engineer have a name?"

"John Hanson. He's a nice guy, Kayli."

"Well, tell John for me that I'm sorry I already had plans. It sounds like a wonderful evening out. Where'd you meet John Hanson's sister?"

"At the opera in the park. She was walking her bulldog. It caught my attention. Her brother seems like a real catch, Kayli. Stop chasing after the next Mel Gibson. You don't get married only on feelings."

"Good advice!" Mrs. Heiden called from the back room. "Your pie is burning."

Kayli gasped. "See you, Robert! I have to run." She sprinted to the back ovens and opened to see her pie a perfect golden brown. The pie had bubbled over and spilled onto a protective cookie sheet, filling the room with a luscious caramel aroma. "Perfect."

Mrs. Heiden came behind her. "Yes, it looks fine, but I miss the cow."

"I did these fall leaves instead. Don't you think that's pretty?" Kayli tilted the pie toward Mrs. Heiden and with dread watched as it slowly slid off the cookie sheet. Kayli tried to grip it but screamed at the searing heat. The pie landed with a hot splat, erupting with volcanic force, leaving its golden lava on cabinets and in droplets on their pant legs. Kayli sucked on her finger then placed it in a pat of butter on the counter.

Mrs. Heiden said nothing. She lifted her eyebrows in her familiar way and walked off to clean her slacks. Kayli surveyed the mess, unable to believe she'd destroyed another pie. She reached down to clean the counters but realized the filling was still too hot to clean. Sliding to the floor, she decided to wait beside the mess.

"He's going to think I'm a complete idiot." Her forehead

fell into her hands. "Why am I trying to impress this man? He's leaving, he's too good-looking for his own good, and he's building my doom. Could I have worse taste in a man?"

"Kayli, I have seen you talk to yourself more this week than in my entire five years of knowing you. This man is making you crazy. That's the first sign you need to move on. Meet the engineer. He sounds nice. And stable."

"Stable. That's what you want in furniture, Mrs. Heiden. I want something a bit more exciting in a husband." Kayli felt a tear escape down her cheek. She looked at the pie like the remnant of her social life. "Do you really think I'm not capable of meeting a man who sends me soaring? You don't believe there's a soul mate for me? I'm just supposed to settle down with a good selection of sturdy male?"

Mrs. Heiden bent and put an arm around her. "Sure I think someone is out there for you, Sweetheart, but soul mates aren't built on mutual attraction alone. That's all I'm trying to say. I don't want to discourage you, but certainly this pie fiasco is a bad omen."

Kayli began to laugh. "What am I going to tell him?"

"Tell him you have a dynamite tiramisu on special."

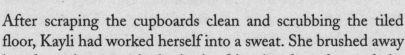

After scraping the cupboards clean and scrubbing the tiled floor, Kayli had worked herself into a sweat. She brushed away her damp bangs with the back of her hands and tossed the final rag into the mop sink. The bell jingled again, and Mrs. Heiden harrumphed. It had to be Adam.

Kayli decided against checking her reflection and made her way to the front counter. Her pants were still splattered with apple remains, and she pulled herself up at the shoulders.

Adam's eyebrow lifted, and he crossed his arms.

"I'm taking it this means my pie isn't ready."

"It's been postponed." She jutted her chin forward, forcing a confident stance. "There was a little trouble with the oven." *I put an apple pie in it,* she added silently. "I have incredible chocolates available. Why don't you take a truffle or two?"

He shook his head. "I'm not much of a sweet eater anyway. It's just that apple pie brings thoughts of home. I thought it might be nice to try yours."

Yes, wouldn't it, though?

"It's not a big deal, Kayli." Adam shifted uncomfortably. "I'll be going home soon for a visit. I can have one then."

Kayli stamped her foot. "I'm determined to make you an apple pie."

"Even if it blows up your business?"

Kayli squinted. "I have a beautiful apple and peach tart here. It's certainly not me. It's your order that's jinxed."

"You know, there's a Baker's Corner up the street. I can pick up a pie there."

Mrs. Heiden gasped. "You're throwing pearls before swine, Kayli. He isn't good enough for your pie—if he could eat a corporate pie and compare the two."

Kayli looked at her employee, thankful for the offered support. But at the sight of Mrs. Heiden's cuffs filled with apple sludge, the comments did more harm than good. It only brought attention to the fact that Kayli had painted everything a sticky apple brown.

Adam laughed. He tried to cover his mouth, but his shoulders started to shake. He put a palm in the air. "I'm sorry," he said between choking laughter.

"You are taking home chocolate, and I don't care if you're

allergic to the stuff. You are going to eat it, praise it, and know I am the finest baker in Palo Alto." She watched him through her narrowed eyes, daring him to continue laughing.

His shoulders soon stilled, and he took out his wallet.

"Put it away. This is on the house. The compliments, however, will cost you. Write them down if you have to."

He shook his head rapidly. "That's okay. I'm sure I'll remember them."

Kayli took out a gold foil and wrapped a slice of tiramisu and one truffle. "There's enough fat in here to keep you going for a week. I expect you to eat both."

"Are we still on for tomorrow night?"

"Absolutely. You owe me, Adam Harper. I have made exact replicas in chocolate of the Eiffel Tower, Mount Rushmore, even the White House. Your pie will not beat me—do you understand?"

"I think so. Am I going to get the red earth of Tara speech now?"

"Adam Harper, you take this chocolate and devour it. Then pick me up tomorrow with compliments at the ready." Kayli raised her eyebrows playfully. "I'll get your pie one of these days."

"I will wait until I go home for Thanksgiving. It is not important."

"Oh, yes, it is. It's very important now that you think I can't do it."

"Andrea couldn't make an apple pie. I almost married her."

"I can make an apple pie, the best pie you ever tasted, in fact. My timing is just off. This has undermined my confidence. But I'll get it back, and you'll be begging me for another slice."

He came around the counter. Mrs. Heiden threw him daggers through her glances, but Kayli noted Adam didn't appear to notice. He placed his solid hand on Kayli's shoulder, and she gulped at his touch.

"I'm terrible with words, Kayli. That's why I work with my hands. I don't care about the pie. I only ordered it so I could see you again."

"But I really can make an incredible pie. I want to prove it to you."

"How about you prove that you're there under all that sticky film? Would you do that for me?" His green gaze upon her caused her heart to stir again. She closed her eyes.

An engineer would be so simple, a man who wanted to settle down, have a dog, maybe a couple of kids. Adam Harper wanted too much: a life in the country, corporate money to build his cabin, and a woman like his own mother. Kayli could fulfill none of that criteria, so why didn't she end this here and now?

"Kayli?" he whispered.

"I'll clean up. We'll enjoy ourselves tomorrow night. I'll get into Mike Williams's command center, and we'll get out for an evening. One night out of our lives—it's a fine deal."

He frowned. "That's not exactly what I meant."

"No, but it's best for both of us." Kayli watched as Mrs. Heiden turned the open sign around in the shop window and locked the deadbolt.

"I suppose you're right about that." Adam looked back to the door, taking his hand from her shoulder. "I'd better go. I'll pick you up tomorrow at six."

Mrs. Heiden stood at the door, a warden in the waiting. Adam strode toward the door, and she unlocked it with a grimace. She closed it with fervor behind him. "Good riddance to him."

"I think you like him, Mrs. Heiden. You're as taken in by

his charms as I am."

"Tsk." She clicked her tongue. "That will be the day. If you go out with him tomorrow night"—she wagged her forefinger—"well, you deserve to fall in love with the likes of him."

Kayli grinned.

Chapter 5

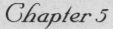

A dam adjusted his tie and buttoned the lower button on his sport coat. Satisfied this was as good as it would get, he started toward his Jeep. He had thought the rugged vehicle would be out of placc in high tech Silicon Valley, but plenty of engineers were driving Jeeps and foreign SUVs. Most had leather interiors and never touched a dirt road, however. Adam had seen plenty of mud on his four-wheel drive, and the shredded seats were testament to the fact his vehicle had visited plenty of job sites in its day. He hoped Kayli wouldn't be embarrassed to show up at Mike Williams's mansion in such a chariot.

Adam sighed thinking about Kayli. Her fresh-looking skin and dark hair mesmerized him. Her dark brown eyes were al-most a russet color, big and wide and completely unaware of their effect on him. When he first looked into those eyes, he nearly forgot all his reasons for being in Silicon Valley, casting aside the fact that he would be going home someday soon. The warmth in those eyes arrested his attention and wouldn't let him go. Even though he knew he should before he got in too deep.

He smiled about the pie. He never doubted her abilities, but it touched his heart she couldn't complete the task, which had to be simple to her. For every pie she annihilated, Adam had one more reason to come back to her pleasant European bakery. He would have known Kayli was a believer even without the fish in the shop window. Adam's spiritual gift of discernment told him the Holy Spirit dwelled within that shop. Comfort and a feeling of home emanated from the place, something Mike Williams's monster restaurant would never be able to duplicate.

He drove up to Kayli's apartment. It was obvious which was hers. A small cluster of lights lined the walk, each of them a cappuccino cup holding a tiny bulb. The stone path led to a bright red door with an intricate beveled glass window at the top. He rapped on the door, and Kayli opened it immediately.

Adam felt his jaw drop at the sight of her. He groped for words, trying to take in her beauty, which was so contrary to fashion. Black seemed to be the only color a woman wore out at night in the Bay Area, but Kayli wore a simple linen sheath in bright apple green. It wasn't a color most women could wear, but on Kayli it looked radiant. She would be the envy of every woman in the room, with her slender figure in the simple dress. Neither sequins nor diamonds nor designer labels would equal the picture Kayli created.

"Excuse my stunned silence. You look amazing." He stammered over the words. How many men with fancy words must have told her the same thing? He probably sounded like some backcountry farmer to her. He felt perplexed by her beauty, unable to wrestle his tongue free to say what he thought. He swallowed hard and forced a shaky grin.

She blushed, turning away. "You mustn't spoil me with such sweet words. I may begin to believe them, and then where will you be?"

"I hope you do believe them. I can't be the only man who's ever told you, but I am the most sincere."

She turned her chin upward, gazing at him with a look that nearly stole his breath. "I wish I could believe you, but you have all the charm of William Holden." She fiddled with her hands. "William Holden starred in *Sabrina*. I'm an old movie fan." She cleared her throat. "I'll get my sweater." The closet door swung toward him.

It took all his will not to reach out to her and put her at ease. He planted his feet in the doorway, determined to fight the rising feelings within him. He longed to kiss her, to take her away from California forever, and bring her back to his Montana home. But that was barbaric and ridiculous. He barely knew her, and when she found out his reason for going home, she would disappear like the loose flour in the bakery. Yet he saw them together, watching classic movies and growing old together.

"Are you nervous about seeing Andrea tonight?" she asked.

"No, as a matter of fact, I hadn't thought of it until you brought it up. I loved Andrea once—for all the wrong reasons. The next time I fall in love, it will be for the right reasons."

"Which are?"

"A woman who loves me despite my bank account. A woman who can deal with what I must grapple with in Montana, and one whose beauty lies both inside and out."

"I hope such a woman exists."

"I'm sure she exists. The question is, would she have anything to do with me?" They both laughed.

Kayli came close to him, turning her back to him and handing him her sweater. He felt the electricity from her. It was as if being next to her created its own current. He placed the sweater around her shoulders, leaving his hands there for a moment longer than necessary. Almost unconsciously he embraced her, putting his head beside hers, and whispered in her ear. "I wish I could explain what I feel for you so suddenly, Kayli, but I think that might be hazardous."

He heard her swallow. "We should be going." She walked quickly, her heels clicking on the entryway's tile. She waited for him to exit and locked the door behind them, keeping her gaze from matching his own. Why had he been so forward?

Once in the car, their conversation stalled. Adam didn't know what to say, but he also didn't feel it necessary to speak. Kayli beside him said enough. A short drive deposited them on the tree-lined streets of Los Altos Hills, an elegant enclave of mansions. Each bigger and more elaborate than the one built below it on the hill. Even in the dark night, the city was lit up like a thousand stars.

Driving up the long drive, Adam's stomach churned. Kayli would only realize how different he was from her, how he didn't belong here. He hoped she wouldn't hold it against him—at least not for the evening. He wanted tonight to go perfectly.

The house lay before them like a mighty Mediterranean fortress. A rose pink, it practically glowed in the carefully planned landscaping, even though night had descended. Sixteen million the house cost to build, and not nearly enough of it had gone into Adam's pocket. He felt almost ashamed he'd been part of its construction. Once he thought it would be the flagship of his company, a testament to his building skills. Now it felt like disgusting excess.

"There it is, Silicon Valley's newest tribute to the almighty dollar."

Kayli placed a hand on his. "It's a beautiful house, Adam. You should be very proud of your work."

He didn't feel proud; he felt mortified, but he tried to justify himself. "I'd like you to see the inside. Outside is quite tacky, but not a detail within has been left unturned. I used every bit of experience I'd gleaned to build this house. If you can overlook its size, you'll see it really is very homey—once you get into the actual living area, the parts of the house that aren't for show."

A hired man opened the car door and let Kayli out. Adam pulled the tie loose from his neck and came around to grasp her arm. "You're shaking."

"I'm a bit nervous. I've never been in such a mansion as this, and I'm fearful of meeting Andrea. What will you tell her about me?"

"I'll tell her how fortunate she is to live in such a well-built house and to excuse me for bringing in a woman who will outshine her."

Kayli playfully hit him. "Oh, stop. You will do no such thing."

"I won't, but I should. You'll surpass every woman here in that dress."

"It was twenty-nine dollars at the clearance store," Kayli whispered. "The sweater was free with purchase."

He laughed. "A woman after my own heart. It goes to show you—beauty can't be purchased."

"From the looks of this house, I'd say it can."

"You can't buy taste, Kayli. This house, though big, is tacky. Admit it."

"No."

"You'll admit it when you see the brass and beveled glass elevator inside."

"Tell me you're kidding."

"Apparently carrying the poodle up the stairs got to be too

much for them." Adam shrugged, and Kayli giggled. The sound of her laughter carried infectiously into the night air. He couldn't tear his gaze from her, until a familiar voice broke the spell.

"Adam, what a pleasant surprise." Andrea met them in the elaborate foyer and held out her diamond-laced fingers. "Who's this?" Her voice held a tinge of disapproval, but Adam shot her a look of warning.

"Andrea Williams, meet Kayli Johnson. Kayli is a European pastry chef in Palo Alto."

Kayli shook hands with Andrea, gripping the jeweled hand in both of her own. "Your gown is exquisite, Mrs. Williams. I appreciate the honor of being able to see your new home."

"Be sure Adam shows you everything. He's full of surprises."

"Hardly," Adam quipped. "I'm pretty stagnant. You've said so yourself, Andrea."

"I think you're full of surprises, Adam." Kayli's voice told him she believed it with her whole heart.

"Mike is around here somewhere. You wouldn't be the little baker on University Avenue, would you, Kayli?" Andrea craned her neck, searching the small crowd. "My husband says he intends to hire you."

Much to her credit, if Kayli was reacting within, she gave no outward sign. "I think your husband intends to hire everyone at some point, Mrs. Williams." Kayli smiled sweetly. Too sweetly.

"How is Rachel, Adam?" Andrea looked to Kayli and this time got a reaction.

Adam winced at how the words affected Kayli. She questioned him now. Why shouldn't she? He hadn't been exactly forthright. Maybe he was full of surprises.

"Rachel is doing fine. Thank you for asking." Adam placed

his palm at the center of Kayli's back, guiding her away from Andrea and her meddling ways.

The strained look in Kayli's expression made him want to spill everything. But what good would that do? In two months' time he would be gone from California for good. This was a date. Nothing more. So why did it feel different? Why was he so drawn to this beautiful pastry chef?

"You have interesting taste in women," Kayli said from out of nowhere.

Adam laughed. "I suppose you mean because I dated Andrea, but that was a long time ago. I've grown up a lot."

Kayli lifted her eyebrows. "So I see."

They entered the main area of the home. The expanse was incredible, with marble making up nearly every surface. He processed thoughts of how troublesome the heavy material had been to move. All of the furniture had that distressed look, making him feel as if he'd entered an ancient tomb. He should feel proud of his work, but in reality he felt humiliation for building a circus tent.

Well-dressed people milled about, sizing up Kayli and Adam, deciding if they were worthy of a conversation. Most would have probably decided no, but Kayli had an aura about her, a light that shined outward, attracting people easily, especially the single men.

"Hello. Alexander Peyton." A hand was thrust toward Kayli. She grasped the hand and returned the greeting, which technically should have been extended toward Adam, but chivalry was dead in Silicon Valley.

"Hi, I'm Kayli Johnson, and this is Adam Harper. He built this beautiful house."

"It's very nice, and what a coincidence—I did all the art."

Alexander nodded toward him. "Adam, would you mind if I showed Kayli my work? I'm so proud of the gallery. Come with me." Alexander Peyton gently guided Adam's date away.

Adam blinked in surprise before noticing Andrea grinning proudly. The tap of her heels echoed on the marble flooring, and the crowds around him felt nonexistent. Like a caged animal he longed to rip off his tie and escape before this hunt continued.

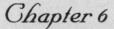

Chapter 6

Alexander Peyton appeared to have little interest in whether Kayli enjoyed art. It didn't take a genius to figure out Alexander's tour had ulterior motives. Andrea Williams had a distinct and current interest in Adam Harper, and Kayli was merely a barrier. The gallery owner, Alexander, represented nothing more than a pawn sent to do Mistress Williams's bidding.

Kayli eyed Adam warily. Was he a part of this? He didn't seem like the type to use a woman, much less carry on some type of affair with a married woman. Whatever secrets Adam held, Kayli couldn't believe they had anything to do with Mrs. Williams. But maybe she was only casting wishes. His handsome features blurred Kayli's reality a bit.

"Have you known Mrs. Williams long?" Kayli asked the hulky gallery owner.

He spoke in a foreign accent Kayli couldn't place. He was incredibly handsome but appeared very aware of that fact with silver blond hair and brilliant, icy blue eyes. While he explained each art selection in the home, his attention seemed to drift continually to his preferred piece: the mirror.

"Mrs. Williams began shopping my store before she had

the husband to pay for such works. She has a fantastic eye, and it's only right she should have the money to pay for such beauty. Do you like this one?" He stopped in front of a large painting. "It is my favorite."

Kayli focused on the artwork before her. She cocked her head, trying to make heads or tails of the colors. Surely the artist was trying to say something, but Kayli thought it must be something about misery because that's what she felt staring at it. "I'm not an art critic, but the colors depress me. I studied quite a bit of artwork when I lived in Paris, and I never was too fond of the abstracts. I guess my taste runs to the more simplistic landscapes and portraits."

"All people say that at first. It is not for everyone to understand, but with time and depth, you would understand."

"What should I understand about this piece?" Kayli moved closer to the barrage of color. She eyed it thoughtfully, trying to see the message.

"Besides that it's worth twenty thousand?" he asked with a haughty laugh.

"Yes, besides that," Kayli answered, unimpressed that anyone would waste money on this callous piece of art when they could have fed thousands with the money. "What do you think the artist was trying to convey?"

"Well, I don't know, Kayli. What does it say to you?"

Kayli crossed her arms and drew in a deep breath. "I find it simplistic and drab. I believe the artist must have been saying he's at a low emotional point in his life, and he needs some spiritual guidance. Perhaps you might lend him a Bible."

The gallery owner exploded into laughter. "And you say you aren't a critic. It goes to show you that everyone's a critic. Mrs. Williams finds this piece contemplative and earnest."

"I think I would be more contemplative about spending twenty thousand dollars on a piece of art. No offense—I realize that's what you do. I hear all the time how ridiculous it is that a truffle should cost two dollars."

Alexander grinned. "I think, my dear Kayli, that this ex-boyfriend of Mrs. Williams has done far better for himself. But you didn't hear that from me. But I do hope to see you in my gallery one day." He excused himself and went to greet more potential buyers.

Kayli turned to see Andrea whispering in Adam's ear. Kayli felt the hair on the back of her neck rise. Whether or not Adam had any interest in Kayli, she wasn't about to sit back and watch him carry on with a married woman. As a Christian she answered to a higher authority. At least that's what she told herself was the reason for interrupting the tête-à-tête.

Marching deliberately toward the cozy couple, Kayli watched Adam straighten and pull away from Andrea. He pulled at his sleeves and jutted his squared jaw toward Kayli. Her resolve weakened a bit watching the action. He was uncomfortable and appeared almost grateful for her presence.

Kayli put a smile on her face. "Mrs. Williams, I've had quite an interesting encounter with your gallery owner. Alexander is a fascinating man and went on about your impeccable taste. I find it very different from mine but can appreciate your theme here." Kayli grasped Adam's arm and tugged him slightly away from Andrea. "Clearly we have the same taste in some things."

Andrea's eyes flashed. "Alexander failed to show you the gallery up on the landing. That is where his work is seen at its finest. Why don't you run along and catch him?"

"While I love the art of an artist, there is no artist like

God. Don't you think? The human biceps are a work of magnificence." Kayli ran her fingertips down Adam's arm and casually pulled him away from the married woman. It took willpower to keep from digging her nails into his powerful arm. "Keep walking," she whispered.

Away from the crowd, Adam pulled her into an empty room. He found a light and turned it on to reveal a complete theater with rows of seats and a large screen.

"What was that about?" Adam raised his brows.

"Listen." Kayli felt her hands shaking. "What you do with your time is your business, but if you profess to be a Christian, it's best that you not be seen on the arm of a married woman. It's inappropriate, not to mention that your boss, and her husband, certainly wouldn't appreciate it." Kayli crossed her arms to stop the trembling and flopped into an oversized theater chair. She looked around her and sniffed. The room was almost eggplant in color, a deep purple resembling a big, ugly bruise.

Adam pulled her back to her feet. "Are you accusing me of something, Kayli?"

Kayli felt her eyes fill with tears, and she blinked them away. "I'm just saying if you invite a woman to an event, it's appropriate to stay with her. I believe you cowfolks would say, 'Ya got to dance with the girl that brung ya.'"

Adam's smile made Kayli's tears more insistent. He brushed one away from her cheek. "You're absolutely right," he whispered.

"Don't sweet-talk me, Adam. I'm not a fool. If you brought me here as your cover, I will not play that game."

"Kayli, you've got this wrong."

"I won't be played like a pull toy. Whatever disgusting thing you and Andrea have going, keep me out of it. I may not like Mike Williams, but I wouldn't hurt him this way."

He cupped her face with his roughened hands. "Do you really think that's what I'm doing? Kayli, look at me."

Kayli's shakiness became obvious, and she clenched her jaw, which only caused her teeth to clatter. "I don't know what you're doing, Adam. Unlike you I don't have much experience with dating. I guess in my mind I made you out to be something you're not."

He let out a small laugh. "What is it you think I am?"

"I have no idea." Kayli pulled free and turned away from him. "I thought you were a cowboy out of his element in Silicon Valley, longing for a taste of home, but you seem to work this town just fine. Better than I do, that's for sure."

Adam came behind her, resting his hands on her shoulders. "I am a cowboy. Just longing for an apple pie."

"You seem to know your way around this mansion pretty well."

"Kayli, I built it."

"Well, that's no excuse." Kayli lifted her chin.

He whirled her around. "You're jealous." He forced her gaze to his, and she squeezed her eyes shut, rather than face those gorgeous clear eyes. Eyes that appeared so true and sincere.

"I'm not jealous," she railed. "What do I have to be jealous of? And no offense, but if you're the kind who would carry on an inappropriate friendship with a married woman, well, I wouldn't want you anyway."

"But I'm not the type to do that, and you know it."

She gulped. "No." She shook her head. "No, I don't know it. I wish it, but I don't know it at all."

"Let's get out of here. I'll take you anywhere you want to go, but, Kayli, something is here between us. I can't describe it, but I feel it. When you're next to me—don't get me wrong—it isn't lust; it's this unimaginable feeling that I'm destined to know you. I can feel you next to me."

"So you can leave for Montana and let me battle it out with Mr. and Mrs. Williams and their giant conglomerate bakery?"

"You're avoiding the real subject. You live in one of the most expensive areas in America. You can imagine how everyone wants a piece of the pie, as they say."

"Except these people own the whole pie already, and now they want to dip into a little tiramisu too."

"Competition breeds better product," Adam said confidently.

"Is that how you justify what your building will do to me?"

"I can introduce you to any of these people here tonight, Kayli. You could make enough on the gallery owner's openings alone. You just have to look for other resources."

"What makes you think I want to? I like my business the way it is. I'm not going to change everything into a catering business to assuage your guilt."

"Kayli, stop it." Adam grasped her shoulders. "I didn't ask you out to assuage my guilt, and I'm not going to leave and forget everything I've done to the city of Palo Alto. I'm certainly not going to forget you. Stop avoiding the real issue. What is it between us?"

Kayli felt the undeniable chemistry between them both. An invisible pull that said everything and nothing at all. "You're attractive," she shrugged. "I find you attractive—that's perfectly understandable. You're a fine-looking man." Kayli rambled in her most unaffected voice—when in reality she wanted to explore why she originally thought this man might be her soul mate.

Adam bit his lip, clearly fighting his mirth. "Why were you jealous of Andrea?"

"Because I'm not fond of a man who invites me somewhere

and pawns me off on a gallery owner—who is quite handsome, by the way. What if I went off with him and left you alone at this soiree?"

Adam clicked his tongue. "You're absolutely right, and that would prove my country roots. An educated man would never leave the most beautiful woman in the room for an unavailable tyrant of a woman. Just wouldn't happen." Adam shook his head.

Despite herself Kayli smiled. Squaring her shoulders, she added, "What if I get to know you, like what I see, and you fly back to Montana without looking back? Love is a decision—haven't you heard that?"

"Then you leave me no choice, Kayli."

Adam approached her, and she felt her heart pound. This kind of attraction wasn't healthy. Maybe she needed to go home and call Robert, retreat to the safety of a friendship and the calm life she knew. She couldn't take this kind of attraction forever; it couldn't be good for her heart. Adam bent as though he might kiss her, and Kayli closed her eyes waiting for his lips to mesh with her own.

"Well, there you are." Andrea's firm voice invaded Kayli's dream, and Adam pulled away.

"You have the most impeccable timing, Andrea."

"Countless remodels are out there waiting to speak to you, Adam."

"Let them wait, Andrea. I'm not taking on any additional jobs, so I appreciate the thought, but—"

"Rachel awaits," Andrea added.

"Among other things."

Kayli felt breathless, torn between her emotions for the man she wanted to trust and driven by fears of who he might actually be.

Chapter 7

The party continued well into the night, but it ceased to be fun at the return of Andrea. To his credit Adam stole Kayli away immediately, escorting her to his Jeep without an explanation.

"Come to dinner with me tomorrow night." Adam's voice broke the darkness of the car.

"No," Kayli forced herself to say. "I know what I feel, but I also know what I think. I can't throw my brain out the window. That's how women end up married to men who don't keep promises. They believe them when they know they shouldn't. Well, not me. I listen to my instincts."

"Let me tell you about Rachel. I don't want you to question my motives."

Kayli grabbed his hand on the stick shift. "No. Don't tell me a thing. It's better that I just remain ignorant; then I can go on about my life remembering you only as the man who helped Mike Williams seal my fate. This long evening will fade into a distant memory."

She recoiled at the sight of his sad eyes under the map light. "Is that what you want?" His low voice resonated, and she felt the vibrations in her chest.

"Absolutely," Kayli said before truly answering the question in her heart. It wasn't what she wanted at all. But how did she tell this man she barely knew that his absence would hurt her. That his allegiance to Andrea Williams and an unknown woman named Rachel sent an ache through her soul. How sane was that?

"Fine. I don't need a two-by-four through the head. Consider yourself left alone, Garbo. But it's not my choice, Kayli. It will be solely yours." Adam pulled up to the side of the road, and the little cappuccino lights suddenly looked ridiculous to Kayli. She took no pleasure in her quaint decorations. They made her look that much more naïve.

She sat frozen, knowing she must move. *Get out of the car*, her brain said, but her heart feared reaching for the door. Walking out of Adam's life forever was a big step, and she wasn't sure she was ready for it. *No, I must stick to my resolve.*

"Is something the matter, Kayli?"

"No," Kayli said too quickly. "I'm leaving." She shivered. "It's a little chilly tonight."

"It's seventy-four degrees."

She shrugged. "Must be the dress."

"It certainly does give one chills." He focused out the window as he said it. His structured profile was outlined, illuminated by the street light. The portrait, so like a great piece of Roman art, sent another flutter through her stomach. He turned to face her, and even in the darkness she could see the intensity of his eyes. Those eyes. "You can run, Kayli, but if you don't see this through, you'll never know."

Oddly she didn't need to ask what he meant. She knew. It was the crazy soul mate thing again. Is this what the Lord had for her? All these wild butterflies in her stomach and searing looks from a handsome stranger? It's what she wanted. She'd always said it. Since she was a little girl, she wanted a man to love her with a fiery intensity. Like Christ loved His church. The older she became, the more outlandish such a prayer seemed. Yet Adam seemed to be asking her about that very subject. Dare she ignore it when she longed for the answer?

"I'll make you dinner tomorrow night. Complete with an apple pie," she blurted out.

He smiled, letting out a long breath. "Thank you. I'll bring a Bible and lead a devotional after supper. It will keep us out of trouble."

"I would like that. Why don't we see a movie afterward, so we don't get too comfortable?"

"Perfect." Adam brushed the back of his hand along her cheek. "May I kiss you good night, Kayli?"

She nodded. He came closer, and she felt his breath upon her cheek. He brushed his firm lips against hers, and it seemed over before it began. He stepped out of the car and walked her to the doorway.

"Pray about it, Kayli. I don't understand it either."

"I will." She opened the door and closed it quickly behind her. "What am I doing, Lord? He's going to leave for Montana." She dropped her head against the door. "I know I always said I wanted this passionate, immediate kind of romance, but now I'm not so sure, Lord. Now it just feels dangerous."

The phone rang, interrupting her heartfelt prayer. "Hello?"

"Kayli, it's Robert. How was your date?"

"Different. How about yours?"

"Weird. She didn't talk much. I'm not used to being the one who talks."

"That's because you are usually with me, and I have an opinion on everything," Kayli admitted.

"Very true."

"Are you going out with her again?"

"Yes, sometimes things get off to a slow start. I prayed about it, and she has a solid faith, a good family. I think it's worth pursuing."

"Do you think it can start out fast?"

Robert groaned. "What do you mean, Kayli?"

"I mean, what if you were thrown into this short amount of time, and you felt this urgency to get to know someone."

"God doesn't work on a time line. It sounds dangerous."

"It feels dangerous, Robert."

"Then get out."

"It feels dangerous, but it feels right. We're both committed to purity. That's not the issue. My fear is that I'm ready to fly off with a man I hardly know and live amidst the cows. What's wrong with me?"

"Desperation maybe. Your business is in trouble, and it's been a long time since you've seen anyone seriously. Maybe you're not thinking clearly."

"What about arranged marriages? Sometimes brides and grooms never even see each other before the wedding."

"What on earth are you talking about, Kayli? It was just a date. One evening out and a few weeks of your trying to out-bake his mother. I think rambling about marriage is a little frightening. Our pastor says you should know someone at least a year before you contemplate marriage."

"You're right. You're totally right. And besides, no one is asking me to marry him. For all I know, he's got a couple of ex-wives and eight kids. I'm not thinking clearly."

"Right."

"Coffee after church tomorrow?"

"Sure, at our regular place." Robert clicked the phone, and Kayli breathed a sigh of relief at the steadiness of her friend. Of course she was imagining things. It was desperation over her business, nothing more. It had been a long time since she'd had a date. It felt good to be thought beautiful. That was it: flattery.

Adam pulled up into his driveway, confused and a bit numb. He felt as though he'd met his wife. He knew it in his heart. Yet how could he explain this fact to a complete stranger? *Hi, God sent me to California to find you. Now please come back to my little cabin in the wilderness and live in a place where they've never even heard of tiramisu.*

He laughed at the thought. He needed to tell Kayli about Rachel. That would seal it. Kayli would run for protection, and he would know how ridiculous these thoughts of marriage were. He wasn't the marrying kind. Hadn't his solitary life taught him that? Andrea said he would never learn to be a partner to anyone. He thought too much of himself. That was probably true, but then again Andrea wasn't exactly a great judge of character.

His eyes narrowed in disbelief. Andrea stood on his front porch. Her long, violet gown sparkling under the porch light. He sighed and stood tall. This was going to end. "What are you doing here, Andrea?"

"I see you didn't bring your date home. I knew you wouldn't. Still living the monk's life, Adam?"

"What do you want?" He unlocked the front door and walked past her. She followed him in.

"I think you know what I want."

"Is this a joke? You didn't want me when I didn't have the money to pay for your lifestyle."

"Don't be ridiculous. You dropped me, and you know it."

"Lot of good it did me. Look—it's inappropriate for you to be here." Adam remained cool, but his heart pounded. He and Andrea had never had more than a casual friendship with a slight crush. She made it sound like something vulgar and obviously remembered scenes that had never taken place. Living with Mike Williams had changed Andrea, and it wasn't for the best.

"Inappropriate. That's what you said when I tried to talk to you at the party."

"And it was inappropriate then. I fail to see how meeting me alone at my apartment would be any more suitable. You're a married woman, Andrea. Act like it."

"I'm not going to make a bigger fool out of myself, Adam. I came here because I want to know how much it hurt you when I left. I want to hear how you cried when I married Mike. You give me that, and I'll let this go. But if you continue to pretend I was never the one, I won't let it die. I'll let Mike know exactly what we were to each other. What we are to each other."

"What are you talking about?" Now he truly questioned her sanity. Before she seemed bitter and unrepentant toward her husband, but now she seemed incapable of living in reality.

"He's worth more to me divorced than married. That house alone could pay for my lifestyle for an eternity, and I wouldn't have to put up with the slobbering idiot."

"Andrea! Don't say such a vile thought out loud. I haven't been paid for this job yet, and I won't let you imply there's anything between us."

"Why? Because Rachel might find out you were less than a Boy Scout?"

"Because it isn't true. You would let Rachel suffer for your own ego?"

"Tell me how I was the one for you, Adam," she cooed.

He felt his cheek flinch. His mouth would never form such words. But thinking what it might cost Rachel back home in Montana, he swallowed roughly, trying to rid his throat of the terrible lump. "Why would you want me to say that? You belong to another man—that's how God ordained it."

"That's how I ordained it, Adam. I gave up true love for money. You might have thought that was a mistake, but now I can have both. I know you've thought about it. All you have to do is tell me, Adam. Did you think I brought you to California for my health?"

He stared at Andrea with a man's eyes. She was beautiful on the outside, the peak of fitness with elegant, luminous skin, but inside her heart was dead. Frosted over by years of ignoring God's call and neglect by a husband who bought her affections, but now cared little for what she did. Adam tried to keep the contempt from his face and tried to see her as the pathetic figure she was. Cheated on by Mike Williams, who apparently thought she was nothing more than a possession. She was ripe for vengeance. Adam seemed to hold the key to her retaliation.

"I think you brought me to California on a lie. What we had was a long time ago, Andrea. It was special when we were younger, but that was a lifetime ago. You don't really love me. I'm a builder. I will always be a builder. I know you don't respect that."

"But it doesn't matter now, Adam. I have enough money for both of us."

He reached for her hand. "If you think I ever cared about money, you never really knew me."

"I know you need the money now. I know Rachel needs it, and if you want payment from Mike, you'll do what's right."

"No." Adam shook his head. "I would never do what you

consider right. I love Kayli."

She cackled. "You can't possibly love Kayli. You've been on what, one date?"

"I don't expect you to understand it. I don't understand it."

She placed a key in his hand. "The guesthouse. Make your choice, Adam. You've got until Tuesday."

Chapter 8

Adam watched Andrea drive away in a black Mercedes. He knelt and prayed vigorously for her. They had been childhood friends, high school crushes, and that's where it should have ended. His ignorance showed in coming to California. He should have known God wouldn't have appreciated the easy route. The fast buck. He would pay for his mistake now. Worse yet, so would Rachel.

Andrea's threat was useless and without merit. Mike Williams was no fool. He would pay up on his contracts or face court. Adam would get his money—eventually. The question was, how long would it take? A scorned husband could make it harder than Adam had time for. He couldn't afford a battle or his boss thinking he'd had anything to do with Andrea's schemes. He prayed over the matter and called Kayli. He wanted to hear her voice. To know all women weren't capable of such lying and wicked games, that a woman out there still enjoyed the simple things in life. One who took joy in decorating the front walk or placing a tiny cow of dough on an apple pie.

The phone rang twice, and Adam breathed a sigh of relief when Kayli's voice sounded alert. "I didn't wake you?" he asked.

He heard the smile in her voice. "No, you didn't wake me.

I was reading a novel. How are you doing? You don't sound so good."

"Andrea was here."

"Andrea—was at your house?" Kayli stammered, and Adam felt the heat flare into his face.

He shouldn't have told Kayli. She'd think he had something to do with it, but the alternative was worse.

"She's really a hurting soul." Adam sounded as though he were justifying Andrea's behavior, and he quickly recanted. "I would feel sorry for her if I didn't fear what she might do."

"You should fear what she might do, Adam. Women don't find their way into Mike Williams's heart without a plan. And they don't find their way out without a better one."

Adam scratched his head. "You couldn't have discerned all that from five minutes of meeting the woman."

"Adam, you must be kidding. We women see so much you men don't. First off, women committed to their husbands don't find a way to be alone with another man at a party. Second, a woman of Andrea's means should have nothing to fear in the likes of me. Andrea has a distinct plan, Adam, and you'd be smart to get out of the way if you value your reputation."

His stomach turned. "Are you saying you think it's time for me to leave?"

"No, I don't want you to leave." She let out a breath. "I want you to stay and tell me more of the beautiful rivers running through Montana. I want to hear about the trains to the old mining camps and exploring the ghost towns."

"How much time do you have?" He heard a thump.

"My book just got boring."

They talked of childhoods and dreams and shared hopes until Adam made the mistake of returning to a hard subject.

"Listen, about Andrea."

"I don't care about her, Adam."

"But you need to know. She's up to no good, and I don't want you to believe her." He didn't add that Andrea planned to thwart his payment unless he cooperated. Kayli wouldn't have believed any woman capable of that.

"Adam, one thing I've learned about you in these two weeks. You are not a man who takes the easy route. You have yet to see an apple pie, but you keep showing up, somehow believing one day it's going to be there. "

"It will be. I'm certain of that because I believe in you, Kayli."

"You'd be smarter to believe in God and let Him handle the rest." Her tone had a chill in it, and Adam started.

"What?" Adam looked into the phone, unsure of what Kayli was trying to say.

"You're leaving, Adam. I've got you what, two months, tops? I feel as if for once in my life, I have someone whose opinion I really value. Someone who makes me feel like a princess. Let me live in my little world. Don't remind me you're leaving. Don't remind me a woman named Rachel is waiting back home."

"Rachel is—"

"No," she said, stopping him. "Don't tell me. I told you I want to live in my little world. In two months I'll go back to being Kayli Johnson, struggling pastry chef. Today I want to be Kayli Johnson, princess, or none of this is worth it. I want to be the woman who arrives on the arm of Adam Harper, rugged builder and envy of Mike Williams. A modern-day prom queen."

He felt stunned and tense. What was Kayli telling him? Why did she want him to play this charade? He didn't toy with women's hearts. He was steadfast and true. Yet he looked at the trail of women around him: Rachel, Andrea, and now

Kayli. What did it matter if he saw himself as steadfast when others saw him as divided and noncommittal?

"I can't join you for dinner tomorrow night, Kayli." *I'm not worthy.*

He thought he heard a small whimper, but her resonant voice came back to him. "It's just as well." A light click followed.

Kayli arrived at the coffee shop after church. Robert wasn't there yet, so she ordered a nonfat double mocha, anxious to thwart the pounding headache she attributed to caffeine withdrawal and a long night on the telephone.

She wouldn't give Adam Harper the benefit of knowing it was he who caused her pain. Why would she get involved with a man like him anyway? She'd only listened to that chemical fusion between them, their shared hopes for three children and a mom who stayed home. She hadn't given any credence to the facts. She was sure she'd heard God's voice and that He'd been in favor of the courtship; yet she supposed today was proof He wasn't.

"Hey!" Robert waved at her, bringing in another woman. Another era ended. Their Sunday mornings at the coffee shop had been sacred, a time to regroup, and Robert had never allowed someone else to invade their time.

"Hi!" Kayli forced a chipper tone. "Who's this?"

Robert's eyes reprimanded her, forcing her to be polite. "This is Joanie Hanson."

Kayli tried to smile. Joanie was entirely too bouncy for someone who hadn't had coffee yet. "Nice to meet you, Kayli. I understand you and Robert have been friends a long time."

"We have," Kayli said flatly. "But apparently not long enough." She flashed her eyes, and he pulled her by the waist.

"We'll just order coffee, Joanie. Why don't you save our table? Latte?" The redhead nodded. "Great." He drew Kayli into line and stood behind her. "So you want to tell me why you can't be decent to my friend?"

"Robert, this is our time. What's she doing here?"

"I saw her at church after our date last night, and she asked to come along. You can't have your way forever, Kayli. You made your choice about me a long time ago."

"What does that have to do with our friendship?"

"It has everything to do with it. I'm not going to turn down the opportunity for a girlfriend and possibly a spouse in order to be at your beck and call anymore. Your heart was apparently stolen overnight, so you'd best not chastise me."

Shame washed over Kayli like extra foam through a latte. The reason she understood Andrea's actions had nothing to do with being a woman. It was being a woman like her.

"My heart was not stolen." Kayli crossed her arms. "It was temporarily misguided."

"Things are working out with Joanie and me. Why can't you deal with that?" The cut in Robert's words hurt her. Was she so selfish as to deny her best friend a woman of his own? Simply because no man wanted her?

"I suppose I have to." Kayli's coffee came up, and she reached for it. "Tell Joanie I said good-bye. No sense being a third wheel." She turned, making her way through the tables of countless people reading the Sunday paper. She heard Robert call after her, but she ignored him. She offered a phony smile and a wave to the sweet little redhead who'd captured Robert's attention and made her way out the door through the sidewalk tables.

She stopped where she was. That's it! As owner of a local small business, she could get Robert to approve sidewalk tables and café rights before Mike Williams opened his business. The city wouldn't allow two such businesses within a block of one another. Kayli dashed home, determined to beat Mike Williams to the punch and force thoughts away of a dashing builder who made her feel like abandoning thoughts of the future as she knew it: as a successful business owner.

A wife and mother, she sniffed as she walked home balancing her coffee. *I'm not meant for that lifestyle. I'm meant for a higher calling—destined to bring European delicacies to the American masses.* She smiled to herself. That had to be it. That's why the Lord had allowed all of this to happen. Kayli was allowed to feel like putty in Adam Harper's arms so she could know that was a mere whim and wasn't supposed to be her destiny.

She rushed home to make an apple pie. She needed to purge her system of all thoughts and dreams of Adam Harper. Finishing her assignment was a necessary part of flushing him from her mind for good, but not before he knew what he'd be missing.

Chapter 9

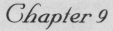

S unday afternoon smelled of cinnamon and warm apples, all the comfort of a familiar quilt. Such a homey scent. Kayli wished it felt that way. The air only reminded her that apple pie was Adam Harper's favorite. He didn't care for her white chocolate truffle or elegant apricot tarts. He enjoyed the simple things in life. Kayli enjoyed the extravagance of life: the different and unique. But would she ever feel the same about excess when Adam enjoyed apple pie in Montana?

Fresh, warm apple pie reminded Kayli of her own mother and the afternoons spent baking. Hot, stinging tears sprang to life. She instantly understood her disdain for apple pie and the reason her bakery had never created one. Some memories were too painful. Her mother died young and with her, those cozy afternoons. Adam Harper seemed to bring all that emotion bubbling to the surface.

She let the pie cool a bit and placed the disposable pie tin in a custom-made basket. Looking a bit too much like Little Red Riding Hood, Kayli set the pie on her front seat and placed some books around it to prevent its shuffling. Then she squared her shoulders and started her car. She took out Adam's business card and noted the scribbled address on the back. She was on a mission. Adam was about to learn that even the simple things in life could take on an added dimension with Kayli at the helm.

Kayli studied the address on the card then the boxy units in front of her. Adam lived in an old yet desirable part of town. His apartment was on the first floor of a tired-looking building with perfectly manicured lawns. Enough upkeep and neighborhood to keep his rent high, she supposed.

She knocked on the door, not expecting him to be home on such a bright and sunny afternoon, but he answered swiftly. "Kayli." She couldn't tell if he was happy to see her or not, but it didn't matter. This was the end.

"I brought you your pie." She pulled out the tin with a towel. "It's still warm so be careful. You can keep the towel." Turning to leave, she felt him grasp her forearm with his free hand.

"I don't want the towel."

She faced him. "Fine. I'll take it." She reached for the towel, but he wouldn't relinquish it from his grip.

"I have to go back to Montana." His voice held no inflection. "It's Rachel."

The game stopped. "You're leaving? You said two months."

"What does it matter? I take it this is my good-bye gift regardless of what state I'll be in." He raked his hand through his hair, his glass-green eyes fighting back emotion. It broke her heart to watch this steely man lose his normally unnerved stature. His tie from church draped near the phone carelessly, his face blanched. Kayli now understood the freshness of his pain.

"Adam, what's happened?"

"My mother took a turn for the worse."

"Your mother?"

"Rachel. She's the woman who married my father when

my mother walked out on us. Technically she's my stepmother, but in my heart she's the only mother I ever had."

"Rachel's your mother?" Kayli's relief could not have gone unnoticed. She nearly cried from the joy that permeated her heart. Perhaps she wasn't there to say good-bye after all.

Adam continued, "She would never take the name of Mother from me. She hoped my mom would return to me someday. She kept that hope alive in me, though I know now she's my mother. She's in a rest home in Montana." He dropped his head. "I knew I should have taken care of her. I should never have left, but I couldn't make any money to care for us, Kayli. I had to work. The rest home costs are tremendous."

Kayli searched for the words. He'd done so much. Didn't he understand that? She didn't have to know the details to know he'd done everything he could. She reached for him and pulled him into an embrace. "It will be okay," she heard herself say. "Mike Williams won't withhold payment when he knows the circumstances." But even Kayli didn't believe that.

Adam shook his head. "I didn't listen to my conscience once. I won't ignore it now." He stood tall, gazing at her with a look that said more than words ever could. He squinted, the worn lines from his constant smile reminding her of his capacity for joy. How did she know what this man meant with only his eyes?

"Yes, you need to go." What was she saying? She didn't want him to go. Her business, her condominium, her bills, her future—suddenly none of it seemed important. None of those things made her feel the way Adam did.

He shrugged. "Tom can take over for me until I get back. I have to pray for the best." He stooped and kissed her cheek then found her lips and pressed his firmly to hers. Nothing prepared her for what coursed through her body. This was it. She'd never hesitated before when she knew what she wanted. No man would ever make her feel this way. Of that she was certain. Her soul mate did indeed exist, and she felt numb thinking he might walk out of her life forever. She couldn't let that happen.

"Are you coming back?" She clutched his forearm, as if to force him to stay.

A black luxury car rolled into the apartment drive, and Kayli separated from Adam immediately. Andrea Williams got out of the vehicle, dripping with platinum baubles and wearing an orange silk pantsuit. Kayli swallowed hard, stepping in front of Adam protectively. This might be her last moments with Adam, the only opportunity she would have to tell him to return to her, and Andrea was stealing what belonged to her. This precious time.

"What do you want?" Kayli asked rudely.

Andrea lifted an eyebrow. "Since I'm not at your house, suffice it to say, I don't want anything from you. It's my employee I wish to speak with."

"Andrea, go home," Adam said.

Shock registered on Andrea's face. "Adam, we have business to discuss, and it won't wait until Tuesday."

"We have nothing to discuss. I work for your husband. If he has something to say, tell him to call me in Montana."

"Montana? You can't leave for Montana! You have a restaurant to finish."

"I have other, more pressing responsibilities."

"Adam," she said in a low, threatening tone, "you don't want to do this to me."

Kayli lost the momentum to breathe. "What do you mean, Andrea? What do you think is between the two of you?" An uneasy swirl started in Kayli's stomach and moved to her throat, stifling any further words.

"I'm the one who got away—isn't that right, Andrea?" He sniffed. "The one who didn't wither under her seductive glance. She doesn't want me. She only wants to feed her ego, to know I'm still hovering about, wishing I could have her." Adam tossed his head.

Andrea's eyes widened, as if she didn't know what Adam might be talking about. "That's not it, and you know it."

"Well, Andrea, I don't wish it. As a matter of fact, I count my blessings every day that the Lord saved me from you. I'm a man who knows what he wants, and I knew a long time ago that I didn't want you." Adam flinched, as though such ugly words pained him, but he obviously felt the cost necessary.

Kayli swallowed hard, wishing there was something she could say, support she could offer.

Andrea looked to Adam with venom. "You needn't bother coming back to California, Adam. If you leave for Montana, Mike will never take you back. It's obvious he can't trust you."

Adam crossed his arms in front of him. "With all you've seen Rachel go through, you would let her be thrown out into the street to satisfy your own vengeance? I can't believe it, even of you, Andrea."

"Rachel told me I'd never amount to anything, and I find it interesting that I should be ultimately responsible for her fate." A low cackle escaped, but it didn't sound as though Andrea took any pleasure in it. A short sob could be heard soon after, and Andrea's cold expression mingled with pain.

"Don't do this, Andrea. It's been over for a long time, and you know that. I love Kayli, and whether you admit it or not, you love Mike."

The fire returned. "You can't possibly love her. You don't know a thing about her."

"I know I've been given a message about her, that she loves the Lord and is committed to the sanctity of marriage."

"Five years of my life I devoted to you, waiting for you to ask me to be your wife."

Adam visibly swallowed. "That was wrong. I was wrong. I knew when we wrote to each other in college. A man knows, and I was too weak to say good-bye. I hope someday you'll forgive me, that you and Mike will work things out." He grabbed her hand, and Kayli wished she could crawl under a nearby rock rather than witness Andrea's soul-piercing cry. Adam's words threw Kayli's heart into turmoil as well. Yes, she loved him, too, as ridiculous as it sounded. But would he play her for years on end as he'd done with Andrea? She shivered.

"You would commit to this woman after knowing her two weeks?"

Kayli's heart pounded waiting for his answer. Was he committing?

"It's not knowing her for two weeks; it's what I know about her." Adam rested his gaze on Kayli. "She loves the Lord, she's committed to Him, and everything she does rises out of that. I know. I have a leading, and I know." They shared a look, and Kayli knew she would never forget that intensity. Whatever happened in her lifetime, another man would never look on her with such overwhelming devotion.

Andrea laughed derisively. "Do you expect her to live in the sticks with you, Adam? She lives in one of the most cosmopolitan areas in the world. Does she love you enough to live in a log cabin near Glacier? Where the clothes come only in flannel?" Another evil laugh followed. "You're dumber than I thought."

Kayli thought about all the luxuries of life: her little convertible, her carefully decorated condominium, her taste for espresso met on every street corner. How would she survive in some little backwoods town with a man she barely knew? She needed to pray, to get away from this and the emotion. Her entire future hung in the balance.

"I need to go home." Kayli gathered her basket and darted for the car. She didn't look back, fearing where it might lead. If she looked into those green eyes again, she would throw out reason, casting away her doubts. Doubts were important; they protected a person. Look at Andrea. She hadn't listened to her doubts, and now she was desperately pursuing another man after her marriage. That was exactly the kind of crazy thing a heavenly man like Adam caused one to do.

"This is all too complicated. I'm a pastry chef, nothing more. Why did I think that some handsome prince was going to sweep me off my feet? I have more smarts than that." The car wanted to steer itself back to Adam's, but she forced the wheel to her condo. This was a time for prayer. Deep and strenuous prayer.

The next day, work pacified Kayli, tearing her mind from the reality that Adam might be gone for good and why she should care. He was a stranger. Nothing more.

Mrs. Heiden remained quiet in her comments. So quiet it unnerved Kayli.

"You might as well say what you're thinking, Mrs. Heiden. He's gone now. Your opinions were apparently right."

"He'll be back."

"What do you mean?" Kayli stopped brushing her pastry and focused on the older woman.

"A man doesn't look at a woman as Adam looked at you and forget it. He knows."

"He knows what?"

The elder woman busied her hands with a wet rag. "My husband used to say that a man knows when he meets his wife. All the rest is merely formality."

"Mrs. Heiden, I can't believe you would believe in such a romantic notion. It's preposterous."

"Maybe, but I can only go on what my husband said, and I think Adam is the same kind of take-charge man. He saw what he wanted. I'm certain of that."

"So if that's true, where is he?"

"Preparing for marriage."

Kayli laughed out loud. "You're right. I suppose he's ordering his tux as we speak."

"That's not what I mean. I mean he's taking care of business, so he can focus on caring for a wife. Open your eyes, Kayli."

"His married ex-girlfriend is still after him, pursuing him with a vengeance. You don't see a problem there?" Kayli asked.

"Only for her."

"I can't believe you're saying all this, Mrs. Heiden. You're usually so practical. Where did that common sense of yours go? And I thought you said he was too good-looking for his own good."

Mrs. Heiden sat down at a small table near the front of the store and stared out the window. "I had forty-three years with my husband, Kayli. It wasn't long enough. I don't want to see you waste your time. If you seek the Lord in this, you'll know you knew from the first day that this is who you wanted."

"Wanting something doesn't make it the right thing." Kayli was arguing for argument's sake.

"True enough, but ask your heart, Kayli."

The shrill tone of the phone's bell reached her, tearing such thoughts from her mind. Adam's warm, familiar voice met hers.

"I miss you," he growled.

"When are you coming back?" Kayli asked unwillingly, afraid of the answer.

"Rachel went home to the Lord, Kayli." Her heart clenched at the sorrow she heard in his voice.

"Oh, Adam, I'm so sorry!" Kayli wished she could embrace him and soothe his pain away, but his distance felt like a world between them.

"God was gracious. I got to see her, to tell her what she meant to me, how much I loved her. She would have loved you, Kayli." He sighed and lowered his voice. "I told her all about you, and she smiled through the whole description, nodding her head."

"It's a compliment that you think she'd like me." Her comment sounded so vacant. She longed to let him know she'd been praying, that she cared, but she came off as austere and disconnected. "What's next for you?"

"I'm coming back to California. We'll decide then."

"Decide?" Kayli choked, her heart throbbing at the possibilities.

"On marriage. I've wasted enough time in my life. You're welcome to say no or wait or whatever you feel, but I'm certain of this, Kayli. I'm coming home to marry you if you'll have me. Rachel told me to act if I was sure. I'm sure."

"Home is where?"

"California. There's nothing to keep me here now. Only bitter memories and a real mother who never loved me. Maybe someday I'll have the strength to tackle that problem, but not yet."

"I'll be waiting," Kayli whispered through stiff lips, afraid to hope he meant what he said.

"I know you're thinking this isn't the best time and I've been through a trauma, but I know, Kayli. I'll be there in a week, and we'll make plans. I'll call you tonight."

"Adam?"

"Yeah?"

"Are you sure?"

"I've never been more certain about anything. I love you, Kayli Johnson. Become Mrs. Harper and make me the happiest man alive."

Her eyes filled with tears. "You'll have to ask me in person if you're serious."

"Until tonight." He clicked the phone, and Kayli sobbed from pure emotion, leaning her face against the door post and mourning a woman she never met. A woman who shared her love of Adam. Mrs. Heiden surrounded her with a comforting arm.

"I remember it well, Kayli." Mrs. Heiden's own eyes filled with tears. "There is no rational explanation for such a bond."

The two women laughed together. Kayli wondered at what her future would hold but no longer feared it.

Chapter 10

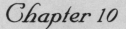

A dam took a deep breath. Flying over the golden hills of California, along the deep blue ocean, brought a renewed peace to him. No, the landscape wasn't nearly as dramatic as his beloved Glacier, but the Golden State was now his home. He'd tossed phone cards out like they were scrap metal from a wrecking yard, but in return he'd learned Kayli was a mystery he would continue to discover in their life together. His first inclination was correct: Kayli's dreams and aspirations matched his own. Whatever path they took, they'd take it together.

Landing smoothly at San Jose International Airport, Adam stepped onto the tarmac, breathing in the cool Bay Area air. Then he saw her. Kayli's deep brown hair flowed in the afternoon breeze, her soft highlights echoing the sun's rays. She waved, her smile growing larger, and his stomach lurched.

He breathed in deeply, but he halted at the sight of Andrea standing beside Kayli. Andrea crossed her arms, anticipating his arrival with seemingly precise motives. Free of carry-on luggage, Adam quickened his pace, meeting Kayli's rustic brown eyes with joy. Momentarily the world around them disappeared, and he pulled her into his arms. The scent of her hair with a mixture of coconut and suntan oil forced a grin. He was home.

"I missed you," he whispered the words into her hair, lacing his fingers through the soft mesh of tendrils. "But I'm free, Kayli. I wish Rachel was here to meet you, but I know she's smiling on us. She had a solid faith and taught me to love God in the darkest of circumstances." He looked at his feet for a moment. "If I didn't know better, I'd say she released herself so I could go on with my life. She was that type of woman."

"She must have been if she raised you."

"How's business?" Adam asked avoiding Andrea's gaze and crossed arms.

"It's okay. I have more business now that I'm putting the tables out, but I fear Mike Williams's Sunday hours are going to hurt me. I won't do that, though it costs me big financially." She waved a hand in the air. "It's not important. God will provide. If Rachel believed that, I have to as well."

To her credit Andrea let them have their moment together before she approached. "Quite a cozy greeting. It makes me all tingly inside." Andrea let her eyes roll back in her head to show her sarcasm.

"I heard the restaurant is coming along nicely. Mike sounded pleased when I talked to him on the phone." Adam smiled.

"I'll leave you alone, Adam, but I need one last favor."

His grin died. What would Andrea say in front of Kayli? He uttered a silent prayer, hoping for the best. "I'm fresh out of favors, Andrea."

"Please. I thought about what you said. I do love Mike, as much as it pains me to say so. I want to be his wife. But I want him to want me as well. I thought maybe if I had another man's attention, I'd get his."

Adam placed his arm around Kayli's waist, pulling her

closer. "I want the same thing for you, Andrea, but you're going about it wrong."

"I've made a fool of myself, and we're going to counseling. I came to meet you to ask you not to tell him about the pass I made at you. We have enough to work on for the time being."

Adam looked down at Kayli, grateful they shared a faith in God and a higher calling than simply a secular marriage certificate. "As long as you keep working, my tongue will remain stilled."

"Thank you." She nodded at the two of them. "Sorry to interrupt your time, Kayli. You two are a striking couple." A tear escaped Andrea's eyes, but she turned away quickly.

Adam searched Kayli's expression, and they seemed to share a desire to let the conversation drop.

"So what have I missed?" Adam asked.

"Well, Robert is still dating that woman, and she actually went to the Star Trek convention with him! He thinks I'm crazy for falling for you over the phone, but I know better."

"He's not familiar with my irresistible voice apparently."

"Apparently."

They walked arm in arm into the airport, retrieved the small suitcase, and stepped into her waiting car in the nearby lot. "May I drive?"

"Certainly," Kayli answered.

Adam drove through all the high tech buildings and passed the concert amphitheater, before arriving at the golf course on the San Francisco Bay shoreline. Pulling into a parking spot, they parked before the small lake with several brightly colored sailboards gliding in the wind. He watched Kayli smile and went around the car to help her out. The soothing sound of pure silence permeated the afternoon breeze. The caw of a seagull broke the stillness every few minutes, but otherwise they were completely alone.

He sat Kayli on a bench and knelt before her. "This is crazy. I'm sure you think I'm crazy, but I love you, Kayli Johnson, and, come what may, I'm committed to you. Employed, unemployed, California, or Montana, one thing will remain constant, and that's my love for you."

Kayli smiled, nibbling on her lip nervously. He touched her cheek and pulled out the red-velvet box. It opened with a squeak, and he watched Kayli's expression light up. "This was Rachel's. She wanted you to have it, and I want you to have it."

"I can't take it, Adam. It's for your wife."

"Kayli," he said, laughing. "I'm asking you to be my wife. I want us to be married."

Choking sobs emanated from his future bride. She covered her face, to hide the emotion, but Adam pulled her hands away. "Is that a yes?"

She nodded. Again and again. "It's a yes!" She grabbed his face and covered him with kisses. "Mike Williams can have whatever he wants, as long as I get you."

His throat grew tight, but he wanted to shout with joy. To sing, to dance. Something to show his emotion. So he broke into song to the Lord while Kayli giggled.

"You'll always have my heart, Kayli. Once I tasted that apple pie, I knew life didn't get any better than this."

Kayli smiled, almost an evil grin. "You ate it before you left?"

"The whole thing."

"Well, you little sneak."

"And it was better than my mother's. Rachel laughed contentedly when I told her that."

"You told her?"

"She would have read it in my face if I hadn't. Although she said my taste buds might have been colored by my feelings."

"I certainly hope so."

"Who would have thought I'd have to come to California for American apple pie?"

"America is a lot of things, Adam, but it's certainly like you, sweet as apple pie."

Ellen's Infamous Apple Pie

This recipe is the best apple pie I've ever tasted, and it is a *must* for my husband at Thanksgiving and Christmas. My husband's mother, Ellen Billerbeck, perfected this recipe, and it is incredible! Many thanks to her for sharing this recipe and raising such a wonderful son to enjoy it with.

6 pippin apples (look for brown crown for the best sugared apples)
1 ½ cups sugar (use a tad more if apples are really sour)
dash of salt
½ cup flour
dash of nutmeg
2 heaping tsp cinnamon
¼ stick butter
1 lemon

Preheat oven to 350°. Combine sugar, salt, flour, nutmeg and cinnamon in a bowl. Peel and cut apples in small wedges. Roll out ready-made piecrust, or your own, and place in a 9-inch pie pan. Layer sugar mix, apples, lemon, and butter. Keep layering until all ingredients are used. Then place second piecrust on top, cutting a hole in the top to allow the mixture to breathe. Place a cookie sheet under the pie pan to avoid boilovers and messy ovens. Bake at 350° for one hour; then lower temperature to 300° for 30 more minutes.

KRISTIN BILLERBECK

Kristin lives in the Silicon Valley with her engineering director husband Bryed, their three sons, Trey, Jonah, and Seth and one little princess, Ellena. When not writing, Kristin also enjoys reading, painting, and conversing with her on-line writing groups. She has six published novels with the **Heartsong Presents** line and six novellas in anthologies from Barbour Publishing. Visit Kristin on the web at www.kristinbillerbeck.com

APPLE ANNIE

by Joyce Livingston

Dedication

Several years ago as a surprise for Mother's Day, my youngest son, Luke, took his wife Tammie and me (his three children and his father too) to Apple Valley Farm in Northeast Kansas, where we all enjoyed a marvelous dinner in the Apple Valley Farm Restaurant and a melodrama in the Apple Valley Farm Barn. This yearly trip to Apple Valley Farm has become a Mother's Day tradition, one Tammie and I look forward to every year, and Luke never disappoints us.

Although Apple Annie's story is set in Idaho, many of the things about the restaurant and the barn have been inspired by Kansas's own Apple Valley Farm. With thankfulness and a mother's love, I dedicate this story to Luke.

I'd also like to thank Millie Miller of Edmund, Oklahoma, for giving me the recipe for the Decadently Sinful Awesome Caramel Apple Pie, the specialty of Apple Annie's Restaurant.

Chapter 1

A nnie, Brad's here." The waitress hurried to the window and pulled back the red-and-white-checkered curtain. Her eyes sparkled as the red minivan pulled across the parking lot and came to a stop.

Annie lifted a handful of menus from the big iron kettle and shuffled them in her hands. "That man! I don't know why he refuses to park in one of the handicapped stalls."

"Because it's for handicapped people! I doubt Brad ever thinks of himself as handicapped, or even physically challenged. Isn't that what they call it these days?" the waitress asked. The two women observed the electric lift lowering on the clean van. "I've never seen a man with two legs any happier than Brad. He makes everyone around him feel good. Wish I had his attitude. I'm sure my customers would appreciate it!"

The phone rang, and she scurried to answer it, but Annie lingered at the window. Brad Reed had shown up at Apple Valley Farm the first night of their new season. Several nights a week since then he had returned and always asked for the same table—the table for two, crowded into the far back corner next to the old woodstove. And he always topped off his meal with a wedge of what he called "sinfully decadent" Awesome Caramel

Apple Pie. Even the waitresses had taken to calling the famous pie "sinfully decadent" when they described it to their customers.

Annie smiled. Sinfully decadent. No doubt the apple pie was the only sinfully decadent thing going on in Brad's life. Not with the way he was always talking about God. She enjoyed visiting with the man, but she had to admit he made her feel a pang of guilt sometimes at her own lackadaisical attitude toward God. The guy was too good to be true. Surely something dark and dank lay beneath that winning smile. One would think, from his constant pleasant demeanor, that he hadn't a care in the world.

From the window she watched him struggle to move from the seat into the electric wheelchair, roll onto the steel platform, and lower himself to the ground. Then he pushed the button to return the lift to its place before sliding the door closed. It was amazing how much effort it required for him to get out of his vehicle. With all the trouble it took, it seemed as if he would forget it and stay at home, parked in front of the TV with the remote in his hand. Feeling like a voyeur, she let the curtain drop, lest he see her. The last thing she'd want to do was embarrass him.

As he maneuvered the chair up the ramp, she pushed open the door with her famous Apple Annie smile, the one her customers had come to expect. "You made it. I was afraid with the forecast of heavy rain, you might decide to stay home tonight."

A broad smile lit up the man's face. "A little rain stop Brad Reed? Never. I thought you knew me better than that. Besides, I'd never make it through the weekend without—"

She lifted her hand and stopped him. "I know. Our sinfully decadent Awesome Caramel Apple Pie. You're incorrigible!" She stepped back out of the way while three waitresses left their stations to crowd around their favorite customer, oohing and ahhing over him as if he were a celebrity. *That man is a magnet.* She watched them fuss over him, taking turns arguing about who would serve him.

"As much as I love all this attention, I think you girls better get back to work. You know what a slave driver Apple Annie is." His tone was teasing, and even his eyes seemed to be laughing. "But you're great for my ego. Let's do it again sometime—when Apple Annie isn't watching!" The girls giggled and returned to their stations, glancing over their shoulders and smiling at him.

He shrugged his broad shoulders and lifted his brow at Annie. "Sorry. Some women just can't leave a handsome, eloquent, attractive man like me alone."

The girls tittered and giggled to one another from their places, filling glasses, taking orders and conversing with the customers already seated at their tables.

"Good thing you told my crew to get back to work. I was about to fire the whole bunch of them." Annie smiled and handed him a leather-covered menu. "You're a terrible distraction, you know." She gathered her long calico skirt about her and led him toward his usual table.

"Can I help it? It's sheer animal magnetism. If God created me irresistible, who am I to fight it?" He followed close behind her, the wheelchair's motor making a gentle hum.

"Yeah? You're blaming God? I'd say some men are conceited on their own. And whoever told you that you were handsome and irresistible?" She didn't turn to look at him, but she knew he was smiling.

"Only every waitress who works for you!" His hearty laugh was infectious.

She glanced over her shoulder at him. "You men are all

alike!" The man was a charmer, she had to admit. No wonder he had all the Apple Valley women clamoring after him.

"If I'm such a distraction, maybe you'd better sit down and have dinner with me and keep me out of trouble." She pulled away a chair, and he rolled past her into the space. "They have great food here."

She gave him a nudge then bent and rested her hand on his shoulder. "You should know. I think at one time or another this summer you've tried everything on the menu."

He gave her a sad puppy-dog look that made her laugh. "On the menu maybe, but not your magnificent buffet. I hate to admit it, but in this rolling chariot of mine I have trouble manipulating the food onto the plates and the plates onto the tray and the tray onto my lap and the—"

She tossed her head and held up both her hands. "I get the message! Loud and clear! You need a little help, and you think I'm the one for the job. Right?"

"Exactly. Will you have dinner with me, Apple Annie?" Brad winked then reached out and took hold of her hands. He stroked them gently with his thumbs as he gazed up at her.

She noticed that his eyes were the same color as the thick chocolate fudge sauce they served on the dessert bar. She could never resist that sauce, even though she knew she'd suffer the consequences later for indulging and her bathroom scales would be only too willing to remind her.

He had never touched her before, other than an occasional handshake, and for some reason it unnerved her. She wanted to back away; yet she enjoyed the strong, masculine feel of his fingers closing over hers.

"Dinner? Here? Now?" she asked. She felt awkward.

Her first impulse was to say no. Most days she didn't take

time to eat until after the dinner crowd had gone. But it was still early, and most of them hadn't even arrived yet. With only a piece of dried toast and a hurried glass of iced tea for lunch she had to admit she was a bit hungry.

"Please?"

"Only if you'll let me help you with the buffet. We're trying out a new potato dish tonight, and I'd like your opinion." She pulled her hands from his grasp and adjusted the red satin bow that held her dark, thick ponytail. Why did she say yes? Normally she shied away from eating with patrons, afraid of showing partiality.

"Deal." He stuck out a hand. "Let's shake on it before you change your mind."

She put her hand timidly in his and once again felt the strong, warm touch of his fingers as they squeezed her hand. Then he pulled the lever under his right hand, and the chair backed slowly away from the table. "Lead the way. I'm famished."

Annie crossed the restaurant to the buffet line and lifted a green tray from the tall stack. "What kind of salad would you like?"

Brad rubbed his chin and surveyed the enticing array of salads. "I've never tried the red cabbage. Is it good?"

She laughed and spooned a small bowl full and placed it on his tray. "You tell me, after you've tasted it."

"Look—I've got an idea," he said, his gaze never leaving her delicate face. "Why don't you choose the rest of the meal for me? I'm not a picky eater—but I'm sure you know that, as many times as you've seen me making a pig of myself in your restaurant. I'll take potluck—whatever you choose, except for those." He leaned forward and pointed toward a fancy white dish containing bright green Brussels sprouts. "If former President

George Bush can refuse to eat those awful things, so can I!"

She rolled her eyes. "And you said you weren't picky."

"I'm actually more picky about my women than I am my food," he said with a lifted brow and a sideways grin.

"Hmph. What women? I've never seen you with a woman."

He turned up his mouth, his brown eyes riveted on hers. "Umm. You're right. At this time of year most of the good-looking women who chase me are at the beach concentrating on their suntans. And I have an awful time maneuvering this chair of mine in the sand."

A giggle slipped out before she could stop it. "Good excuse."

"Maybe I'd better find me a woman who doesn't want to fry herself and get skin cancer. Want to volunteer?"

She raised her brows and looked at him. "Yes, but only for tonight." Then she laughed, something she seldom did now with the demands of running a restaurant, the Big Barn Melodrama Theater, and the orchards. With all these responsibilities her life had become much too serious and busy.

"Only for tonight?" He inched the chair forward a bit. "I hate one-night stands."

"I thought you said women found you irresistible!"

He threw up his hands. "Maybe I stretched the figures a bit!"

"Well, you've just met a one-nighter." She selected a colorful bowl of fruit salad and placed it on his tray. "Tomorrow you'll have to find a replacement. I don't have time to play the dating game with you."

"Then, sweet lady," he said with exaggerated emotion as his fingertips touched her arm, "we have but one glorious night together. Let us make the most of it."

She gave his hand a swift rap and an accusing grin. "Unquote! Our melodrama actors use that line every night in our theater. You're plagiarizing!"

"Can't blame a guy for trying!" He shrugged then watched her select a thick, juicy slice of roast beef, adding a large helping of mashed potatoes and brown gravy and a beautifully browned cloverleaf roll.

When she was finished filling his tray she followed him to the table. Once his chair was in place, he took the tray from her and removed each item. He kept his gaze on her as she walked back to the buffet line, filled her own tray, and returned.

She set their trays on a nearby table. "I'll get the coffeepot."

Brad laid his hand on her wrist. "No, let me get it. You work too hard. You deserve to be waited on once in awhile."

She wanted to refuse his offer, but she feared she might offend him if she reminded him how much easier it would be for her to do it. So she sat down, leaned back in her chair, and spread her napkin across her lap. "I take decaf."

"You got it!"

Annie watched Brad weave his chair in and out among the tables until he reached the drink station. How would he ever carry that pot back to the table? She jumped to her feet and rushed toward him, not wanting him to be embarrassed by an impending catastrophe. But before Annie could get to him he reached up and pulled a towel from a shelf, wrapped it around the hot stainless steel pot, and locked the coffeepot securely between his thighs.

He gave her a sheepish grin, turned the chair around, and rolled toward her. She stood there gaping. "You didn't think I could do it?"

"I—wasn't sure." Now she was the one who was embarrassed, and she didn't like the feeling.

He lifted an arm, pushed up the sleeve of his polo shirt,

and flexed his biceps. Using that exaggerated deep voice again, he said, "Woman. Me, Tarzan. You, Jane. And don't you forget it!"

Annie relaxed and enjoyed the evening more than she had in a long time. Brad had become like a dear old friend. She had missed male companionship. She hadn't had much of it with boyfriends, but before his illness she'd had her dad, the only real hero in her life.

"Mind if I pray and thank God for our food?" Brad broke in as she reached for her fork.

His question surprised her. Not that she'd been on that many dinner dates, if that's what her college dates to pizza hangouts could be called; but none of her escorts had ever asked to pray before the meal. She glanced around to see if others were watching and, finding them occupied with their own conversations, lowered her fork. "Sure—if you want to."

He reached across the table and took her hands. To her astonishment, instead of bowing his head, he lifted his eyes heavenward. "Good evening, God. It's me, Brad, and Annie is here with me. We're sharing a great meal. We've come into Your presence to thank You—for this food and the hands that prepared it, for the air we breathe, and the life and health we enjoy every day. We may not know how or why things happen the way they do sometimes, but one thing we know. You are in control. Bless this food now and forgive us for neglecting to praise and thank You for all You do for us."

He paused. "Do you mind if I pray for your dad? I've heard he's having quite a struggle with Alzheimer's."

She met his gaze, and the warmth and concern she saw there made her heart tighten with pent-up emotion. She could only nod. His hands tightened around hers, and for a moment she thought she was going to cry. This man was genuinely concerned about her dad.

"And, God, we bring Annie's father to You, asking that somehow You will touch him and heal his mind. And be with Annie and her family as they often find themselves locked out of his memory, and give them comfort as they recall better times. Amen."

She bit her lips and pressed her eyelids shut against the tears that threatened to erupt.

Apparently Brad noticed. "Want to hear the story about the chicken who got hit by a car as he crossed the road?" He unfolded his napkin and grinned.

She wrinkled her nose. Their conversation had shifted abruptly from one of sadness to the ridiculous. "Sounds kind of gruesome."

"Not the way I tell it." He spread the napkin across his lap and smoothed it out with his hands.

She dabbed at her mouth with her own napkin then returned it to her lap, her eyelids still pressing back unshed tears. She was eager to listen to whatever foolish tale he would tell to take her mind off her father's illness. "Okay, I'm game. Tell me about the chicken who got hit crossing the road."

"Well, a man was driving down the road. But before he could stop his car, a chicken ran out in front of him, and he hit it." He wadded up his napkin and let it drop onto the table. "The guy rushed out of his car, scooped up the chicken, and took it to a nearby veterinarian. The doc took one look at the poor chicken and confessed, 'I'm not sure I can do anything for him, but I'll try.'"

Brad folded the napkin in half then rolled the two opposite sides toward the center and held it up for her to see.

" 'This look like the chicken you hit?' The man shook his head. 'I'm afraid not.' "

He folded the napkin in half again, bringing the four rolled ends up together in his hands. He stuck an index finger into the end of each roll and pulled out the loose end, creating four spiraled-out segments.

"The veterinarian held the chicken up and again asked the man, 'Does this look like the chicken before you ran over it?' Again the man shook his head."

With a vigorous laugh Brad held onto the ends of two of the spiraled rolls and let the other two ends drop free. 'Doc!' the man cried out. 'That's the chicken! You fixed him as good as new!'"

Annie's mouth dropped open, and she clapped her hands. "That looks exactly like a chicken, but without the head! How did you do that?"

"My own personal magic!" Brad grinned with satisfaction as she laughed at his ridiculous joke. "I'm full of chicken jokes. Want to hear another one?"

"I'm tempted." She giggled and pointed to their full plates. "But I think we'd better eat first, before everything gets cold. Try those potatoes and let me know what you think."

He scooped up a big helping of the cheesy potatoes and savored them slowly, then waved his fork at her approvingly. "Umm, excellent. With only one leg I'm certainly no Galloping Gourmet, but I say they definitely should stay on your menu."

She nodded. She was glad he liked them, but his comment about his leg took her aback for a moment. "Then they'll stay."

Annie enjoyed every minute of the meal and the light, easy conversation. Most nights she ate alone, after everyone else had finished for the day. Before she knew it she'd cleaned her plate, leaving only an olive and a small piece of bread. It had been months since she'd eaten such a hearty meal. She finished the last of her coffee, folded her napkin, and placed it on the table.

Brad frowned. "You don't have to go yet, do you?"

She pushed back her chair and stood to her feet. "Yes, but maybe we—"

"Maybe we could have our sinfully decadent Awesome Caramel Apple Pie, and then you could go?" He gave her a hopeful look and a wistful smile.

"Sorry, but I have to go now." She hated to leave the man and his wonderful sense of humor. "I was going to say maybe another time, but right now I've got to seat the dinner crowd. I'm afraid you'll have to eat your pie alone."

For only a moment his face lost its resident smile. "I hate eating alone. That's why I come here as often as I do. I may sit at a table for one, but this place is always filled with happy people. It rubs off on me, and I hardly notice only one person is sitting at my table—me."

She detected a certain sadness in his eyes, one she'd never noticed before. "Well, if you're not in a hurry to get home and you don't mind eating late"—she saw his face brighten—"I guess I could have that pie with you after the evening performance in our theater. But it'll be after ten o'clock," she cautioned, glancing at her watch.

He swung his arm across his chest with a flourish and bowed as low as one could from a wheelchair. "Ma'am, I'd be proud and honored to join you in a humble piece of pie—" He stopped and scratched his head. "Or was that a piece of humble pie? Umm, I never can remember."

She gave him a playful swat as a large group of patrons entered, their eyes scanning the restaurant for its well-known hostess. "Brad, I have to go. I guess since you're going to have pie with me later you'll be staying for the melodrama in the barn. I'll see you there."

"Sure, I'll be there. Wouldn't miss it. And, by the way, my mother raised me to be a gentleman, and gentlemen always rise when a lady leaves the table," he told her with a warm smile. "I want you to know I may be sitting on the outside, but I'm standing on the inside."

She smiled too. "You never have to worry about standing up for me. I've always known you were a gentleman. And you're wonderful company. No wonder all those women chase after you. See you later." And she hurried off to greet her customers.

Brad watched as she gathered her skirts about her and made her way through the crowded restaurant. He wondered how beautiful, vibrant Annie Johnson had managed to stay single. At least, she wasn't wearing a wedding ring, and she'd never mentioned a husband during their dinner conversation. Or even a boyfriend. Though he'd known her only a few months, by his standards she was pure gold. If he ever found a woman like Annie, he'd— His glance fell to his empty trouser leg. What woman would want a one-legged, handicapped man?

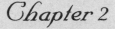

Chapter 2

H ey, Lady, want a ride?"

Startled, Annie spun around. Most of her dinner patrons had headed for the barn to attend the evening's performance of the latest melodrama. She hadn't expected anyone to be waiting when she opened the door.

"I didn't mean to frighten you," Brad explained as he rolled toward her. "I'm sure you've been on your feet all day, and I thought I'd give you a lift up to the barn."

She stared at the man. "Lift? How? There's only a path."

He shot back a smile as he patted his lap, his eyes twinkling. "Right here."

"There? You're kidding, aren't you?" One corner of her mouth turned upward in a slight smile. Thinking back, she couldn't remember ever sitting on a man's lap, other than her father's or her uncle's.

He held out a hand. "No, I'm not kidding. Climb on. I'm a safe driver. I promise not to exceed the speed limit."

Annie watched as he skillfully maneuvered the chair, coming to a stop beside her, facing the barn. Surely he wasn't serious.

"You're afraid I'll drop you or we'll run into a tree, aren't you? Don't worry—I've been driving this little jewel for years."

He patted his lap again. "Come on. I'll bet none of your other boyfriends offered you a ride in a wheelchair. This could be the experience of a lifetime. You wouldn't want to miss it, would you? This baby will do every bit of three miles per hour."

She shifted her purse from one hand to the other. He was right. She was afraid. The path to the barn was up a gentle hill most of the way. What if—

"Annie, you'll be safe." His tone was reassuring. "I promise. It'll be fun."

She accepted his hand but kept her feet on the ground. "Have you ever—"

"Carried someone like this? On my lap?"

She nodded.

"Sure I have. My nephews. My nieces." He tugged on her hand, but she stood fast.

She tilted her head and raised a brow. "How old were they?"

"Well, the oldest niece was seven, but the oldest nephew was—" He paused.

"Brad! How old was your nephew? And be honest," she cautioned. "I want the truth."

"Ah—nine?"

She withdrew her hand and slapped at his arm playfully. "Nine? You've only carried a nine-year-old child on that chair, and you expect to carry me? Forget it."

Brad reached for her hand again and squeezed it tenderly. "Did I mention he was a very big nine year old?"

"You're incorrigible!"

"But lovable, right?" His brown eyes gleamed.

She ignored his question. But, yes, no doubt about it, he was lovable, in a big brotherly sort of way. "You promise you won't drop me?"

"Try me."

She slipped carefully onto his lap, his one arm circling her tiny waist as he pulled her to him. He smelled nice, like shampoo and after-shave, and she found herself melting against him as her arms wound around his thick neck. To her surprise she felt safe.

"Put your feet on the empty footrest," he told her.

"Are you sure it won't crowd you?"

He snickered. "Annie, I need only one footrest—remember?"

She blushed.

"Ready?" His face was so close to hers that their cheeks nearly touched.

She closed her eyes and leaned into him. "Ready, I think. Just be careful, okay?"

Brad adjusted his grip about Annie's waist as his right hand moved to press the lever. The chair moved forward slowly. Annie, the woman he'd fallen helplessly in love with the first night he'd visited Apple Valley Farm, was in his lap, her arms hugging his neck. How many times had he dreamed of being this close to her? Of holding her? Kissing her? The tendrils of her lovely dark hair touched his cheek. If only she were his. If only—

"Brad? Did you hear me?"

"Ah—sure, Annie. I'd never let anything happen to you. I promise."

He maneuvered the chair up the packed dirt trail to the Big Barn Theater, part of the Apple Valley complex. The complex included not only the restaurant and the theater but a large orchard and the family home as well.

"Annie," he asked, feeling the awkwardness of their silence

as they rolled along, "how long has your family owned Apple Valley Farm?"

"Forever. My great-great-great-grandfather homesteaded this ground and started the orchards, but it was my grandfather who started the restaurant and my father who converted the big barn into a theater. Why do you ask?"

He slowed and pushed the lever slightly to the right to miss a rock in the trail before answering. "Just curious. Now you're the sixth generation, and the mantle is being passed on to you? Now that your father is sick?"

She loosened her hold about his neck. He hoped it was because she was feeling more secure and not because she wanted to move away from him. "Yes, he signed the property over to my older sister, Valerie, and me when he was diagnosed with Alzheimer's. He didn't want any problems after he—"

She paused. He knew it was difficult for her to think of her father in those terms, and he almost wished he hadn't asked.

"Sister? I didn't know you had a sister. I've never seen her around the restaurant, have I?"

She shook her head. "She's actually my half-sister, by my dad's first wife. We've never been close. I rarely see her."

Brad stopped at the bottom of the ramp near the theater to let Annie off his lap. Just then the lead actor in the melodrama, the villain, came running toward her.

"What's wrong?" Annie asked.

Between breaths the man told her the pianist had phoned, his car had broken down, and he couldn't make the evening performance. "We have a packed house. Shall I tell our customers we'll give them a rain check? I don't know what else to do."

Annie stared at the man. "I—I guess we'll have to. We have no one else to take his place."

"Is the music score on the piano?" Brad asked.

"Yeah, I saw it there a few minutes ago when I went to check on him, before his call came in." The man was wringing his hands. "Why?"

Brad rolled up next to Annie and tugged on her hand. "I'll play if you want me to. I've seen the play at least ten times. I think I can follow it, if you don't mind a few mistakes and you let the audience know I'm only filling in."

Her eyes widened. "Really, Brad? You'd do this? I didn't even know you played."

"I play mostly by ear, but I can read music too. I'm better at playing country gospel than anything, but I'm sure I can handle the melodrama music."

Annie turned to the man. "Make sure the chair is pulled away from the piano. Brad's going to be our guest pianist tonight."

When it was time for the preshow, Brad skipped the songs the regular pianist played and performed a couple of his favorite ragtime tunes, much to the delight of the audience. Annie took center stage, welcomed each person who had come and introduced Brad.

He nodded, turned back to the piano with a reassuring grin toward Annie and played the introduction to the first act. The footlights dimmed, and the play began. In the semidarkness, out of the corner of his eye, he saw Annie slip past him and drop into a chair only a few feet away. He grinned to himself. *I'd do anything for Annie, even if it means embarrassing myself in front of a crowd.*

Annie watched Brad's fingers move over the keys. He was handling the music score as capably as the regular pianist. How kind it was of him to volunteer. She and the cast were grateful, as was the audience of young and old alike. She laughed as they hissed and booed the villain and cheered the hero and heroine. Brad's fingers never missed a beat, and by the look on his face she was sure he was enjoying himself.

At the conclusion of the performance each actor and actress received well-deserved accolades, but Brad alone got a standing ovation. Annie watched with pride as members of the audience crowded around him to express their appreciation. Without him they would have had no evening performance at Apple Valley Farm.

He waited by the ticket counter until Annie was ready to go back down the path to the restaurant. He beamed as she climbed onto his lap without an invitation.

"Oh, Brad, you were wonderful." She wrapped her arms about his neck and held on tight. "How can I ever thank you?"

A coy smile tilted the corners of his mouth. "Give me time. I'll find a way."

She chattered on, scarcely hearing his answer. He had turned a possible catastrophe and box office loss into a huge success, and she was grateful. Caught up in describing his performance at the piano, she didn't notice the way Brad hung on her every word and drew her closer about the waist.

"You know," she said with a confident smile, "I could get used to this—riding with you. It's kind of fun, and it sure beats walking." Immediately she wished she could withdraw her words. She was sure that staying in the wheelchair, with no other option, was anything but fun for Brad. "I'm so sorry," she said sincerely. "I only meant—"

He pulled back on the lever, and the chair came to a sudden halt, forcing Annie to hold tightly to Brad. "Annie, believe me—you have nothing to be sorry about. I'm sure you think your words upset me. They didn't. I know your heart's right."

"I have a habit of speaking before I think," she mumbled.

Brad smiled and lifted his hand. "Forget it, Annie. I already have." With a little pressure on the lever, the chair moved forward again. "I tried crutches a couple of times, but after a few falls I decided I felt more secure in this wheelchair. Besides, with my hands full, I had no way to carry my briefcase, and a good lawyer can't go anywhere without his briefcase. He needs it to make him look official, even if it's empty!"

She grinned at him, thinking again of the evening's performance. "You're something else, Brad." Then she asked quietly, "Did you ever consider a prosthesis?"

The smile never left his face. "An artificial leg? Never! A buddy I knew in high school had one of those weird things. He never did get used to it. I figured, why bother? I hear those things aren't too comfortable, and I'm a sissy when it comes to pain."

They reached the door to the restaurant. "Hey, I worked up an appetite playing that piano. I'm ready for pie. How about you?"

"You bet. I'm famished too."

The restaurant was empty except for two young women scrubbing the floor. Annie scooted off Brad's lap and waved her hand. "Pick out a table, and I'll get our pie."

Brad selected a table near the front, unrolled his napkin, and waited.

A few minutes later Annie walked to the table carrying two large pieces of pie. "Can you live without coffee? They've already washed all the pots and put them away."

He chuckled and pushed back her chair with his foot. "I'll struggle through, but I could use a big glass of water."

"Done." Annie took two glasses from a shelf, filled them

with ice and water, then returned to the table. "I don't need this pie, you know. If I eat with you very often, I'd have to waddle instead of walk."

"Fat chance," he countered, laughing at his own unintended pun. "That body of yours could use a little fattening up. And I like that comment about eating with me."

She gave him a playful frown. "Thanks for that left-handed compliment."

"Whoops. And you think you have a habit of speaking before thinking? Guess it's my turn to ask for forgiveness. I know it didn't come off like it, but I meant that as a compliment. You have a great shape—" He slapped his jaw. "I'm digging myself in deeper, aren't I?"

Annie picked up his fork and handed it to him with a giggle. "Shut up and eat."

They laughed and talked their way through their pie, Brad being his usual comedic self and Annie his appreciative audience.

"I can't eat another bite," Brad said, rubbing his stomach.

She looked at his plate then at him. "It's a good thing. Your plate is empty."

He gasped. "So it is!" His eyes twinkled.

Annie dropped her fork and stared at her own plate. "I can't believe it. I've eaten all of mine too. I never eat an entire piece of pie. Especially this one—it's so rich." She pointed her finger at him. "And it's all your fault, you and that witty tongue of yours. You kept me laughing so hard I didn't realize how much I was eating." She pinched at her waist. "Yuk! I can feel those pounds creeping on already."

She picked up their dishes and carried them into the kitchen as Brad made his way toward the door.

The two girls had finished cleaning up and left so Annie

turned out the lights and flipped on the burglar alarm. Then she followed Brad out, locking the door behind them.

She extended her hand. "Good-night, Brad. And thanks for a wonderful evening. I've loved every minute of it."

Instead of shaking her hand, he took it and pulled her to him. "Me too. But as I told you, I'm a gentleman, and I won't let you walk to your car alone. Hop on."

She gave him a shy smile, slipped an arm about his shoulder, and slid easily onto his lap. "I thought you'd never ask."

They rode silently to her car with Annie's head resting on Brad's shoulder. He waited while she located her keys and opened her door.

She turned to him and smiled again. "I've enjoyed your company. I hope we can do it again sometime."

Brad grabbed her hand and brought it to his lips. "How about tomorrow night?"

She pulled her hand away and placed it on her hip. "Come on, Brad. Be honest. Is it me or my apple pie you like?"

"Well"—he paused and rubbed his chin—"that's a hard question. But if I had to make a choice I'd pick—"

Annie clamped her hand over his mouth. "Don't say it. I have a feeling your answer is going to be my apple pie."

Brad cupped his hand over hers and gently pulled her fingers away, kissing the palm of her hand. "Annie, as much as I love your Awesome Caramel Apple Pie, it takes a distant second to you." His laugh echoed across the empty parking lot. "But I have to admit—you're both appealing."

Her laughter joined his. "Is that appealing with an a? Or a peeling with two e's?"

"Both. Good night, Annie. Lock your doors and be careful driving."

She slid under the steering wheel and put the key in the ignition. A quick turn and the engine started. "Then I'll see you tomorrow night?"

Grinning, he backed his chair away from her car. "Count on it."

Brad watched the car move out of the parking lot and onto the street before twisting the lever on his chair to the right and heading toward his van. "Well, old buddy," he said aloud as he lowered the ramp and rolled up onto it, "you've done it. Opened your heart to a woman, something you vowed you'd never do." *You know she's only toying with you,* an inner voice told him. *A beautiful, vivacious woman like Annie Johnson doesn't want a broken, incomplete man. A woman like that can have any man she wants, and that man isn't you. You can't even stand up and take her in your arms or walk by her side. You're a fool, Brad Reed—a stupid, gullible fool. And if you don't back away from this woman now, before you fall any further in love, you'll get hurt. And hurt bad.*

Chapter 3

Annie glanced at her watch. Seven-thirty and no Brad. Hadn't he told her he'd see her at the restaurant the next evening? Was he sick? Did he have an accident? She pulled back the checkered curtain and scanned the crowded parking lot for the fifth time.

"Where's Brad?" One of the waitresses stepped behind the register to ring up a ticket. "Several of our customers have asked about him. They thought it was neat the way he played the piano last night. I hear he was pretty good."

Annie glanced out the window again. "He was good. And he said he'd be here tonight."

The waitress walked up beside her and peered out. "Do you suppose something is wrong? He's here every Thursday night—without fail!"

"I don't know," Annie answered, recalling how much fun she'd had riding on Brad's chair. "Maybe he made other plans."

"Maybe he found a girlfriend," another waitress added cheerfully as she joined the two at the window. "He's a great-looking guy, and he's also one of the nicest men I've ever met. A girl would be lucky to snag a man like Brad."

"He's handicapped though," the first waitress reminded them.

"Not every woman could handle that. I'm not sure I could."

Annie listened and for the first time considered what it would be like to date a handicapped man. While she enjoyed riding on Brad's chair, what would it be like to have a boyfriend who was stuck in a wheelchair? To be unable to stand on tiptoes to kiss him or beside him with his arm about her waist. She shook the thoughts from her head. Why should she concern herself about such things? Brad was only a friend, nothing more. Perhaps he'd found a girlfriend. Well, more power to him. A good man like Brad deserved to be happy. She hoped he wouldn't fall for some woman who would toy with his emotions and leave him heartbroken.

It was nearly a week before Brad appeared again at Apple Valley Farm. And although his greeting to Apple Annie was cordial, the old spark she'd seen in him was gone. He sat at his regular table, focused his attention on his dinner, consumed his pie, and left, barely saying good-bye.

Annie watched with heightened interest as he maneuvered his chair across the lot. What had happened? He'd been warm and friendly; now he barely acknowledged her presence. Even the waitresses had noticed. Brad wasn't himself, and everyone was concerned. Had she offended him in some way?

She turned away once the van was out of sight, determined to ask him the next time he came in. If there was a next time.

Brad watched Apple Valley Farm disappear in his rearview mirror. He had promised himself he would stay away, but he'd felt compelled to see Annie one more time, and she was every bit as beautiful as he'd remembered. Much too beautiful to be interested in him. *Oh, God!* He laid his hand on the stub of his missing leg. *Why did You ever let me meet Annie Johnson?*

Annie sat by the bed holding tightly to her father's hand. The nurse was taking his temperature. Today was one of his better days. He had recognized her and called her by name when she walked in carrying a bouquet of daisies. She didn't mind his calling her by her mother's name, but it broke her heart to see him confused and disoriented.

"You're nearly normal, Mr. Johnson. That's good!" the nurse told him with a pleasant smile. She was staring at the tiny numbers on the thermometer. "The sun is shining, and your lovely daughter is here. This must be your day."

The man smiled back and squeezed Annie's hand. "This is my Annie," he told the nurse proudly, remembering her name again.

"You're mighty lucky to have a daughter who cares about you, Mr. Johnson." The woman moved to the window and with one pull raised the miniblinds to the top. Warm sunshine filled the room. "She your only daughter?"

The frail man nodded.

Annie frowned and put a hand on his shoulder. "No, Dad, I'm not your only daughter. Remember? Valerie is your daughter too."

"Valerie?" he repeated. He gazed blankly at the flowers she'd placed in a vase on his bedside table.

"I didn't know you had another daughter, Mr. Johnson." The nurse smoothed his covers then patted his weathered hand. "Is she as pretty as this one?"

Mr. Johnson's gaze never left the daisies.

"My sister, actually my half-sister, doesn't live here. She

lives in New Orleans, so Dad doesn't see much of her," Annie explained.

The nurse filled Mr. Johnson's water glass then gave him his medication. "He'll probably doze off. That pill usually makes him sleepy, but the doctor gave orders for us to give it to him at this time each day."

"I understand, and besides I need to get back to work. I'll stay until he falls asleep."

The nurse stepped over to the door. "You two have a nice visit. I'll be back later to check on him."

Annie thanked her then turned her attention to her father. He seemed to be failing more each day. Only three months ago they'd carried on lively discussions about Apple Valley Farm, politics, the stock market, and a myriad of other things her father was interested in. Now the conversation was one-sided. She talked. He smiled. She wondered how much of what she was telling him was getting through. If only Valerie would contact him—before it was too late for him to recognize her. How many times had she called in the past six months to ask about him? Twice? Three times?

She took a comb from the drawer and stroked it through his thinning gray hair. "Oh, Dad, I need you," she whispered softly. "Running Apple Valley Farm is almost too much for me. Come back to me, please."

For a second she thought she saw a light flicker in his eyes at the mention of his beloved Apple Valley Farm. He was the fifth generation to run the farm, and now she was the sixth.

Not by choice, but by obligation.

I'm going to phone Valerie this afternoon, she promised herself. *Maybe she'll come for a visit.*

It was nearly three o'clock before Annie was able to get

away from her duties long enough to make the call. Valerie answered on the fourth ring.

"Val, it's me. Annie. How are you?"

"What's wrong? Is Dad okay?" the woman asked quickly without greeting her sister.

Annie twisted the phone cord around her finger. She and her older sister had never been close. Annie's father and Valerie's mother had divorced when Valerie was only four. The two girls hadn't even met until Annie was ten, and they rarely saw one another after that. But they had corresponded occasionally through the years, through birthday and Christmas cards mostly. Her father had never talked much about his first marriage, and now it was almost too late to ask him about it. But Valerie was his daughter, and she deserved to know how he was, even if she didn't feel the need to pick up the phone and call.

"He's—fine. At least as fine as a seventy-three-year-old man with Alzheimer's can be. He's failing rapidly, Val. Most days he doesn't even recognize me and calls me by Mom's name. If you want to see him—"

Valerie interrupted. "Funny you should call. I've made plans to come, Annie. I'll be there tomorrow. I already have plane tickets. I need to talk to you about something."

"Oh? What?" *What could she want to talk to me about?* Annie brightened. *Perhaps she wants to help out with his care.*

"I'll tell you when I see you. Can you pick me up at Boise at two? If not, I can rent a car. I think I can find the place okay."

Annie frowned. "Sure. I'll be there."

"Fine. See you then."

The dial tone sounded. Annie stared into the phone. Valerie had hung up.

"What's up with you, Son?"

Brad grinned at the diminutive woman. She was sipping tea from a delicate rose-trimmed teacup. "What makes you think there's anything up with me?"

"A mother can tell those things. There's something going on in your life. Is it a"—she paused and eyed him suspiciously—"woman?"

He felt a flush rise to his face. "Is it that obvious?"

Mabel Reed's eyes sparkled as she reached out her hand and cupped her son's chin. "It is when you've had so few women in your life. Who is she? And when can I meet her?"

His expression sobered. "She's not in my life, Mom. I'm merely her friend. Nothing more on her part. There's no way she'd be attracted to me. Not with—"

Her finger pressed his lips to silence. "Don't say that, Brad. Many handicapped men have full and satisfying married lives. Some women out there are—"

"I don't want any of those women, Mom. I want Annie. But an active, vibrant woman like her could never love me. She needs a whole man." He sighed and leaned back in his chair. "One who can walk by her side, not roll along in a wheelchair."

Mrs. Reed pulled her chair closer to her son. "You've got to get over this, Brad. You're a handsome, brilliant man with a lot to offer. The woman who gets you is going to get a real prize."

"Booby prize, maybe."

"Tell me about her. Is she pretty?" his mother prodded, ignoring his remark. "Does she love the Lord?"

"She's beautiful, Mom. And smart. And witty."

"And what about her relationship with God?"

He glanced down at the table. "I think she's put God in the closet. Her life seems to be too busy for Him right now, what with her responsibilities and all. You've probably heard of her business," he added proudly.

"Oh? What business is that?"

"Apple Valley Farm."

His mother arched her brows. "That wonderful restaurant where they serve some type of caramel apple pie? I've never been there, but several of my friends have, and they rave about it. This girlfriend of yours works there?"

Brad smiled at the mention of Annie's famous pie. "Not only does she work there, but she also owns it. And, as much as I'd like to claim Annie, she is not my girlfriend."

"Have you ever asked this Annie out?"

"No, but we had dinner together at her restaurant. I'm just one of her many admiring customers." Brad leaned over to pick up the teapot and filled both their cups with steaming hot water. "You should see Annie, Mom. Everyone calls her Apple Annie, and she greets each of her customers at the door wearing some sort of fancy long dress with apples all over it and a long white apron. And she has apple things all over the restaurant. Apple tablecloths, apple salt-and-pepper shakers, apple pictures, apple figurines. Even her napkins have apples on them. It's a great place. I'll take you there sometime."

She touched his face affectionately. "Oh, Brad, this is really serious, isn't it? I've never seen you like this. You're really in love with this Annie, aren't you?"

Brad rubbed his forehead. "Yes, Mom. I'm hopelessly in love and can't do a thing about it."

She rose to her feet, bent over her son and wrapped her arms about his shoulders, then kissed his cheek. "You can't not do anything about it, Bradley. You have to tell her how you feel."

He blinked hard then looked into her eyes. "And take a chance on losing our friendship? No, things would never be the same between us if I did that. I'll have to be content with things the way they are."

His mother sank back into her chair and sipped at her tea. "Brad, I can only guess at what life is like for you. To be confined to a wheelchair with no hope of ever getting out of it, and I'm sorry. So sorry. Why did you take a job in the orchard that summer, instead of working at the grocery store? Why did that loader malfunction at that particular time? And why did my son happen to be standing behind it when it did?" She pulled a handkerchief from the cuff of her sleeve and dabbed at her eyes. "You were so young. Only fifteen, with a promising life ahead of you. Why would God let such a thing happen?"

Brad stared at the floor. How many times he'd asked himself those same questions. Why? Why? Why?

"But, despite the pain and suffering and the trials you've gone through, you have such a great attitude. And you've grown up to be a responsible man with a successful business and a promising future. And, best of all, you haven't turned your back on God."

"God has been good to me, Mom. If it weren't for Him and the comfort He's brought me when I've been at my lowest, I don't think I could have made it. That, and the support I received from you and Dad."

Mrs. Reed set her cup on the table, a warm smile on her face. "You deserve the love of a good woman. Don't let this chance at love get away from you, Dear. Ask Annie out on a date. Give her a chance." She gave his arm a little nudge. "You and I both know you won't be content simply being her friend.

You're already in too deep for that. If you love her as I think you do, go to her. Court her. Let her know how you feel."

Brad evaluated her words. Everything she was saying was true. Although he'd never experienced the love between a man and a woman before, he was sure his part of the equation was true love. But dare he let Annie know of his feelings for her?

Maybe.

But not yet.

It was nearly five-thirty before Brad got home from his office. By six o'clock he'd showered, shaved, and with great effort changed into tan trousers and a pale-blue polo shirt. He sat debating about whether he should eat his dinner at the nearby steak house or go to Apple Valley Farm as his heart told him to. He had gone there so often lately that he wondered if he might be wearing out his welcome. Maybe he'd skip a night and go to Apple Valley next week. But, he reasoned, if he did settle for steak instead of going, he'd be missing a chance to be around Annie.

His mind was still not made up when his phone rang.

"Is this Bradley Reed?" he heard a woman ask between sobs. "I'm afraid I have bad news."

"No Brad again tonight?" one of the waitresses asked Annie as she stood in the doorway greeting her customers. "It's past the time he usually comes."

"I haven't seen him," Annie called back over her shoulder as she led a party of six to their table. Where was Brad? Had she offended him in some way? It wasn't like him to stay away like this. Maybe he'd found a restaurant he liked better.

"Hey, is that one-legged man going to play the piano for tonight's melodrama?" one of her regular customers asked when she walked past his table. "That guy sure knows how to play the piano. We really enjoyed him."

Annie shook her head, irritated that he would use those terms to describe Brad. "I'm afraid not. That was a one-time thing. He was kind enough to fill in for our regular pianist. But I'll tell him what you said the next time I see him." *If I see him a next time,* she reminded herself. *Where is Brad?*

Brad propelled his chair from the van and wheeled into his mother's apartment. "Where is she?" he called to the next-door neighbor who was waiting for him at the door.

The woman pointed her trembling hand toward the narrow hall. "In her room. She wouldn't let me call an ambulance. She wanted you."

Brad rolled quickly past her down the hall and into his mother's bedroom. She was sitting on the edge of the bed cradling her arm close to her body, crying.

"I did something so stupid," she said.

He hurried to her side. "What happened? Are you all right?"

"It—it was the electric teakettle," she told him between sobs. "I—forgot to unplug it before I took it—to the table, and when the cord tightened—it pulled out of my hand and threw boiling water onto my arm."

Brad could see the horror written on her face, and he knew she had to be in excruciating pain. He took hold of her hand and carefully pulled it toward him, revealing a scarlet red burn that was already forming watery blisters. "Oh, Mom. You should've let your neighbor call 911. We need to get you to a doctor."

Three hours later Brad was sitting by his mother's hospital bed watching the even rise and fall of her chest as she lay blanketed in white, her bandaged arm on a pillow at her side. The burn was every bit as bad as he'd suspected. The doctor had even indicated some skin grafting might be necessary in the future. But at least she was alive. He shuddered to think what might have happened if the scalding water had splashed onto her face or into her eyes or—it was too frightening to think about.

He stayed with her until he was sure she was asleep. The doctor had said he wanted to keep her in the hospital for several days because of her age, in case of complications with her burns. She was given something to relieve her pain and help her sleep. He had wanted to stay with her, but they'd advised him to leave, saying she would probably sleep through the night.

He checked his watch as he rolled through the hospital's double doors, suddenly realizing he hadn't eaten supper. As he turned into a fast-food drive-through, his mother's words came back to him—the words she'd spoken that very day: "Don't let this chance at love get away from you, Dear. Ask Annie out on a date. Give her a chance. You and I both know you won't be content simply being her friend. You're already in too deep for that. If you love her as I think you do, go to her. Court her. Let her know how you feel."

Valerie's plane arrived at two o'clock the next afternoon, and Annie was there to meet her as promised. After casual greetings and obligatory hugs they picked up her luggage, climbed into Annie's van, and headed for Apple Valley Farm.

"I'm glad you've come. But don't be upset if he doesn't recognize you," Annie warned as they drove along. "Some days he remembers; some days he doesn't." She pulled past a slow moving truck then fell back in line with the other traffic.

"Do you think he'll ever—?" Valerie stopped and fiddled with the clasp on her purse, as if to avoid looking at Annie.

"Get well?"

"Yes."

"No. I wish I could say there was hope for him. But, according to his doctor, he'll get progressively worse and eventually—" She gulped hard, unable to put his foreordained destiny in words.

"That's what my doctor said too, when I described Dad's condition to him."

"It's so sad." Annie's voice broke with emotion. Only recently had she started to accept what the doctor had confirmed about her father's condition. "There's no hope."

Valerie stared out the window solemnly. "It's a good thing he was smart enough to sign the property over to the two of us before he got like this."

Annie smiled. She remembered the day her father had called her into his office and shown her the papers he'd had the attorney draw up, turning over everything to his two daughters. "That's our dad."

"It was all legal, wasn't it? Without any loopholes I don't know about?"

Annie glanced at her sister then back to the road. "Legal? Of course. What do you mean by loopholes? I don't understand."

"I mean, he didn't put any stipulations on it that I'm not aware of, did he?"

"Stipulations?" Annie repeated, wondering what her sister could be implying. "I guess I don't understand your question."

Valerie tilted her head. "I mean, is there any reason why we couldn't sell the farm?"

Annie stepped on the brake. The vehicle slowed and came to a sudden stop on the shoulder of the road. "Sell Apple Valley Farm?" she asked incredulously as she spun around toward the woman. "What kind of question is that?"

"I hadn't intended to bring it up before we got to the house, but I need the money, Annie. And it seems to me we have only two choices. Sell the farm, restaurant, and theater and split the proceeds, or—" The two sisters locked their gazes and their wills.

"Or?" Annie asked, her face burning. The very idea that Apple Valley Farm would leave the Johnson family infuriated her.

"Or we can have it appraised, and you can buy out my half and keep Apple Valley Farm for yourself."

Annie couldn't believe what she was hearing. Sell Apple

Valley Farm? "But—" she stammered, "it's our heritage. We're the sixth generation to run the farm. Our grandfathers—"

Valerie held up her hand between them. "Your heritage, maybe. Not mine. I've barely seen my father since he and my mother divorced. That place means absolutely nothing to me, except for the money it represents."

Annie wanted to slap her. How dare she talk like that? Their father had put his life's blood into Apple Valley Farm. She could understand Valerie's not wanting to pull up her stakes in New Orleans to move to Idaho, but sell the farm? Never! "I can't believe what I'm hearing. If Dad ever heard you talk this way he'd—"

"He'd what?"

Her haughty tone made Annie's stomach turn.

"It's too late for him to do much about anything. He's already turned everything over to the two of us. You can't take something like that back. We're the legal owners now. It's out of his hands. No court in the land would give it back to him."

Annie's hand flew out seemingly of its own accord and hit Valerie's cheek with a loud smack, reeling her back against the seat. She regretted it the minute she'd done it, but it was too late. She had slapped her half-sister.

The two sat staring at one another—Annie grasping for words, her sister holding a hand to her reddening cheek.

"What was that for?" Valerie finally muttered, her face filled with anger.

"How dare you talk like that about our father? He took care of your mother and you all those years. I know. I saw the canceled checks when I took over the book work for him. He paid dearly for that divorce. And from what I've heard, none of it was his fault. Your mother cheated on him." Her accusation was sharp, and like the slap she regretted her words the minute she'd voiced them. Her father had told her those things in confidence.

"My mother cheated on him? That's not the way I heard it!"

Annie drew in a deep breath. She had to control her feelings. Railing at her sister was getting neither of them anywhere. None of what they were discussing could be proven either way. "Let's not discuss this, Valerie. Neither of us was there. And it all happened years ago."

Valerie stared straight ahead, rubbed at her cheek, and remained silent.

Annie fumbled for words. If they were to resolve any of this, the two of them had to get along. "I'm—I'm sorry for slapping you. But you have to realize you're speaking of the loving, caring man who raised me. The man I respect more than any other man I know. I have to defend him, even from you, his other daughter."

"I'm sorry. I was only telling the truth."

"The truth as you know it," Annie added. "Now could we drop this discussion? Please? We need to hurry to get to the care home and see Dad before I have to head back to the restaurant."

"Okay, but I want my share of the money, Annie. And I want it as soon as possible. Let's go see Dad, and we can discuss this later. But, believe me, I'm serious about this. I want out of Apple Valley Farm."

Annie had to clasp both hands together to keep from slapping Valerie again. She bit her lip until she nearly drew blood to avoid saying the things she had on her mind. No way would she let Apple Valley Farm leave the family. But how would she ever keep it? She was barely breaking even as it was. A few dollars one way or the other would put her either in the red or in the black.

Unfortunately, in the early stages of his illness, before they knew he had Alzheimer's disease, her father had let the farm lapse into disrepair. Then, to cover his losses when the stock market dropped, he took out several big loans, which now needed to be repaid. But, by the time Annie discovered the poor financial condition, the harm was done, and she had no other choice but to try to set things right and repay the loans. If her father had been in his right mind, he would never have let things get out of hand like that. There was absolutely no reserve to buy out her sister's portion.

"As you said, we'll discuss this later." She pulled the car back onto the road, and they continued in silence toward the care home and their father.

Their visit was pleasant enough. Their father was slightly more alert after his afternoon nap, and once he even called Valerie by her name. But in his next sentence he called her by Annie's mother's name, which didn't set too well with his elder daughter.

No mention was made of selling Apple Valley Farm, for which Annie was grateful. Not that her father would have understood anyway.

She drove Valerie to the farmhouse, with her assurance that her sister would walk to the restaurant for dinner later, then hurried to greet her customers as Apple Annie. Only tonight Apple Annie found it difficult to smile. The mere thought of losing Apple Valley Farm set her nerves on edge.

It was nearly eight before Valerie showed up at the restaurant. Annie selected a small table in the far corner of the restaurant, the same table for two where she and Brad had eaten dinner, where they could talk without being interrupted.

"You've done wonders with this place," Valerie conceded as she ate her dinner salad. "Where in the world did you find so many apple things? Everywhere you look are apple pictures, apple figurines, apple this, and apple that. I'm amazed. And your customers seem to love it. And that garb of yours!" She pointed toward Annie's costume and laughed in a way that Annie sensed was slightly mocking. "That's priceless!"

"It's all part of my long-range marketing plan, Valerie. I went to college for four years to learn marketing. I figured I'd put that education to good use," Annie explained. She was proud of what she had done to build up the restaurant's clientele. But Valerie made it sound like a big joke.

Valerie stabbed a cherry tomato on her fork and waved it around. "Well, it's lucky for me—apparently your cute little idea seems to have increased the restaurant's business. That'll mean more money for both of us when we sell it."

Annie grasped the edge of the table with her hands to keep them from flying to her sister's neck and choking her. "We are not selling Apple Valley Farm," she said through clenched teeth. "Positively not!"

"Oh? You have the money to buy out my half?" Valerie raised her brow.

Annie glanced around her, but those nearby were enjoying their dinner and paying little attention to anything else. "Look, Valerie. I am not going to lose Apple Valley Farm. It is staying in the Johnson family. Period!"

Valerie dropped her fork onto her plate, grabbed Annie's wrist, and leaned so close their foreheads nearly touched. She spoke in a hushed but angry voice. "I want my money, and I want it now. I don't care if you have Apple Valley Farm or Joe Blow has it. It means nothing to me. If you want to keep it, fine. But you'll have to come up with my half. I've already spoken to an attorney—one right here in Apple Valley—and he assures me if you cannot buy me out, this place will have to be put on the market. The rest is up to you."

Annie wiped her mouth with her napkin, stood to her feet, and placed her napkin on the table. She appeared calm on the outside, but inside she was seething. Countless words crossed her mind, but she knew she wouldn't change anything by saying them.

Valerie watched her guardedly, as if she expected a thunderous outburst. But when her sister remained silent, she added, "My attorney wants to meet with you at ten tomorrow morning—at the restaurant. Then I'm flying home."

Annie took a deep breath and let it out slowly. Valerie hadn't come to see their father. She had come only to lay claim to her half of the farm. She was thankful her father would never know that. "I'll be there," she said dryly as she turned and walked away, leaving her sister at the table.

It was nearly eleven before Annie returned to the farmhouse. She was glad the door to the room she had given Valerie was closed. She'd had enough confrontations with her already. Carrying on a congenial conversation was impossible now. The battle lines had been drawn. Only the weapons had to be chosen.

She set her alarm for six and was out of the house before the door to Valerie's room opened, although she was sure she could hear her moving around inside.

At least she could have managed to see our father again before she left, she told herself angrily. She climbed into her van and headed for the care home. *But it seems all she's interested in is his money.*

"Well, you're up early," one of her father's caretakers said as Annie passed her in the hallway. "Your father had a good night, and I'm sure he'll be glad to see you."

Annie nodded and hurried into his room where her father greeted her with a big smile. He was sitting on the edge of his bed drinking a glass of juice.

"Hi, Daddy," she said cheerfully, hoping she wouldn't have to explain why Valerie wasn't with her. "I love you." She kissed his forehead then hugged him.

"I love you," he returned, taking her by surprise.

"I came to see you yesterday. Do you remember?"

He nodded, but his face held a vacant smile.

"The nurse said you had a good night."

Again he nodded.

Oh, Daddy, I need you, she said in her aching heart. *I don't know what to do, and there's no one to talk to about this.*

"Is she here?" he asked, his expression still wearing its pasted smile.

Annie's heart sank. He remembered Valerie's visit. "No, sorry."

"When did your mother leave?" he asked as he took another sip of the juice.

"Mother? Leave?" It suddenly hit her. He wasn't talking about Valerie after all. He was thinking about his wife. "She—she's been gone a long time, Daddy. Don't you remember? We buried Mama in the Apple Valley cemetery several years ago."

He placed his glass on the tray, raised his legs onto the bed, and leaned back into the pillows. "I'm going to see her, you know. She's waiting for me. She's with God."

Annie blinked then shut her eyes. "I know, Daddy. I know."

She pulled her chair up close and stroked his fragile hands until he drifted off. "I miss you, Daddy," she told him in a whisper. "I promise you I won't let Apple Valley Farm get away from us."

Brad was awake and up long before his alarm sounded. All he could think about was his mother. He entered her room at Apple Valley Memorial Hospital before seven and sat watching her sleep, wishing somehow he could bear her pain for her. When she began to stir he pulled the white blanket up about her shoulders as best he could then put a kiss on the tip of his finger and transferred it to her cheek. She looked so small, so helpless, lying in that sterile bed surrounded by a dozen bouquets sent by her friends and neighbors. He had been extremely concerned about her, but the doctor had assured him she was doing well but should remain in the hospital for a few more days.

He moved her glass of water where she could reach it more easily, then turned and rolled toward the door. It was time to get to his office.

"Brad?"

He spun around to find his mother's eyes open. "Yes, Mom?"

A faint smile played at her lips. "Are you going to see that young woman of yours tonight?"

"I thought you were asleep." He rolled up beside her bed. "I've put your glass where you can reach it. Is there anything else you need before I leave?"

"You're not answering my question."

Brad thought it over before responding. "Yes, I am. I'm going to her restaurant for dinner."

"Court her, Son. Like your father did me. No woman can resist a loving, caring man like you. Don't let your handicap keep you from her. Even if she says no and turns you away, at least you tried. Nothing ventured—"

"Nothing gained. I know. Dad used to tell me that all the time. It's the reason I finished my college education. He drilled it into me."

"Go to her," she said softly, her words drifting off. Her eyelids closed, and she fell back into a deep sleep.

Brad smiled at his mother. In many ways Annie was like her. Beautiful. Tenacious. Ambitious. Gentle. Caring. He could go on and on about the attributes of the two women he loved. He closed the door behind him and headed for his office.

He had been at his desk for only a few minutes when his cell phone rang.

"Brad Reed."

"Oh, Brad, I'm so glad I reached you. This is Annie. I got your number from one of the waitresses. I need you. Can you come to Apple Valley right now?"

Chapter 5

B rad smiled into the phone. Annie Johnson was the last person he'd expected to be on the other end of the line. "Now? You want me to come now?"

"I'm in trouble, Brad. I didn't know who to turn to, with Dad so ill. I've been so busy running things here since I've come back home that I've hardly taken time to make friends with anyone."

"Sure, I'll come—if you need me." He glanced at the stack of unopened mail on his desk and the pile of call slips left over from the day before when he'd stayed with his mother at the hospital. "Give me thirty minutes."

"Oh, Brad. I can't thank you enough. Please hurry."

Brad placed the phone in the receiver then called his secretary. "An emergency has come up. Call and reschedule my appointments." He shoved a few file folders into his desk drawer, put his cell phone in his pocket, and rolled toward the double doors leading to the elevator. "If you hear anything from the hospital or my mother's doctor, call me on my cell phone."

His secretary hurried to keep up with him. "But where are you—"

The elevator doors opened, and Brad rolled inside, calling

back before they closed, "I'll check with you later. Please take care of things for me, okay?"

It seemed to take him forever to reach Apple Valley Farm. The traffic was unusually heavy for a weekday morning. Finally, he drove into the parking lot and pulled up near the front door. Annie ran out to meet him. She was wearing a light pink pantsuit, instead of her Apple Annie costume. To Brad, she was the most beautiful woman he'd ever seen.

"I'm so glad you're here." Her face was pale, and her breath came in short gasps. "I knew I could count on you."

"It isn't your father, is it?" Brad asked, his own mother's accident fresh on his mind.

Annie stood beside the door of the van as the ramp lowered his wheelchair onto the pavement. Her eyes were puffy and red from crying, and he wanted nothing more than to take her in his arms and comfort her.

"Let's go inside where we can talk." She grasped one of the chair's handles and walked along beside him. "We don't have much time."

Talk about what? And why don't we have much time? he wondered.

They reached Annie's office then, where they wouldn't be disturbed by the employees who were getting ready for the lunch crowd.

He took her hands in his. "Okay," he said gently. "I'm here. Tell me what's upset you so much."

She glanced nervously at her watch. "My sister and her attorney will be here at ten. That's less than an hour away."

He frowned. "Your sister? Her attorney? Why are they coming here?"

Annie pulled her hands from his and started pacing the

room. "I probably should have a lawyer representing me, but I don't know any lawyers in Apple Valley. That's why I called you. I thought perhaps you could help me find a good one—someone who wouldn't bleed me to death."

He leaned toward her and took her hands in his again. "Annie, settle down," he said calmly. "Breathe. It can't be that bad. Tell me what's going on."

Annie drew in a fresh breath of air and swallowed. "She's demanding her half of everything on Apple Valley Farm. The restaurant, theater, orchards, the house—all of it," she blurted out. She let go of his hands and sat down in the chair beside her desk.

"How can she do that? Your father is still alive. Doesn't he own everything?"

Annie shook her head. "No. When the doctor diagnosed Alzheimer's, Dad had papers drawn up giving everything to my stepsister and me. Equally. He knew he would reach the point where he would be unable to make a decision and wanted everything to be clean for us girls."

Brad rubbed his hand across his forehead. "I didn't even know you had a sister."

"Half-sister," she said. "By my father's first wife."

"And she's decided she wants her half now?"

She nodded again. "She gave me two choices. Sell everything or buy out her half." She lifted her tear-filled gaze to his. "I can't raise that kind of money, Brad. I'm barely scraping by as it is."

"She sounds pretty selfish."

Annie bit her lip. "She is. And she barely said hello to Dad when we visited him yesterday." She glanced at her watch again. "Oh, Brad, I'm sure I'm going to need an attorney to represent me. I wish I'd known which one to call. That's why I phoned you. I need someone here with me who's on my side."

Brad rolled his chair up next to hers and slid his arm about her shoulders. "You have an attorney, Annie. One who'll fight for you like a mad dog."

She turned and looked at him. "Who?"

"Me."

Annie stared at Brad. "You? I don't understand."

He smiled at her. "Do you realize you've never asked me what I do for a living? And then the night I told you I don't think you heard me. I'm an attorney. I have my own law firm." He gave her a jaunty salute. "Brad Reed, attorney-at-law. At your service, Ma'am."

Her eyes widened with surprise. "You're an attorney?"

"You bet," he said, pulling a business card from his inside pocket. "And a mighty good one, if I do say so myself."

Her expression sobered. "I don't have much money to pay you."

He took her hand, lifted it to his mouth, and kissed it. "I'll take it out in Caramel Apple Pie."

Annie let out a sigh of relief. "You're incorrigible."

"I think you've told me that before." Brad kissed her hand again then became serious. "We have work to do. Tell me everything you know about this so we'll be prepared when they arrive."

For the next twenty minutes they discussed her sister's demands and Annie's options.

"I have one final question for you, Annie." Brad placed his pen on the legal pad where he'd been taking notes. "I want you to think it over carefully and make sure your answer reflects how you feel."

Her eyes widened.

"You've been to college to prepare for a career, and from what you've told me you'd never intended to come back here to live. Then your father got sick, and you were forced to come back."

"I wasn't exactly forced." She twisted her ring on her finger. "I mean, Dad needed me. That was reason enough."

"But once your father—" He hesitated. "I hate to say it, but we have to face reality. Once your father is gone, or he's lost his mental faculties, your obligation will be fulfilled. Isn't that right?"

She nodded. "I guess so."

"Then this is my question, and I want you to think about it long and hard before you answer. Are you sure you want to stay on Apple Valley Farm for the rest of your life?"

Annie's mouth dropped open, but no words came out.

"One more thing, Annie." He cupped her chin in his hand and looked into her eyes. "God has a plan for your life. He allows us to make our own decisions—He's given us a free will—but His way is always the best." He slipped an arm about her shoulders and gave her a firm hug. "I'd like to pray with you about this. Okay?"

She nodded then bowed her head.

"Lord, it's me again. Annie has a real problem and needs Your guidance in this matter. You know the details, and You know what's best for her. Help her make the right decision."

He drew her close to him, and for the first time in a long while she felt secure. She was no longer alone. Brad was there.

"And, God," he continued, "most of all, draw Annie close to You. Reveal Yourself to her and help her want to draw near to You. I praise Your name. Amen."

Annie rested her head on Brad's shoulder. He asked so little of her yet was willing to give so much. Who was this man who had come so suddenly into her life? And why was he willing to drop everything and run to her aid when she called him? She knew she should pull away. Their prayer was over, but something about his nearness comforted her. She didn't want the moment to end.

It was Brad who moved away. "I'm going to get us some coffee while you consider my question. Take your time. Your answer is very important." He rolled to the drink station and filled two cups, placed them on a tray on his lap, and rolled back. Then he pulled his chair up beside her.

Annie added cream to her coffee and stared into the swirling mix. She had never thought about it that way. She realized that any decision she made now would influence the rest of her life. Was keeping Apple Valley Farm in the Johnson family that important? Important enough to dedicate her life to it? To give up the career for which she'd spent four hard years preparing?

She watched Brad out of the corner of her eye. Strong, handsome, confident Brad. Life had dealt him a terrible blow; yet he'd succeeded in spite of it. Would she be strong enough to stand by the decision she must make with such grace and style as he had?

He remained silent, occasionally jotting a few notes on his legal pad, other times looking away as if in deep thought.

Annie placed her elbows on the table and cradled her chin in her hands, her eyes closed. Was it pure stubbornness that made her want to hold onto the farm? Was it her hard feelings toward her stepsister, who hadn't raised one finger to help her since their father had become ill? What were her motives?

She turned toward him, her eyes misty with confusion. "What would you do, Brad? If you were me?"

He took her hand. "I'm not you, Annie. This has to be your decision. You're the one who will have to live with it."

"But committing to something for the rest of my life at my age? I've barely begun to live. There's so much out there I haven't experienced."

He pushed a lock of hair from her forehead and smiled into her eyes. "Many people make a lifetime commitment when they're much younger than you. Marriage is a lifetime commitment too."

Marriage? Annie pondered his words. What an unusual parallel. He was right, though. But how many of those marriages ended up in divorce? Over fifty percent? And couldn't she sell the farm later?

"Annie, I'm not saying your commitment has to be forever. Of course, you could decide to sell the farm later on. What I'm saying is, no lender will even talk to you about financing unless you are committed to a long-range plan. Your age will go against you. You've run the farm in the absence of your father, but other than the few months you've been on your own, you don't have a track record with the business."

She drew back at his words, tears clinging to her dark lashes. "Are you saying I don't have a chance to keep this place?"

"No, Annie, I'm not saying that at all. But you have to be prepared for the battle ahead of you. Not only the one with your sister, but the one you'll have finding someone to finance your sister's half. If you intend to keep this place, you must be committed."

Why does life have to be so complicated? she wondered.

"Think what you could do with the money your half of the sale would bring. You could write your own ticket. Establish your own marketing firm. Wherever you choose. Be your own boss."

She looked at him. "Now are you saying we should sell this place?"

"No, not at all. I want you to consider all the ramifications before you make a decision."

An awkward silence filled the room. The only sound she heard was an occasional bang or thud coming from the kitchen.

"I want to keep Apple Valley Farm," she said finally. "It's my heritage. I've already used my marketing skills here, and they're paying off." She leaned back in the chair and smiled at Brad. "I'm sure of it. I could never let this farm out of the family without at least making a stab at keeping it for my children. If I'm ever lucky enough to have children."

"Oh, I'm sure you'll have children one day," he assured her.

Annie smiled. "I'll have to find a man who'll have me first."

"You'll find him all right. In fact, he may be closer than you think."

She scarcely heard Brad's words as she started to think of ideas for building up Apple Valley Farm's business.

"I'll be there for you, Annie—if you want me to represent you as your attorney. You know that, don't you?"

She suddenly realized how difficult it must have been for him to get away from his office on such short notice. "Can you? I mean, don't you have other clients you should be taking care of? I don't want to cause—"

"You let me worry about that, okay? Right now you have my full, undivided attention."

A faint smile crossed her lips. "Thanks for praying with me. It helped."

"My pleasure. But, Annie, you need to be on praying ground with God to expect answers to your prayers. Are you?"

His question stopped her. "When you put it that way,

I'm—not sure," she answered hesitantly. She felt uncomfortable with the direction their conversation was taking. "Do we need to discuss religion now? When we should be concentrating on—"

"Annie, dear Annie. Nothing is more important than having a right relationship with God. I brought this up now because you are probably facing one of the most difficult battles you'll ever encounter in your life."

He put the cap back on his pen, slipped it into his shirt pocket and smiled. "Keeping Apple Valley Farm is going to take a miracle from God."

"There you are!"

The two at the little table turned quickly at the sound of Valerie's voice.

Chapter 6

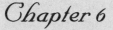

Annie feigned a smile and hurried to greet them, but her heart wasn't in it. Her sister's threatening words kept ringing in her ears: "I want my money, and I want it now. I don't care if you have Apple Valley Farm or Joe Blow has it. It means nothing to me."

"I hope you've decided to sell, Annie," Valerie said curtly as she gestured toward the short man behind her carrying a large briefcase. "It would simplify matters."

Annie ignored her remark and gestured toward Brad who had rolled his chair up beside her. "Valerie, this is my friend Brad, and he—"

"You're going to need more than a friend, Annie," Valerie said sharply. She looked at the handsome man then the chair. "You're going to need a good lawyer."

"Looks to me like she's already got one. The best one in the state, I'd say." The man behind her crossed the room to Brad and extended his hand. "Nice to see you again, Brad."

"Yes, as I was about to say when you interrupted me, Valerie—Brad is not only my friend but my attorney. He'll be representing me in this matter."

Valerie cleared her throat nervously then nodded toward

the man. "I see. Well, Ben Calhoun will be representing me."

Annie motioned to one of the servers to bring a coffeepot while they sat down around one of the restaurant's larger tables. Once everyone's cup had been filled, Brad began.

"As I understand it," he said, enunciating each word as he looked directly into Valerie's eyes, "you've given my client two alternatives. Sell the entire estate known as Apple Valley Farm and the two of you divide the proceeds evenly. Or you expect Annie to buy out your half. Is that correct?"

Valerie nodded.

Annie smiled to herself. Her sister seemed intimidated by Brad's authoritative manner. And to think two hours ago she didn't even have an attorney.

Brad placed the yellow pad on the table and studied it for a few moments. "I also understand you have done nothing toward the maintenance or operation of Apple Valley Farm. Is that correct?"

"Doing those things was impossible for her. I want to remind you she was living out of state," Ben Calhoun interjected.

"How about the care of your father, Ms.—"

Annie felt a flush rise to her cheeks. She hadn't told Brad her sister's last name. "Malone," she whispered, leaning toward him.

Brad smiled at Annie, and she felt her heart grow warm. Then he nodded toward Valerie. "Ms. Malone."

Valerie bristled. "No. As Ben said, I live out of state. Taking care of him was impossible."

Brad narrowed his eyes and leaned forward in his chair. "Was my client also living out of state when her father became ill?"

Valerie hesitated, glancing about the room. "I guess. She was attending college. But—"

Her words dwindled off while the three of them waited for

her answer. "I was—ah—busy. I couldn't be here," she mumbled.

"Oh? Your employer wouldn't give you time off?" Brad prodded, his eyes never leaving her face. "You were holding an important position of some kind?"

Valerie fidgeted with a button on her blouse. "No. I mean— I don't work—outside the home, that is."

"May I ask what kept you so busy that you couldn't come when your father needed you?"

"I—ah—" She looked helplessly at her attorney, but Ben Calhoun sat listening, apparently as interested in the answers to Brad's questions as he was.

Brad pressed on. "You were saying?"

"I have—social obligations," she blurted out, avoiding his penetrating gaze. "And I have headaches."

Brad leaned back in his chair and locked his hands behind his head. His smile seemed almost, but not quite, threatening. "Then, of course, you'll want to make sure my client is reimbursed for taking the full responsibility of the maintenance and operation of Apple Valley Farm, as well as the constant care and responsibility of taking care of her ill and aging father."

Valerie grasped her attorney's arm. "Do I have to do that? Can they make me?"

But before he could answer, Brad spoke. "We can't make you do anything, Ms. Malone. But I assure you, if this is taken to court, which my client is prepared to do, any judge will look favorably on the person who has abandoned her own life to take care of her father and do whatever was necessary to keep his business in operation. Especially a business that has been in the family for six generations."

Valerie shoved herself back against the chair and crossed her arms. "It isn't fair."

"That's what I thought when you came waltzing in here yesterday demanding your half of Apple Valley Farm," Annie blurted out while trying to keep her tears from surfacing.

Brad lifted his hands. "Look—I don't think anyone here wants to take this thing to court. Between the four of us we should be able to find an equitable solution."

He turned to Valerie. "I'll do some figuring and come up with what I feel is a reasonable amount for the services Annie has provided. Of course, that'll come off the top of whatever is determined to be a reasonable fair market value of the estate. And it will include the wages Annie could have earned at some New York marketing firm with the degree she received in college."

Valerie hit the table with her fist. "But that could be thousands of dollars!"

"Yes, I'm sure it will be, Ms. Malone. Must I remind you she's done it all without your lifting one finger to help? I'm sure the nursing home has kept a record of all your father's visitors over the past year. How many times has your name appeared on that list?"

Annie wanted to stand up and cheer. Brad was saying all the right things. Things she'd wanted to say but hadn't had the courage. But she was sure the nursing home guest register was something he'd made up to frighten Valerie. She had never seen such a list.

"Aren't you going to say anything?" Valerie yelled at her lawyer.

Ben Calhoun shrugged his shoulders. "Brad is only saying what any judge would say. I thought you wanted an equitable settlement. That's what he's talking about. What more do you want?"

"I want what's rightfully mine!" she shouted, her face red

with anger. "Half! And I want it now!"

"I'm sorry, Ms. Malone," Brad told her in an even voice. "The wheels of justice don't roll that fast. I can assure you that coming to an agreement with my client will facilitate matters much more quickly than any court hearing." He capped his pen and put it in his pocket. "Your attorney can expect to hear from me in a few days."

The two men shook hands; then Brad extended his hand toward Valerie. "You'll have to excuse me, Ms. Malone. If it were possible, I'd rise to shake your hand, but unfortunately I'm not able."

Valerie backed away, refusing his hand and not saying a word.

Annie moved quickly to her sister's side. "Please, Valerie. I have no idea how I can raise that kind of money, and I can't fathom the idea of selling Dad's beloved Apple Valley Farm. Won't you reconsider? I could send you a check every month. Everything above the actual cost of running the place. Wouldn't that help?"

Valerie put her hands on her hips and glared at her sister. "Like I told you, Annie—I want what's mine, and I want it now! Put up or shut up!" With that she turned around and headed for the door, knocking over two chairs on her way.

Ben Calhoun said a hasty good-bye, grabbed his briefcase, and followed her out the door.

Annie leaped onto Brad's lap and threw her arms about his neck. "You were wonderful! I couldn't have asked for a better lawyer."

"Don't get too excited, Annie. It isn't over yet," he reminded her, making no attempt to pull away from her grasp.

Annie suddenly realized how foolish she must look, plunking herself onto his lap like that, but she couldn't help herself.

Only a few hours earlier she had been terrified, with no one to turn to for help. Then Brad had come to her rescue. Warm, comfortable Brad. He always seemed to appear in her life at the right time. She leaned away from him, looked into his eyes, and found she didn't want to turn away. Something about Brad was so—manly. Yes, that was the word. And he always smelled nice. As if he'd come fresh from a shower. His gaze held her captive.

Brad pulled her to him and cradled her head on his shoulder. "I'd do anything for you, Annie. Absolutely anything," he murmured as his lips sought hers.

"Sorry—I forgot my hat."

Annie pushed away from Brad to find Ben Calhoun hovering over them.

"I—didn't mean to interrupt," he stammered awkwardly. He grabbed his hat from the table and hurried back toward the restaurant door.

Brad burst out laughing, and Annie blushed as she pushed herself off his lap and stood, smoothing the wrinkles from her shirt.

Then she turned and smiled at him. "Will you be my guest for dinner tonight? I feel like celebrating."

"You bet I will!"

Brad spent the afternoon in his office. He worked on the proposal he would present to Ben Calhoun, setting aside the papers of his more important clients for later. Right now Annie was his prime concern.

By four o'clock he was sitting beside his mother, holding her hand, and reading to her from the Bible. Afterward he told her about his morning with Annie.

"I'm anxious to meet this woman," she told him as he prepared to leave. "Any woman who can put that kind of smile on my son's face has to be some kind of woman. I've never seen you so happy, and it's about time."

"I'm in love, Mom," he confessed as he filled her water glass. "Hopelessly in love." He paused then leaned forward and lifted his empty trouser leg. "But Annie could never love me. She has one invalid to care for already. Why would she want two?"

His mother frowned and patted his hand. "Don't use that word, Son. You're not an invalid. You've always taken care of yourself. And since your father died, you've taken care of me. I'm sure your Annie doesn't think of you as an invalid. Don't let that stand in your way. Let her know how you feel. At least you'll find out for sure where you stand with her."

Brad grinned at his mother. "Where I stand? Was that an intended pun, Mom?"

She swatted at him with her uninjured hand. "You! That's another wonderful thing about you, Brad Reed—your delightful sense of humor. I can't even remember a time, since right after your accident, that I've heard you complain. About anything! You can't say that about most men. Any woman should be proud to be your wife."

"You are my mom. You are supposed to say nice things about me."

"Brad, be serious. You love this woman, and I can't imagine her not loving you. Don't let her get away."

"What I'd like to do is ask her to marry me," he said shyly, avoiding his mother's eyes. "Foolish, huh? Guess I'm a dreamer where Annie is concerned."

"Then ask her. Before some other man does. If she's as

good a catch as you say she is—well, don't wait too long."

"I wish I had the courage."

Mrs. Reed pointed toward the door. "Be gone with you. Go to that young lady of yours and show her how much you care." She smiled. "And I'll be praying God will give you courage."

He kissed her hand and called back over his shoulder as he rolled toward the door. "You and God? With a team like that, how can I miss?"

Annie spent more time than usual fixing her hair and applying makeup. She hadn't been able to get Brad off her mind all day—the professional way he'd handled Valerie and her attorney, and the ridiculous way she'd thrown herself into his lap. She smiled as she flipped through the menus, making sure each one had the nightly special attached to it.

"You're mighty happy tonight," one of the waitresses told her. "Is that a new pair of earrings?"

Annie reached up and touched her ears. "No, not new. I only wear them on special occasions."

A second waitress joined them. "Special occasions? Is this your birthday?" She gave Annie's arm a playful pinch. "Maybe you have a date!"

Before Annie could respond, the door opened, and Brad rolled in, a bouquet of red roses in his lap.

Both waitresses glanced from the flowers to Brad to Annie then disappeared, whispering and giggling as they went.

"Hi." Brad grinned and handed the bouquet to her. "These are for you."

Annie buried her face in the lush, red-velvet blooms and breathed in their fragrance. No one had given her flowers since her college days. "I love them. Thank you, Brad. You are so thoughtful. I'll put them in—"

Suddenly they heard a loud rumbling noise from the parking lot.

Annie hurried to the window, pulled back the curtain, and peered out. "It's that motorcycle gang again!" she groaned. The waitresses and some of the customers dashed to the window too.

"What motorcycle gang?" Brad asked as he rolled up beside her and stretched forward to see.

"They were here earlier this summer and caused a lot of trouble. I think they'd been drinking. They knocked over chairs, threw food at each other, and used words I'd never heard before. Most of my customers feared for their safety and left. I had to call the sheriff to get them out, but they nearly wrecked the place before he arrived."

Brad's eyes widened. "He arrested them, didn't he?"

She shook her head and shouted over the noise. "No, he told them if they left, he would let them go. And he did!"

The room became quiet as the rumble of motors ceased. Annie watched the gang members stalk across the parking lot to the door of the restaurant.

"I'm not going to serve you again," she said to the rough-looking man who was apparently their leader. She stood in the doorway, her arms folded across her chest. "You and your friends are not welcome here."

He stuck his thumbs in his belt loops, jutted out his jaw, and stared at her. "You sure that's a good idea? Me and my men are hungry. Our money's as good as theirs." He gestured toward the customers who sat in their chairs like statues.

She lifted her chin. "As I said, you are not welcome here. Now go."

Staff and customers alike watched the scene before them, but no one moved to help Annie.

"What if we don't want to? What're you gonna do about it? Hit me with a wet noodle?" He threw his head back and let out a boisterous laugh. "Or maybe call my old pal, the sheriff?"

Brad rolled toward the man. "Look, Frank. Why don't you and your men find another place to have your supper? Miss Johnson has already told you you're not welcome here."

The gang leader ran his hand over his face. "Hey, Brad, old boy. How you doin'? Ain't seen you since—"

"Since my client sued you for damages, right?"

The man rolled his eyes. "You got lucky. The judge was on the take."

Brad tightened his jaw. "Frank, turn around and get out of here, okay? No one wants you here. Crawl on your cycle and take it on down the road."

The man he called Frank leaned into Brad's face, nose to nose. "And who's gonna make me? You? I can take half a man like you with both arms tied behind my back."

Annie caught her breath. "Brad! Don't antagonize him. I couldn't stand it if anything happened to you because of me."

Without turning to look at her, still nose-to-nose with the burly man, Brad told her calmly, "Don't worry. Frank and I understand each other. Don't we, Frank?"

The man backed away. "That mean you're gonna tell your little woman to let us stay?"

"Nope, I'm telling you to get out of here. Now."

Frank narrowed his eyes beneath his shaggy brows, his rowdy laugh echoing through the room. "Guess that means you're gonna make me, right?"

"You wouldn't fight a one-legged man, would you?" one of

230

the male customers called out. "That would be mighty cowardly."

"If I fight you and win, will you and your men leave?" Brad asked Frank, ignoring the other man's remark.

"How could I fight you? You can't even stand up!" he said, scowling.

"Brad, don't!" Annie rushed to his side.

He turned to her and smiled briefly. "Clear off that table behind you, Annie," Brad instructed. "Take everything off, even the tablecloth."

Frank frowned at him.

"How about arm wrestling, Frank? That sound fair to you?"

The man rolled up his sleeve and flexed his huge biceps. "Sure you want to tangle with this?" he asked with a smirk.

"I win—you leave," Brad said.

Frank laughed bitterly. "But what do I get when I win?"

"I'll buy your supper," Brad said as he rolled up to the table Annie had cleared. "Steak, lobster, whatever you want. I'll even throw in a piece of Annie's Awesome Caramel Apple Pie."

Annie could hear her heart pounding in her ears. How could he joke at a time like this?

Brad motioned to the chair opposite him. "Come on, Frank." And with a wink toward Annie he added, "Put up or shut up!"

Frank stepped over to the chair.

Chapter 7

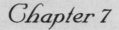

Annie tried to swallow around the lump in her throat. What was Brad thinking? She guessed Frank weighed at least thirty pounds more than Brad, and he was probably taller too. And it was obvious by the size of the man's muscles that he worked out regularly and was in great shape. He could take Brad in—she refused to think about it.

She stared at Brad. He was sitting at the table looking calm and cool, waiting. He was fit too. But how could he ever expect to hold his own against that man? She glanced at the phone. Should she call the sheriff before things got out of hand? He didn't do anything the other time—why should this be any different? Why waste her energy?

Frank pulled out the chair, threw his long leg over its back and sat down, his huge hands gripping the table's edge. "Hey, Man. Last chance to back away. Sure you want to do this? I'd hate to see a grown man cry," he taunted. "Especially in front of your little girlfriend."

Brad leaned back and locked his hands together over his chest, keeping his eyes on the man. "I'm sure someone will give me a tissue if I break out in tears. Don't worry yourself about it." He leaned forward again, nearly touching Frank's nose with his, and narrowed his eyes. "I think the question is—are you sure you want to do this? I'm the challenger—remember?"

Frank shot a look at his comrades who stood watching in silence. "One of you guys keep your cell phone handy. Old Brad here is gonna be needin' an ambulance. I owe him big-time. Twice!" he added, holding up two fingers.

"Aren't you ready yet?" Brad asked impatiently. "Let's get this show on the road."

Frank appeared to be not only up for the challenge but eager for it. He cracked his knuckles then placed his right elbow on the table, holding his muscular, tattooed arm in an upright position. "You wanna do two falls out of three? Or go for broke with one?"

Brad's gaze never left Frank's. "I issued the challenge. You decide."

Annie couldn't remain silent any longer and rushed to Brad's side. "No, don't! Please. Stop this right now. I don't want—"

"It's okay, Annie," Brad reassured her. Still looking at Frank he reached out and touched Annie's hand. "Frank and the boys have promised to leave when this is over. Everything's going to be fine. Trust me."

Frank laughed coarsely again. "Sure about that, Brad, old boy? I think the best advice you could give your little girlfriend would be to start getting a table ready. I'm gonna have me a nice big steak after I beat the—" He stopped and grinned at Annie. "Excuse me, ma'am. I nearly forgot I was in the presence of a lady."

"Let's get on with it," Brad told him. "One? Or three?"

Frank sized up his opponent before answering. "I'm not sure that arm of yours would hold up for more than one round." He nodded his head and scowled then stationed his elbow on the table. "Let's make it one."

Brad smiled, and Annie wondered if this was his strange way of psyching out the competition. It certainly wasn't a smiling matter to her. Frank could break Brad's arm. Then where would he be?

One of the waitresses stepped up to her. "Don't let him do it. He'll get hurt, and losing could devastate him. Think how embarrassed he'll be with everyone watching. You've got to stop this."

Annie's shoulders drooped. She couldn't bear the thought of what might happen to him if he lost. "I've tried. Brad won't give up, and I'm sure Frank won't either."

Frank motioned to Annie. "We need a starter. You're it."

She gasped and stared at the man. "No, I couldn't!"

"Do it, Annie," Brad told her, his gaze still locked on Frank. "All you need to do is count to three and say go!"

"But, Brad—"

"Do it, Annie. Now." His tone was firm.

Annie moved to the side of the table, her heart pounding furiously, as the two men adjusted the position of their elbows on the table and locked hands. "Oh, Brad, be careful. I couldn't stand it if he hurt you. You're too important to me."

Brad stared into Frank's dark gaze. He had faced him once before as an opponent—in a courtroom. The man had been charged with beating up an innocent bystander and stealing his car. He had won the case, and Frank had ended up in jail. He knew Frank carried a grudge against him and was out to get him, and he knew the man was strong. Men in prison spent much of their time working out. But he was strong too.

And he had to protect Annie. He might not be able to stand toe to toe with Frank, but at least he had a chance of defeating him hand to hand.

God, he breathed out to his Father in prayer, *if I ever needed Your help, it's now. I can't let Annie down. Give me the strength to defeat this vile man. He can't win. Please, God. I know I can't have Annie, but I have to do this for her. I love her.* He tightened his jaw, lifted his chin, and nodded for her to start the count.

Annie's eyes widened with fright, as did most of the on-lookers'. She reached over and squeezed Brad's shoulder then started counting.

"One."

Brad swallowed.

"Two."

He sucked in a deep breath and held it.

"Three."

His fingers tightened about Frank's.

It seemed as if she would never say it.

"Go!"

Brad felt Frank's paralyzing grip on his hand, and the two men began their struggle for victory over the other.

The restaurant was silent.

It seemed as if the clock on the wall had stopped ticking.

Men stared.

Women hid their eyes.

Annie cried.

One second it seemed as if their locked hands were going Frank's way. The next second, Brad's. Back and forth they went. On and on, each hoping to outdo the other.

Annie caught her breath then wrung her hands as the minutes ticked by.

Brad watched Frank's eyes for any sign of weakness, but all he saw was dogged determination. He suddenly became aware of all Frank had to lose. He was the head of the gang. For him to be defeated would be a disgrace. Especially by a man in a wheelchair. *God, give me strength. With Your help I know I can do this!*

With one powerful grunt that seemed to come from the deepest part of his being, Frank gave a hard lunge of his wrist, and their hands moved toward his side of the table.

Then Brad saw what he had been looking for, a flash of satisfaction on Frank's face. A quick window of weakness. With all his might and one final gasp of fresh air to fill his lungs, he pushed Frank's hand across the imaginary line, and it was over. Frank's arm hit the table. Hard.

Brad had won!

Annie rushed to Brad's side, jumped onto his lap, and threw her arms about him. "Oh, Brad, you did it! You did it! And you're all right. I was so afraid—"

"I did it for you, Annie." He took a deep breath and looked into her eyes, his face covered with perspiration. "I told you I'd do anything for you. Doesn't this prove it?"

She kissed his cheek, and Brad breathed a prayer of thanks to God. For he knew without God's help he could never have defeated Frank.

Brad looked across the table into the man's face. Frank hadn't moved. He was still sitting there, staring at him, dazed.

"I'm sorry you went down like that in front of your friends," Brad told him so softly that only the three of them could hear. "I hope now you'll keep your end of the bargain and leave without any trouble."

Frank stuck out his hand. "I may be a troublemaker, but

my word is good. You beat me fair and square." He gave him a slight grin. "Both times."

"I had the advantage, you know."

The man frowned. "Advantage? What advantage?"

Brad gave his hand a hearty shake. "I asked God for help."

Frank looked at him. "That so? Me and the man upstairs aren't exactly on speaking terms. Guess he liked you better."

Brad smiled. "Mind if I send you a Bible? I have your address, unless you've moved since your trial."

Frank stood to his feet and shrugged his broad shoulders. "Sure. Send it to me. I can always use a little kindling for my fireplace." He turned and headed for the door alone. His gang was already in the parking lot starting their motorcycles and heading out.

"I guess this cost him his place as a leader. I doubt his men will have much respect for him after this."

Annie leaned her head on his shoulder and patted his cheek. "Oh, Brad, you were wonderful. My brave Brad. My hero!"

Brad beamed. He'd never been called a hero. If it would impress Annie, he'd fight Goliath, even without the help of a bag of stones. "God helped me," he said. He enjoyed the attention she was lavishing upon him.

"But Frank was so strong. I never thought you'd stand a chance of winning!"

He pulled a handkerchief out of his pocket and wiped the perspiration from his face. "I neglected to give Frank one small bit of information he might have found useful."

She leaned back with a puzzled look. "Information? What?"

He grinned. "I've been the YMCA's undefeated arm-wrestling champion for five years in a row. And I've taken first in the state competition the past three years. I've whipped several men bigger and stronger than Frank."

She cupped his chin in her hand and looked into his eyes. "Even if you'd lost, you'd still be the winner to me. No one has ever stood up for me the way you did. I lo—" She stopped herself, a shy smile on her face.

Just then a dozen or more of the restaurant's male patrons gathered around Brad to congratulate him. As much as he enjoyed their praises, he felt sadness when Annie slid off his lap and stood.

After the men had returned to their tables, Brad rolled into the rest room and washed his face and combed his hair. He smiled at his reflection in the mirror. He had won!

Annie was waiting for him at their little table, her heart filled with admiration. His damp hair lay in ringlets over his forehead, and his face was flushed from all the effort he'd put into defeating Frank. He was the handsomest man she'd ever seen. Why hadn't she noticed it before? Her heart did a somersault as he rolled up beside her. What a strange feeling she had in the pit of her stomach at the mere sight of him.

What was happening? Yesterday he was her friend. Today he was— She smiled warmly as their elbows touched. What was Brad to her? Her attorney, of course. Now her defender. But he was more than that. Much more. Brad was—Brad! The most wonderful, caring, unselfish man she'd ever met, and she found herself wanting to spend every minute with him.

They enjoyed a relaxed dinner together. For once Annie let her staff do the work while she lingered beside Brad. Since it had been such a hard day, she decided to go home and let those helping at the theater close for the night.

"Hop on—I'll give you a ride," Brad said at the door.

She climbed onto his lap immediately and put her arms about his neck. When they reached her car she kept her head on his shoulder. She felt as if she wanted to stay there forever. It was a beautiful moonlit night—a perfect night for lovers. She smiled inwardly. *Lovers? The two of us?*

"I guess you're tired," Brad said finally, breaking the spell. "I'm going to meet with Ben Calhoun in the morning. I'll call you after we've talked."

Annie kissed him lightly on the cheek and stood to her feet. "Thanks, Brad—for everything."

"You're welcome." He waited until she started her car then rode the lift up into his van and waved good-bye.

He watched the taillights of her car disappear in the distance and then turned the key in the ignition. He had nearly blurted out how much he loved her but was glad he hadn't. Sure, Annie was grateful for what he'd done to Frank, but admiration and gratitude were a far cry from love. Why would she want him when she could have her pick of men? Whole men. Not a half man like him—as Frank had called him.

No, he had to prepare himself. As soon as Annie and her sister's estate was settled she would have no more use for him. He'd better start distancing himself from her now. He wasn't sure he could handle her rejection. Yes, it was time for him to get out of Annie Johnson's life.

It was nearly ten o'clock when Brad entered the Apple Valley Farm restaurant two days later. Annie was finishing her bank deposit and hurried to meet him. "Oh, Brad, I've barely slept the last two nights. All I could think about was you and the way you stood up to Frank. I was so proud of you."

He pointed to his half-empty pant leg. "Stood up? That's a stretch of the imagination, isn't it?"

Her hand covered his, but he pulled away. "Why do you always put yourself down? You're a wonderful man. You needn't apologize for anything. Look what you've done with your life. Look what you've accomplished despite—" She stopped.

He rolled up to a table and motioned for her to sit beside him. "I've brought bad news. I presented the figures to both your sister and Ben Calhoun. And while she didn't dispute them, she made it very clear she wanted the farm sold and her half of what was left after all your expenses were taken out. She was adamant about it. I don't think she'll back down."

Annie stared at the table, unable to speak.

"And I've checked with several of the banks where I regularly do business. None of them is willing to lend you the money to pay her off, considering your outstanding loans. I tried—I honestly tried. It looks as if you have no choice but to sell."

He felt like a villain as he watched the look of horror spread over Annie's face. "The worst part is that your sister already has a buyer. Someone has placed a firm bid on Apple Valley Farm. And it's a good one. I think she had that in her pocket before she came here."

Annie leaned against the table and held on to it for support. Her stomach churned. "A buyer? So soon?"

"Yes, and you have only three days to accept, or their offer will be withdrawn."

Annie rubbed at her temples. "Is—is it really that good an offer?"

"I'd say it's an exceptionally good offer, considering the last appraisal your father had on the place," he conceded. "Even taking the portion out for your expenses, you'll both come out extremely well, but you'll lose the farm."

She lifted a misty gaze to his. "And you think we should sell at that price?"

He stroked his chin. "I'd say it's probably as good as you'll get, considering the economy and the reluctance of the lenders to finance you. It's your decision." He reached into his pocket and pulled out an official-looking document. "I've brought the signed contract. All you have to do is read it and sign it. I've read every word. It's a legitimate offer. But the final decision is yours."

Annie reached for it with trembling hands. "There's no other choice, is there?"

Brad lowered his head and answered softly, "No, I'm afraid not."

Annie dropped into a chair and through bleary eyes scanned the words. With Brad's assurance that he had read the document, she took the pen he offered and signed her name.

"I'll take this to Ben this afternoon. As you no doubt read, I insisted on the closing to be three months from now. That should give you plenty of time to wrap things up here and re-move your personal items. Your sister has agreed to those terms." He took her hand in his and slowly rubbed his thumb over it. "I'm sorry, Annie. I had hoped we'd be able to dissuade Valerie."

She turned her head away and blinked several times. "You did all you could. I know that. And I can never thank you enough."

Brad stared at her for a moment then withdrew his hand,

backed away, and moved toward the door. "I guess that does it for us. It's been a pleasure knowing you, Annie. You take care now." And he rolled out of the door.

Annie stood frozen to the floor. Whatever was he talking about? "It's been a pleasure knowing you"? What did that mean? His words sounded so—final! As if it were over between them. She pulled herself back to reality. As if what were over? Nothing was going on between them, was it?

She hurried to the window. The platform on Brad's van was lifting him inside. She had to catch him!

"Brad! Brad!" She rushed outside and across the parking lot, her apron strings waving behind her. "Wait! I love you!"

Brad rolled down the window and leaned out, a questioning look on his face. "Annie? What did you say? I couldn't hear you."

She rushed to the window, cradled his cheeks in her hands, and kissed him on the mouth. "I said I love you, you silly goof. I'm losing Apple Valley Farm, but I can't lose you too! Did you think I'd be stupid enough to let the only man I've ever loved get away from me that easily?"

Brad stared at her. "You? Love me? Really? Are you sure?"

She let go of him, rushed around the van, opened the passenger door, and then clambered onto his lap. "Quit talking and kiss me." She slipped her arms around his neck.

Brad sighed and laughed at the same time. Then, reaching alongside his seat, he released the lever and pushed the seat back as far as it would go. "Whew, it was pretty close quarters there for a moment. I don't think the engineer built these seats for two!"

She grinned and kissed him again.

Then he sobered. "Don't toy with my emotions, Annie. Please."

She leaned back against the steering wheel and stared into his eyes, wondering if she'd misread his attentions. "You–you mean you don't have feelings for me? I was so sure—"

He tightened his lips and swallowed. "Oh, I have feelings all right—I've tried to hide them. I think what you're feeling now is gratitude because I've helped you through some rough spots. What I want and need is—your love. Real love." He paused and turned his head away. "A love to last a lifetime. Not your pity."

"Pity? Why would I pity you? You're the most together person I know." She touched his chin, forcing him to turn back to her. "I want that same kind of lifetime love. And I want it from you."

His hand went to the stub of his leg that had been left behind after his accident. "I'm not the man for you. Not with this."

Annie's fingers ran down his arm to his hand, to the stub veiled by his trousers. "This is one of the reasons I love you. I think what you've gone through with the loss of your leg has made you more of a man than the most whole man I know. But—" She frowned.

"But what?"

"But I wonder if I'm enough woman for you. Maybe you don't love me as I've hoped you do. I mean, you're so close to God, and I feel"—she swallowed—"separated from Him. I'm not sure He'd accept me, the way I've turned away from Him all these years."

Brad pulled her close. "He's only a prayer away. All you have to do is ask for His forgiveness. It's that simple."

"I will, and I'm ready. I've seen Him working in your life, and I want that same closeness you have with Him. I know He loves me, but—I need to know how you feel about me. Do you think you could ever love me, Brad?"

He nestled his face in her hair then let his lips trail across her cheek and finally rest on her lips. "Love you, Annie? I'm so crazy in love with you that it hurts. I've loved you since that first night I came to your restaurant and—"

"And tasted my sinfully decadent Awesome Caramel Apple Pie?"

Brad pulled away long enough to murmur with a mischievous smile, "Exactly."

That evening a smiling young woman, dressed in her freshly starched Apple Annie costume, pushed open the door for her favorite dinner customer, Brad Reed. Only this time, instead of handing him a menu, she sat on his lap and kissed him—to the applause of the staff and other patrons.

Brad considered the setting and decided this was the perfect time to propose. He pulled a small, black-velvet box from his jacket pocket, opened it, and held out a beautiful diamond solitaire ring. "Apple Annie," he said, speaking slowly to make sure she understood every word, "will you marry me?"

"Yes!" she exclaimed and held out the ring finger of her left hand. "I thought you'd never ask!"

Everyone in the restaurant clapped again.

Brad grinned. "Now can I have that piece of pie?"

The next week was filled with mixed emotions for Annie: deep sadness when she told her employees of the sale of Apple Valley Farm and great joy as she planned for her wedding to Brad.

Brad. Dear, sweet, lovable Brad. How could she have ever

hoped to face her future without him? Her only regret was that her father wouldn't be alert enough to get to know the wonderful man she would be marrying. They'd decided to put their wedding on hold until after the closing of the farm, wanting nothing to cloud their special day.

Annie heard Brad's van pull into the parking lot. She glanced at the apple-shaped clock on the wall then watched him make his way to the restaurant's door. Why was he here at ten in the morning? He'd told her he had an early appointment at his office. She filled two cups of coffee and walked over to a table, motioning him to join her. Something was wrong. She could see it on his face.

"The deal on the farm fell through," he blurted out as he reached for her hand and pulled her onto his lap. "I'm sorry, Annie. Ben assured me the man's credit was impeccable. He couldn't raise the money."

She leaned against him and sighed. "What does that mean? Where do we go from here?" The words were scarcely out when she heard loud thuds coming from outside the restaurant.

Brad slipped his arms about her and held her close. "A man is putting up a for-sale sign. Your sister insisted on it."

Annie's hand went to her chest. "Is that—necessary?"

"She seems to think so, and legally we can't stop her."

Annie looked at the sparkling diamond on her finger. "This will delay our wedding, won't it?"

Brad nodded.

"It isn't that I wanted to leave Apple Valley Farm," she said with a sigh. "I just wanted the whole sordid mess to be over. Will this never end?"

The next week several prospective buyers paraded through the restaurant. None of them fit the description of the kind of person Annie would want to take over her beloved farm. Each day her sadness about leaving the place seemed to offset the joy of her engagement to Brad. Her life was a roller coaster of highs and lows. The brightest spot in her day came when her wonderful Brad entered the restaurant for his supper. His mere presence caused her gloom to disappear, if only for a few hours each night.

"Annie!" He rolled through the door toward her, waving a piece of paper in his hand. "Look! A new offer!"

She hurried to him, took the paper, and began to read. But what she read didn't make sense. Her name, Anastasia Johnson, was listed on the buyer's line.

She looked up at him. "I don't get it. What does this mean?"

Brad patted his lap, and she climbed onto it. "You're buying Valerie's half of Apple Valley Farm! It's all yours—lock, stock, and apple!"

She scanned the paper again. "But I've been turned down by all the banks. How could this be?" His laugh soothed her heart. How could she be sad when she was engaged to a man like Brad?

"Hey, Sweetie, you're marrying a lawyer. Haven't you heard all those lawyer jokes? We're a bunch of smart cookies."

She jabbed her elbow into his ribs. "Cut the funny stuff, Reed. Explain in plain English, not lawyer terms."

"I had misgivings about that first offer when it came in. I did a little checking on my own, and from what I found out I was reasonably sure the deal would go sour. So I called a few of my close friends who owed me favors and had a little money lying around, and I offered them a good use for it. With what I had and what we collected, we've made up an association of investors. We even have a name for ourselves—AARP."

She raised her brow. "AARP? Now that's original. Seems I've heard of another organization with those initials."

Brad grinned. "Apple Annie's Rescue Partners. Catchy, isn't it?"

She sobered. "You're serious, aren't you? You've done this!"

"As I told you in the beginning, dear Annie, I'd do anything for you. I love you with all my heart."

"No joke?"

"No joke. This is the real thing."

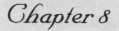

Chapter 8

I t was a beautiful fall day. The sky was blue, and the birds were singing in the trees. Annie Johnson-soon-to-be-Reed was very happy. She stood in the window of her upstairs bedroom and gazed out at the rows and rows of lush green apple trees in their orchard. The trees stood like soldiers. Their branches, now relieved of the weight of the fall crop, were lifted heavenward toward their Creator.

Annie felt a peace with God she hadn't dreamed possible. She was grateful to Brad for his patience in explaining the Scriptures to her and leading her to his Lord. She was grateful to him also because now, with God's help, she possessed two very important things in her life: the wonderful man she was about to marry and her beloved Apple Valley Farm. Only one other thing would complete her happiness.

Babies!

The young couple had been so busy taking care of the farm and the restaurant, visiting with their parents, and planning their wedding that they'd scarcely had time to sit down together and enjoy one another's company. They had discussed financial and personal affairs, but the subject of children had never come up.

Annie thought she knew why. She suspected Brad didn't want children because he feared he might not be the father he'd like to be, confined to his chair, unable to run with them or play sports with them. Perhaps she had avoided the subject because she didn't want to face the answer. If that's the way it had to be, fine. She would learn to live with it. Brad would be enough for her. But she had to know now—before they exchanged their vows. She hurried to her bedside table and dialed Brad's number. He answered on the first ring.

"Are we going to have babies?" she blurted out, barely giving him time to say hello.

"Babies?"

"Yes. Are we?"

"Don't you think we should get married first? I'm kind of old-fashioned, you know."

She could almost see him smiling over the phone. "Brad, be serious. Do you want babies?"

"Do you?"

"Of course, I do. I want your babies. Oodles of them!"

"Umm, oodles? I'll have to think about that one. By the way, how many would oodles be?" She could hear the laughter in his voice. "How about only a dozen?"

She smiled into the phone as she twisted the cord about her finger. "Then I take it you do want children?"

"If you promise they'll all look like you."

"I'd rather they look like you."

"Well," he said, his tone more serious, "I can promise you they won't be born with only one leg. It's not hereditary, you know—not in the genes!"

"I love you, Brad Reed, you crazy nut!"

"That's why you called me? To ask if I wanted children?"

"Isn't that enough?"

"Don't you know it's bad luck to speak to the groom on the phone on his wedding day?" he asked. She could hear muffled laughter in the background.

"That isn't what they say, and you know it!"

"Lady, anything you say or do is good luck to me. The kind of luck God brings, not the world."

"I know. I love you. See you at the church in a few hours."

"Church? Is today our wedding day? I was going fishing."

"You're—"

"I know. Incorrigible." He paused. "Annie? This is going to be our wedding night. Our first night together. Some things may seem a little—uh—strange. Are you sure you're up to it?"

Her grip tightened on the phone. He would never admit it, but she knew he was concerned that she might find the stub of his leg repulsive. "Sure, I'm looking forward to it. You needn't worry. Everything will be fine, the best night of our lives."

She heard a chuckle on the other end.

"Whew, I'm sure glad to hear that. I guess it's okay then if I bring my teddy bear and wear my funky nightshirt. The one with Big Bird on the front."

She laughed into the phone. Life with Brad would not only be wonderful; it would be funny. And their children would have a loving father.

The little country church was filled to overflowing. Even Annie's father was there, seated by Brad's mother, who had offered to keep an eye on him. Huge clay pots of blooming lavender chrysanthemums with big white satin bows decked the front of the sanctuary. White and lavender satin bows graced each end of the old oak pews, where the couple's friends and family sat waiting for the wedding to begin. On either side of the lectern, tall brass candelabra stood, each holding twelve tall lavender candles, their wicks glowing, filling the church with a warm amber glow. Everything in the room spoke of peace and serenity.

Everything but one.

The groom.

He watched the closed door to the foyer, anxiously waiting for his bride to appear, sure she would change her mind at the last minute.

The music began, and the audience stood as Annie stepped into the open doorway. At that moment Brad knew if he'd had two good legs he could not have contained himself. He would have rushed down the aisle and pulled her into his arms. She was so beautiful. He couldn't believe she was going to be his—for as long as they both should live. Squinting against the tears he felt rising to the surface, he lifted his face and thanked God for the wife to whom he was about to pledge his life. He was sure no man had ever been happier than he was at that moment.

Annie, in her mother's wedding gown of antique white satin, checked off for the hundredth time the items a bride should have at her wedding: a blue garter, a handkerchief borrowed from Brad's mother tucked into the tip of her sleeve, the old comb her grandmother had worn in her hair, and a brand new pair of white satin slippers. She was ready.

She stepped into the doorway of the chapel, tears of happiness welling up in her eyes. She gazed with love at the man seated at the other end of the long white runner on the floor.

The runner seemed to draw a path right to him as he sat there smiling at her. She wanted to lift her skirts and dash to him, slip into his lap, and hold him close to her. But she knew such unorthodox behavior would throw their wedding into pandemonium. Instead she fought the impulse and fell into the expected one-slow-step-at-a-time bridal march.

Since neither Brad nor Annie had young relatives, they had no flower girl or ring bearer and chose rather to meet one another at the altar. Annie had wanted her father to give her away, but because of his illness she felt it best for him to sit in a pew and watch. Her maid of honor was her old college roommate, and Brad's best man was an attorney friend.

As they repeated their vows to one another, Annie thanked God for bringing Brad into her life at the right time, a gift above all others.

Finally, after the soloists had sung and the couple had exchanged vows, Pastor Moore challenged Annie and Brad to live their lives for each other, putting God first in all things. Then he pronounced them husband and wife.

Annie gave her bouquet to her bridesmaid then slipped onto Brad's lap for the traditional bridal kiss. Brad lifted the shimmering veil that covered Annie's face, pushed back a lock of hair, and kissed her. Lightly, at first, but then the kiss deepened—as if neither one remembered the audience looking on, witnessing their happiness. Annie and Brad would remember that kiss for the rest of their lives.

Pastor Moore turned to the friends, family, staff, and business acquaintances who filled the church and with a broad smile said, "It is my pleasure to introduce to you, Mr. and Mrs. Bradley Reed."

The groom drew his wife close and pushed the lever forward, and Brad and Annie Reed rolled up the aisle in his wheelchair, love for each other shining on their faces.

"Are you ready to go home, Sweetheart—to Apple Valley Farm?" Brad asked tenderly when they had reached the privacy of the church's foyer.

"Oh, yes, dearest love, my precious husband." She longed to be alone with him as his wife.

The wheelchair came to a sudden stop, and Brad snapped his fingers. "Oh, no!"

Annie stiffened. What could have happened to cause him such anxiety?

"I have to go back to my apartment!" he exclaimed. "Now!"

"Whatever for?"

He grinned. "I forgot my teddy bear and my Big Bird nightshirt!"

Sinfully Decadent Awesome Caramel Apple Pie

This terrific recipe was given to me
by Millie Miller of Oklahoma City.

INGREDIENTS:
   1 high-quality, ready-made, deep-dish apple pie
      with lots of apple filling
   1 small jar of caramel ice cream topping
   1 cup of chopped pecans

DIRECTIONS:
Bake the pie for 20 minutes according to the package directions. Remove from oven and make deep holes in the top, filling each hole with a spoonful of caramel topping. If you have any topping left, spread it over the top. Sprinkle chopped pecans on the topping. Return pie to oven for approximately another 20 minutes and bake until the topping bubbles and apples are tender. Serve and enjoy!

NOTE: Be sure to put a large piece of foil or a cookie sheet
   under the pie when baking since it may boil over.

JOYCE LIVINGSTON

Joyce is a real Kansas "lady" who lives in a little cabin that her husband built overlooking a lake. She is a proud grandmother who retired from television broadcasting, but she keeps very busy lecturing and teaching about quilting and sewing. She is also a part-time tour escort, which takes her to all kinds of fantastic places. She has had books and articles published on sewing, quilting, crafts, cooking, parenting, travel, personal color, and devotions—you name it. In 2000, she was voted **Heartsong Presents** favorite new author and her book *The Bride Wore Boots* was named favorite contemporary book of the year. She invites you to visit her website: www.joycelivingston.com and to email her at: joyce@joycelivingston.com

APPLE PIE IN YOUR EYE

by Gail Sattler

Chapter 1

"A re you sure about this, Lynette?"

Lynette Charleston had never been so sure about anything in her life.

"Yes, Mrs. McGrath. Plenty of other people in the congregation can serve on the gardening committee besides me."

"Then what are you going to do with yourself?"

"Nothing, at least for awhile. The church has grown so much in the last few years. Close to six hundred people attend here now. Let's give someone else a chance to participate."

Over the ten years since her father had become pastor of Good Tidings Fellowship, Lynette had been a part of almost everything that needed doing in the church at one time or another. She had served in the nursery, typed the bulletin, played guitar for the worship team, organized events, even cleaned the washrooms. She'd served on the construction committee when they converted some of the storage area into classrooms. She'd actively participated in organizing the social club at Christmas and holiday events. She sang in the choir. She'd occasionally been asked to find and arrange for guest speakers for the ladies' ministries luncheons.

Lynette couldn't remember a time when she hadn't been

actively involved in something. Now, at twenty-six years old, she needed to stop being the pastor's daughter and simply become a member of the congregation so she could take some time to focus on her relationship with God.

No more teams, no more council sessions, no more meetings. Especially no more committees.

"I guess I'll see you on Sunday then," the elderly lady said, patting Lynette on the shoulder.

Lynette reached up and patted Mrs. McGrath's hand, as Mrs. McGrath continued to pat her shoulder. "Yes, Mrs. McGrath. I'll see you Sunday."

"Oh, no! Look at that! Do you think it's because of the storm last night?"

At Sarah's voice Rick Meyers glanced at the puddle on the floor of the foyer then looked up. Nothing was dripping now, but the telltale stains on the open beam ceiling told him where the water had come from.

He turned to Josh. "Go get the mop and bucket from the lockup and wipe this up before everyone starts arriving. Ryan, we've got to see what happened to the roof." He turned to the group of girls. "Can you young ladies see if there are any more spots like this and clean them up? Then find buckets or something to catch more drips in case it starts raining again."

Sarah tugged on his sleeve. "What about our practice for the drama?"

With the dark skies and winds still gusting, Rick knew they should prepare for more rain that morning. "I've got to check the roof first. Get whoever isn't busy cleaning up to help set everything up and start without me. I'll be there as soon as I can."

As he walked with Ryan to dig the ladder out of the storage shed, Rick unclipped his cell phone from his belt and dialed Pastor Chris's number. Since there was no answer, he knew the pastor was already on the way. He was amazed he'd arrived before the pastor on a Sunday morning, especially since he'd picked up some of the youth group members on the way.

While he climbed the ladder, Rick thought of last night's storm. He had picked up pieces of soffit and vinyl siding from his backyard this morning. Not all had come off his own house. Many houses in his neighborhood had suffered damage either from downed trees or simply from the force of the wind and heavy rain.

Ryan steadied the ladder in the wind while Rick climbed up. Once he reached the eaves and surveyed the wide expanse, his heart sank. The roof on the old church building hadn't been in the best condition to start with. In addition to many shingles being ripped and broken off, some sections of shingles were missing entirely. In more than one place he could see strips of black tar paper flapping in the wind, exposing bare wood beneath.

He calculated from his present perspective which one of the gaping spots caused the puddle in the lobby.

And this was only one side of the roof. He doubted the other side was much different.

A car entered the parking lot on the other side of the building.

"It's Pastor Chris!" someone called out.

Rick made his way down the ladder and jogged into the building, where he found Pastor Chris in the lobby staring up at the ceiling while Josh wrung out the mop into the bucket.

"Quite a storm last night. I was worried about this. Josh

says you were on the roof. How bad is it?"

Rick rammed his hands into his pockets. "Bad."

"Can it be fixed? I got a few drops of rain on the windshield on the way here, so more rain is coming any minute."

"Yes. The forecast said we'd have more rain this morning, but not as much wind. As to fixing it, I don't think it's possible. For now we can patch it, and a few spots will have to be tarped, but it will only be temporary. We need a new roof."

"We don't have money in the kitty for this. This is a major expenditure."

"I know we've got a few members who are roofers. Between them and a few volunteers from the congregation I bet we could do the work for nothing."

"Yes, but we need something to work with. Do you have any idea how much the shingles and tar paper to do a roof this size will cost?"

Rick shook his head. "I'm guessing it would be in the thousands for materials alone."

Together they watched the small group of teens scurry to clean up and prepare for the Sunday worship service.

Pastor Chris folded his arms across his chest. "We're going to need a few fund-raisers, not just within our own church. We've got to reach out to involve the whole community for this kind of money."

A few more members of the youth drama club walked in. The main door closed behind them with a bang.

"Hey, Pastor Chris! Rick! Wicked out there. Sorry we're late. We had to pick up some stuff that got blown down before we could leave."

Silence hung in the air until the echo of rain started on the roof above.

Rick and Pastor Chris turned toward each other. "Uh, oh," they mumbled in unison and looked up.

"I hope those girls found a few buckets," Rick muttered as he pushed the mop bucket to where he thought the water would most likely come down.

Pastor Chris checked his watch. "It's time for me to start preparing for the service. It looks as if I have a few extra things to pray about."

Rick nodded.

As the pastor retired to his office, Rick gathered the drama team to run through their production as best they could before the congregation arrived.

Throughout the service, water dripped into the buckets, distracting and disturbing many of the members. At the close of the service, because of the obvious need, everyone agreed that something had to be done quickly.

Most of the church members stayed behind for an emergency business meeting. A group of volunteers came forward to patch and tarp the roof as soon as the rain stopped and it was safe to do so. The same people also volunteered to follow the guidance of their two professional roofers to save the labor costs when it came time to put the new roof on.

Then came the hard part. Money.

Pastor Chris stood. "I don't suppose I have to say that now we need a fund-raising committee."

Mrs. McGrath raised her hand. "What about the conference? Can't they give us the money?"

The pastor shook his head. "They gave us money less than a year ago to expand the Sunday school classrooms. They have a limit as to how much they can spend on one congregation, and we've already exceeded our allowable expenditures."

Everyone in attendance nodded. Rick remembered what a difference the new classrooms had made. He also remembered how they'd barely raised the money in the first place. The pastor was right; they couldn't ask for more money until they tried to raise it themselves and fell short.

The pastor smiled weakly. "Everyone here knows how committees usually run."

He paused. Many people smiled and nodded, mostly the elders and others who were more involved in activities requiring group organization.

Pastor Chris continued. "The more people on a committee, the longer each decision will take. And as long as it takes to make a decision, it takes even longer to get the project moving. We don't have time to waste now. We need a committee, but we also need to move things along quickly."

Mrs. McGrath raised her wrinkled hand and stood. "Your daughter, Lynette, has the most experience with committees. If anyone can get things moving quickly, Lynette can. And Lynette isn't on any other committees right now."

All heads turned to Lynette.

Rick's heart started pounding.

Lynette.

He couldn't remember a time in his adult life he hadn't loved her. When her father became pastor of Good Tidings he had been eighteen, and she'd been sixteen. The first day they met he'd immediately developed a massive crush on her that grew with every passing week. By the time he turned twenty, he was hopelessly and helplessly in love with her and had been ever since.

But Lynette didn't know he existed. At least, she didn't know he existed beyond the realms of the group functions of the church. Many times he'd joined a committee or volunteered for a special event simply because he knew Lynette would be involved. He'd asked her out on a number of occasions, but she had simply replied that she didn't date members of her father's congregation, changed the subject, and gone on to business as usual. Sometimes he'd been part of that business; sometimes he hadn't.

Over the years Rick had tried to forget about Lynette, but he couldn't when he saw her at least once a week. Being one of the few single men in the congregation, many women made it more than obvious that they wanted to get to know him better. But every time he went out on a date he found himself wondering what it would have been like if he'd been with Lynette. Such thoughts were not fair to the other women who would never be Lynette and could never take her place in his heart.

Therefore, unless a woman could be content simply to share a friendship, he chose not to have an active social life. This also gave him the opening to devote all his time and energy to the youth ministry. He would never forget the day he turned his life over to the Lord, because that was literally the day he knew his life had been saved by grace. When he was a child, the constant conflict between his parents had been difficult. When he reached his teen years, the fighting and battles for control of each other and their family had come to the point where he didn't think he could make it through another day. Then a friend had brought him to a youth group meeting. That had become a turning point in his life and made him want to be there for other teens who needed Christ, whatever their reasons.

Through both his leadership and his friendship he'd seen many young people build a firm relationship with Jesus Christ before they were thrown into the adult world. He had been the youth leader for five years, and Rick never wanted to do anything else, unless it was pastoring a church of his own. For that reason he'd been attending Bible college at night school, taking courses as he could squeeze in the time between his job and his part in the youth ministry.

In many ways he envied Lynette for having been born into a church family. However she had chosen to be involved in adult ministry functions rather than with the young people.

One of the senior deacons raised his hand and stood. "I've seen Lynette in action, and she does get results fast."

A round of mumbled yeses echoed from the large group. Almost everyone nodded in assent.

Pastor Chris smiled at his daughter. "Lynette? Will you head up the roofing fund-raising committee?"

Lynette's eyes widened, and her face paled. "Committee?"

Except for the plop, plop, plop of water dripping into the buckets and the drum of rain on the roof, silence filled the room.

The pastor lowered his voice. "We need you, Lynette."

Eyes still wide, she scanned the entire congregation.

"Come on, Lynette," one of the ladies called. "I'll help you."

"Me too!" someone else called.

Many people called out with offers to help. However, Rick did note that no one volunteered to actually lead or let Lynette off the hook. He wondered if he'd been the only person in the congregation who'd thought that Lynette seemed tired lately, and less enthusiastic than in the past. A number of times he'd tried to ask her if anything was wrong, but when the conversation became personal, she'd changed the subject.

Pastor Chris raised his hands. "Wait, everyone! I appreciate so many volunteers, but in this case I don't think we should have more than two or three people involved, at least at first, until we get something in place. Maybe before we go any further, we should discuss some ideas as to how to raise this much money and then accept volunteers."

People started calling out their ideas, not waiting for a show of hands.

"Bake sale?"

"Bottle drive?"

"The junior youth could do a car wash?"

"A fund-raising dinner with prizes to draw people?"

"Maybe we could sell hot dogs outside the grocery store one Saturday?"

"What about a craft day for children in the neighborhood? People from all over come to do things with their kids."

Rick frowned. While those were good ideas, none of them could provide the amount of cash needed in a short time—unless the church could combine them.

Rick raised his hand and stood. "I wonder if we could have an event inside the building and extend it into our parking lot, something big that would reach out to the whole community. Then we could do all those things in one day. We could advertise to draw people."

"Yes! The youth group could run the whole thing. A youth fun fair!"

"Uh, I didn't mean—"

Before he could finish his sentence, the group applauded.

"That's great, Rick. Thanks for volunteering with the youth group. And what about you, Lynette? Rather than have a whole committee, how about if you and Rick organize the whole thing? I'm sure it would be much smoother, and faster, with only two people running everything. I know this is rather short notice, but as you can see we're desperate."

All heads once again turned to Lynette, who sat in her chair stiff as a board.

Water continued to drip into the buckets as rain pelted the roof.

"I guess I could. . ."

"Wonderful! Thank you, Lynette and Rick. Do you think you can have a proposal put together for the church board meeting on Wednesday?"

"Wednesday? This Wednesday?"

Rick turned and focused his attention on Lynette. At the same time she turned to him. They stared at each other, not breaking eye contact.

Rick forced himself to breathe. For the first time ever he would be spending time alone with Lynette. Just the two of them and no one else. For years he had prayed for the opportunity to be with her and not be surrounded by a crowd, but he had never in his wildest dreams considered or wanted circumstances like these. This would not be a leisurely chat over a cup of coffee. This project meant hard work, intense brainstorming, and careful planning. As their plans progressed, it would also mean strict supervision of the teens, who would be in their charge.

It was far from the ideal situation, but this gave him the first opportunity in ten years to spend significant time alone with Lynette. Up until now, for all the times he'd tried to talk to her in varying situations, both alone and in a group setting, he'd failed.

If God was leading him toward Lynette, then conversely she should have been as drawn to him as he was to her. He couldn't help but feel she liked him, which was encouraging.

But every time he steered the conversation from neutral topics to something more personal, everything changed. She had drawn some kind of unseen line he couldn't cross, because suddenly, instead of drawing closer, she would pull away. For a few weeks he wouldn't see her at all except for church on Sunday, and even then it would be at a distance.

Now, since they were forced to work together, if he handled this correctly he could discover if what had burned in his heart for her all these years was God's will for him—and for her. His questions would finally be answered. But he would also have to accept it if her answers were not the ones he wanted.

Rick swallowed hard. Whatever happened between them now would affect his entire future and the direction of the path for his entire life.

Slowly Lynette nodded at him.

Rick nodded back and turned to the pastor.

"Yes, I think we can have something before the board on Wednesday."

Chapter 2

Lynette hit send to reply to Rick's E-mail confirming their meeting after supper. When the words disappeared from her screen, she rested her elbows on the edge of the desk and buried her face in her hands. She didn't know which was worse, working with another committee or working with Rick.

She didn't think asking God for a little time off was a bad thing. Yet, not only was she expected to work on possibly the most important project of the church's history, she had to do it with Rick.

Over the years she had seen a number of church members fall to the burnout syndrome from pushing themselves too hard for too long. For all Lynette did, so far she hadn't succumbed. Up until now. She had started to feel herself falling into the pattern. Because of her experience in dealing with people, she thought she could pull herself out of the downward spiral before too late. She needed to retreat and spend some time with God, and that meant being away from people for a little while. After some time alone, she could face another committee meeting for the Lord's work and do it with enthusiasm.

The saying that God didn't give people more than they

could handle echoed through her mind. For the first time she had to trust that was true, because deep in her heart she didn't know if she could handle so much responsibility one more time. At least not now.

But then, Rick had come up with the community Fun Day concept. Therefore, he had to already have a workable idea in mind or he wouldn't have made the suggestion. As tired as she was, she had to trust Rick to shoulder most of the workload while she did what she did best, which was the behind-the-scenes organization of the project.

Lynette stared at the computer screen so long the screen saver came on.

Rick.

Many of the single ladies in the church had a crush on him, yet to everyone's dismay he remained single. Lynette had always been fond of Rick. He had asked her out a few times, and she was tempted. However, before she agreed to go out on what was obviously meant to be a date, images of what happened to her mother flashed through her mind. In the nick of time her good sense returned, and she turned him down.

Lynette rose from her desk and prepared a simple supper for one. Rick had asked if she wanted to go out to grab a quick bite so they could get down to business, but she wasn't ready for that. She didn't want to be near Rick when she was weak and unsure of herself. Yet now she had been obligated to spend time with him with no one else present.

Allowing herself to give in to what she'd worked so hard to maintain would be a recipe for disaster, both personally and spiritually. She was tired, and it would be easy to let her good judgment wane. Until whatever day they selected for the event, Lynette prayed for God's strength to guide her, because she couldn't do it on her own.

The doorbell rang at the exact second she finished her dinner. She tucked the plate in the dishwasher and ran to the door.

Before opening it, Lynette paused to remind herself not to stray from the topic of church business, regardless of Rick's charm. They were together to raise money for the new roof, and that was all she could ever allow.

When she opened the door, Rick stood smiling in the doorway. "Hi, Lynette. I'm glad you could find the time to do this tonight. You looked so tired yesterday that I was almost surprised you agreed to it."

Lynette tried not to be impressed with his sensitivity. "I know, but I always find it so hard to say no when people ask me things. I suppose I have to learn."

He nodded. "It's hard, but I've found it's okay to say no. People do understand."

Lynette wasn't so sure. She had been involved in so many things for so long that people expected these things of her. But Rick wasn't there to discuss people's expectations. He was there to start work on the fund-raiser.

Lynette directed him into the living room. When he sat on one end of the couch, she sat at the other end.

"So, Rick, what do you have in mind? Have you selected a day? How many of the youth will be involved?"

"Uh—so far I have no idea what we're going to do, I don't know what day is best, and I haven't talked to the youth group because our meetings are Wednesday and today is only Monday."

"You're kidding."

He grinned. Little crinkles appeared in the corners of his bright green eyes. All of a sudden the supper she thought so delicious didn't sit too well in the bottom of her stomach.

"Nope. I was just as unprepared for this as you."

Lynette shook her head to bring her concentration back to the problem at hand. "What are we going to do?"

His smile disappeared. "I have a number of ideas. We only have to get a proposal to the church board by Wednesday—not the whole complete plan—but we have to be realistic about this. We can't waste time because the next time the rains come we'll be in serious trouble. I'll phone the older members of the youth group about whatever we come up with today; then we'll discuss it again. By Wednesday we should have a good idea about what we're capable of producing."

"I think I should warn you that Dad has already found a supplier for the shingles and made a tentative order, pending financing. He's getting a good price through Jeff, who's going to be heading up the actual work."

Rick cringed. "Great—no pressure." He let his sarcasm hang for a few seconds then cleared his throat. "He's right to do it now, but we have to be prepared. I was thinking we should pick the Saturday before Labor Day weekend. That way people will be antsy to go out and do something, but not be out of town or otherwise have made plans."

"That's a good idea. What do you have in mind?"

"I don't know. When I got home after church yesterday, I wrote down what I could remember." He twisted, not rising from the couch, extended one leg, and pulled a crumpled paper out of his jeans pocket. He tugged on the paper to straighten it then began to read. "Bake sale, bottle drive, car wash, kids' crafts."

"I think someone mentioned selling hot dogs."

"Yes, but none of those ideas can raise the kind of money we need. We have to think big. That's why I thought of a community event, but I have no idea how to put such a thing together."

"I guess that's what I'm best at—putting things together. But I usually don't come up with many good ideas by myself."

His grin froze her thinking process. "Don't we make a great team then?"

Lynette jumped to her feet. "Let me get a pen and paper, and I'll start making notes too."

Once in the kitchen Lynette tried to stop her hands from shaking as she dug through the drawer. She didn't want to be a great team with him, although she had to admit they worked well together. In the past when they'd served on the same committee, she had admired Rick's creativity when they needed to get a job done. He came up with good and unique ideas, most of them workable if she set her mind to organizing the details and mechanics.

Then, when the time came to ask for volunteers, especially with the more difficult tasks, Lynette was more likely to be silent and do whatever was required herself. Rick, on the other hand, was good with people. No matter what task lay ahead, very few people could say no to him. As well, whoever ended up helping did so cheerfully and graciously. His gift for the Blarney made Lynette wonder if he had a little Irish in his background. As much as she didn't want to, she couldn't help but like him.

By the time she made her way back into the living room, she found Rick leaning over her coffee table and scribbling more illegible notes on the small paper.

"I think I've come up with a few more ideas," he said, still writing. "We could make it into a mini-fair. Our parking lot is certainly big enough." He stopped with the pen still touching the paper. "Did you know that the Robindales know someone who has a hobby farm and does a side business of a traveling petting zoo? Since we're a church, I wonder if they'd let us use their portable pen and some animals for free if we let them display their signs in a prominent place on the day of the fair."

For the first time since she heard of the project, a rush of excitement fluttered in her stomach. "I don't know if we could charge money for that, but it certainly would be a drawing feature for the community."

Rick nodded. "We can't have rides or anything, so I'm trying to think of stuff I usually see at the smaller country fairs, like bake sales, displays, and contests with prizes."

The excitement waned. "That would mean we'd have to buy prizes. I don't know if we can afford that kind of expenditure."

Rick shook his head as he wrote something else. "We don't have to. I'll make a few phone calls tomorrow and see if I can get a few donations. I have an uncle who runs a motel in Seattle. I could probably get a grand prize of a weekend for two, along with a couple of passes for the Space Needle. Of course, we'll have to decide what kind of contest is worthy of that kind of prize."

Lynette tapped her index finger to her cheek as she struggled to think. "If we're trying to reach the community, we should emphasize kids' and teen activities."

Rick nodded and stopped writing. "I agree. What do kids like to do?"

Lynette grinned. She'd spent enough time in the nursery school and Sunday school to know the answer to that one. "Young children like to draw, and kids of all ages like to throw things. In fact, I know many adults who like to throw things— they just won't admit it. I'm thinking about a paper-plane-throwing contest, with prizes. What about teens?"

Rick's mouth quirked up at one corner. "Teens like to eat,

so my suggestion is some kind of eating contest. The only two things I can think of are hot dogs and pies, but your father is going to be selling hot dogs. We don't want the teens to eat all our profits."

"Then a pie-eating contest is the best choice. One reason I love living in Washington state is because I know so many people with apple trees. Since apples are everywhere this time of year, we could probably get most of the apples for free."

"Sounds good to me," Rick mumbled as he started writing again, which emphasized that Lynette had not written a single thing. She rectified that by picking up her pen and making notes also.

As the evening continued, they discussed everything on Rick's list, which allowed Lynette to make many tentative plans. They also drew a picture of the parking lot and building so they could get a better idea of the space required versus what they had available.

Before she knew it, the clock read 10:30. They still didn't have a concrete plan, but they had come up with a number of good ideas that needed to be discussed with the youth group members before they could present their proposal to the church board.

Lynette followed Rick to the door. "So you know who you have to contact tomorrow?" she asked as she opened the door.

He nodded. "Yes. I'm pretty sure I can get most of the calls made on my lunch break. You're going to call around and scrounge for apples, right? I'll call my uncle about the weekend getaway idea. We should get together again tomorrow. Same time, same place?"

"Yes, I think we should."

Rick smiled. "See you tomorrow, Lynette. Oh, and don't

cook tomorrow. I'll bring something. Since I have to work late, I'll be coming straight here."

She almost said no but couldn't justify why not. His coming over with dinner only meant church business, so they could discuss the matter at hand sooner, and nothing more.

All she could do was nod.

"Good. This has been a great evening, Lynette, in more ways than one."

Before she could respond, he turned and left.

Lynette stood in the doorway, watching as he drove away. It had been a great evening. For the first time in a long time she hadn't minded discussing and making plans for a complicated event. In fact she'd actually enjoyed it, which made her wonder if maybe she wasn't as burnt out as she thought.

Chapter 3

Pizza box in hand, Rick knocked on Lynette's door and waited.

When the door opened, Lynette's beautiful smile nearly made him drop their supper. "Hi," he mumbled as he tried to maintain his dignity.

"Hi. How did everything go?"

"As well as could be expected, I suppose. I couldn't get hold of my uncle, and it appears our other plans may have changed a bit. I don't think anything like this ever happens as it was planned the first time around."

Her smile dropped, and Rick immediately felt the loss.

"You should probably come inside before that gets cold." She turned around and walked into the house. He shut the door behind him and followed her into the kitchen.

She spoke over her shoulder as she reached for a couple of plates from one of the cupboards. "If it makes you feel any better, my quest for apples turned out more bountiful than I could ever have planned. What happened to you today?"

Rick set the pizza box on the table and sat down. "Our impromptu youth group meeting was a lesson in organized confusion. We came up with a million ideas, but nothing concrete.

Everyone volunteered to do something, but no one knows what. The topper came when Sarah Rondstadt said she knows someone who has one of those dunk tanks, and she's going to ask if we can borrow it. You know what Sarah is like once she sets her heart on something. No one can ever say no to Sarah. That means we have to find someone whom people will pay money to try to dunk and who won't mind being dunked. Do you have any idea how hard that's going to be?"

Lynette grinned. "You told me yesterday you could say no to people."

"This is Sarah we're dealing with. That's different."

She scrunched up one side of her mouth as she opened the pizza box. "A dunk tank isn't necessarily a bad thing. But it does change the spin on the other events we can have around it."

He nodded and folded his hands in his lap. "We got the petting zoo, by the way. The owners told me they require four people to be inside the pen with the animals and children at all times, and the teens are all fighting for who gets first dibs to be with the goats. I also found out how they make money from these things. Since we're a church we have the animals for free for the day. It's up to us if we want to charge admission, but I had to guarantee those feed bins will be inside the pens. You know, they're kind of like gum-ball machines, but they hold the feed pellets for the animals. Want to imagine how many quarters go into those machines during a day of wall-to-wall children?"

Lynette's cheeks turned pink. "I've been known to put a few quarters in those things too. But the main thing is the petting zoo will be a draw for the other events where the church will make money."

Rick could well imagine Lynette feeding animals at a children's petting zoo. Her kind and gentle spirit was one of the many reasons he'd fallen in love with her so long ago.

"Ryan suggested the senior teens could do a slave auction, but I turned that down. For our own church members, that's different. But for a community event I'm not going to be sending minors out to the homes of strangers to do work I know nothing about. It doesn't matter how big some of them are; they're still our children."

"Good idea."

"Brad suggested a neighborhood dog show, but we can't have people bringing their dogs if we're having the petting zoo. We can't risk the goats' getting frightened and stampeding or doing whatever goats do when they get scared."

"Oh. I hadn't thought of that. I'd better cross the dog show off my list."

They paused for a word of prayer over their supper then continued to discuss more ideas.

Rick couldn't believe how fast the night progressed, but then he should have expected that every minute he spent with Lynette would pass too quickly.

Before he knew it, he was standing at the door, saying good-bye. "I guess I'll see you at the church tomorrow night. What time? Seven?"

Lynette nodded. "Yes. I'll see you there."

Rick's heart pounded as he stood on the porch. Lynette stood in the doorway, close enough that he could lean over and kiss her, if this had been a date.

Rick blinked and stepped back. This wasn't a date. This was church business, and church business only. While they'd had a pleasant enough evening together, every time he tried to turn the conversation to more personal topics, Lynette had promptly steered the conversation right back to the fund-raiser.

Spending time with her, even in the context of business only, had only intensified what he'd felt all along. Not only did he love her, but more than ever he knew God had put them together.

Now he had to convince Lynette of what God had laid on his heart. Even though she seemed intent on the fund-raiser, he had to move beyond the business at hand and talk about the two of them together—forever, he hoped. Knowing Lynette as he did, Rick also knew he had exactly until the day of the fund-raiser to succeed or fail, because after that she would pull away from him, just as she'd done for years.

Rick cleared his throat. "I guess we'll get together again Thursday night so we can go over what the board says. If they agree with the date we've set, that means we have two and a half weeks to get this whole thing happening."

"That's not a lot of time. Only two days ago it sounded like such a simple thing. It seems to get bigger and bigger as we go on with it."

Rick swallowed and willed his hands to stop shaking. Slowly he reached forward and grasped Lynette's hands, holding them gently within his as he spoke. "I know. There's something else I wanted to talk to you about also."

Within his grasp her hands became rigid. A split second after he spoke, Lynette yanked her hands out of his and backed away. Rick mentally kicked himself for trying to move too fast.

She looked up at him, her eyes big and wide. "Actually, while we're talking about getting together, I think it would be a good idea to meet at the church instead of at my house. That way we'll be right there where it's happening, and we can organize it better. Don't you think so?"

No, he didn't think so, but it didn't appear he had a choice. "I suppose."

She smiled, but her smile never reached her eyes. Once again he kicked himself for trying to move too fast.

"When do you think we should start bringing some of the teens into the planning?" Lynette asked.

If it were up to him, the day before the event. "I don't know. Whenever you think it's best."

She backed up another step, her wide eyes fixed on him like a deer caught in the headlights about to be run over by a truck. "Then let's talk to them right after the church board meeting. I'll see you there. Good night, Rick."

He had barely backed up a step, and the door closed.

Rick wasn't at all sure what had just happened, but he did know one thing. Tonight he would be spending a lot of time deep in prayer.

Rick waited while all the members of the church board read their copies of the proposal. He wondered if Lynette was as nervous as he was, though he didn't know why. Every suggestion they'd made had been outlined into a workable station, and all the stations combined would make a great and varied community fun fair, even without rides.

He'd had no concept of the magnitude of the project before he became involved. The seemingly endless wait for the board's reaction sat on him like a cloud of pending doom hovering above him, emphasizing that he'd jumped in way over his head.

Mr. and Mrs. McGrath, the head deacons, nodded at each other. Mr. McGrath laid his paper down on the table, clasped his hands to rest them on top of the paper, and turned his face toward Rick and Lynette, who were sitting beside him.

"Can you two pull this off?"

Out of the corner of his eye he saw Lynette flinch.

For the first time he had some doubts. For all their great plans, so far they had no viable donations, no prizes, no booths, and no adult volunteers. All they had for sure was a group of overanxious, inexperienced teenagers, an empty dunk tank, a pen of hungry goats, a few bushels of apples, and a list of great ideas. He supposed that if the whole thing fell through, they could still make some money by charging money for kids to feed the apples to the goats. He also feared that the person who'd end up getting dunked was going to be him.

Rick chose not to follow that defeatist line of thought. He turned to Lynette. "We can do this. Can't we?"

His stomach flipped over when she turned slowly, making direct eye contact with every person in the room except him, stopping at her father.

"Yes, we can do this," she said.

Her father crossed his arms over his chest. "Do you have any idea what it will take to get all this together in two and a half weeks? We'll have to advertise beyond our own small community, to match the scope of the fair. Twenty-five thousand people live in this city, and it takes money to reach them. Like the roof, that kind of money isn't in our budget either. But if you say you can do it, we'll okay the additional expense."

Rick's stomach tightened. Attempting to raise money was one thing, but he hadn't anticipated having to spend money to make money.

"I knew that, Dad."

"Okay then. Everyone, I think we can approve this."

Rick forced himself to smile. Of course Lynette would have already figured all the expenses into the big picture. If Lynette thought they could do it, then they could do it. He hoped and prayed he was up to the task.

Lynette stood. "Oh, there's one more thing, which will probably mean more to the success of this fund-raiser than anything else, including our advertising."

Rick's head spun. He didn't need another complication.

The room fell as silent as it had on Sunday when he was nominated for this project, except this time no drips were banging into the buckets.

Lynette smiled at everyone around the room. "Pray for good weather. We're going to have a fair in the parking lot."

Chapter 4

L ynette slipped her key into the lock and pushed the huge wooden door of the church open.

She came by herself to the church often, to be alone with God. Not that she couldn't be alone with God at home, but being in the wide-open sanctuary somehow made the connection more intimate.

In silence she walked through the foyer, pausing to drop her notebook and purse on the table before she entered the sanctuary. Mirroring the shape of the building, the sanctuary consisted of a large rectangular room. As she walked up the center aisle, she ran her hand along the tops of the arms of a few of the pews before she chose a seat in the center.

In turn Lynette took in all the features of this church she loved so much. The old wooden pews showed their age yet were not excessively worn. To the front the simple podium sat before a small raised platform, barely large enough for her father and the worship team of five members. Large narrow windows graced both sides of the long room, letting in the bright sunshine on a summer day or the steady gray of a rainy Pacific Northwest winter.

As she closed her eyes and inhaled deeply, she could still

smell the lingering fragrance of the remaining flowers from the Carrions' wedding last weekend.

This building had done its part in the beginning of many happy marriages over the years by providing a place to celebrate a new joining in God's sight. Also before and after every Sunday service the entire building buzzed with happy voices of children playing as their parents visited with their Christian brothers and sisters.

More important than the building were its people. Her father's congregation had grown to such a point where she no longer knew every regular attender by name. Still, as a body of believers, she loved all the people there with the love Christ had shown her.

Lynette tipped her chin and looked up. The dark wood of the open beam ceiling overhead created an illusion of a greater size to the room, although in practical terms it wasn't the greatest for energy conservation. Often the temperatures were too cool in the winter and too warm in the summer, common for an older building, constructed before people began to think of environmental concerns and the cost of heating. The fact remained that the strength there was the love of the people for each other.

That was why she had to do her best to raise all the money required to fix the roof. These people were depending on her to come through. No one knew her sudden aversion to committees.

In a convoluted sort of way she was glad the committee consisted only of her and Rick. While she had been in group situations with Rick before, she and everyone else knew that performing in the group dynamics of a committee was not where Rick's talents shone. Rick was a leader. Even when she first met him ten years ago, she could see his potential. He had been kind and gentle, but also firm and friendly when it came time to do a job. Years later Rick had matured and met the potential everyone had seen in him in his present ministry as youth leader. Rick loved people, and he loved the Lord. He was everything she could ever want, but she couldn't have him.

Lynette dropped her gaze from the ceiling and stared at the empty podium.

Rick had always held a special place in her heart. For many years she had successfully avoided dealing with how she felt about him, but working so closely with him now made her look at him differently. Over time something had changed so gradually she hadn't noticed, but now she couldn't help but recognize the connection. All they had to do was look at each other, and no words were needed. She knew what he was thinking, and vice versa. As much as she wanted to deny what sparked between them, no matter how hard she tried to fight it, it was there.

Lynette slouched in the pew and buried her face in her hands. "Dear Lord, help me," she said out loud. Her own voice echoed back in the large, empty room.

Before she could collect her thoughts to pray, the thump of the main door closing echoed through the large doorway, along with Rick's voice. "Lynette? Where are you?"

She stood, ran her hands down her sleeves to smooth out a couple of imaginary wrinkles and left the sanctuary. "I'm here," she called out once she reached the table, where she picked up her notebook. Rick approached and came to a stop in front of her.

Lynette jerked her thumb over her shoulder. "Let's go use Dad's office."

Rick's eyebrows raised. "The office? What for?" He stuck one hand in his pocket and extended the other hand, in which he was holding a clipboard with a crumpled note paper attached to it, toward the couch in the lobby. "Can't we sit here?"

Having to share a couch was exactly the reason she wanted to meet at the church instead of her home. "I think we'll be able to write better in the office. With the desk," she said.

With the desk between us, she didn't say.

He brought the clipboard up and pressed it to his chest. "Is there something wrong? I don't understand."

"Nothing is wrong. I just want to use the office."

His eyebrows scrunched in the middle. "But. . ." He shrugged his shoulders. "Okay. Let's go. We've got a lot of things to discuss. I've got some good news and some bad news."

She almost stumbled then kept walking to the safety of her father's office, where the desk would serve as a safe and effective barrier between them. Only after she sat behind her father's heavy wooden desk and Rick pulled up one of the chairs so he could use a corner for his own writing surface could she dare to ask. "I think I want the bad news first."

"Actually that is just an expression. I don't have good news."

Her heart sank, but she didn't say anything. This project had to be successful. Too many people were depending on them.

"Remember I told you about the dunk tank?"

She nodded. "Yes. If the bad news is that we didn't get use of the dunk tank after all, I don't think that's really such a loss. I can't figure out what we would do with such a thing anyway."

Rick shook his head. "No, we've got it for sure. It's just that Sarah told Trevor about it." Rick laid his pen down and started counting the people off on his fingers as he mentioned them. "And he told his brother who told his friend who told his neighbor who told his uncle who told his sister-in-law who told her boss."

Lynette shook her head as well. "I don't understand why you're telling me this. I don't know any of those people."

"Mary's boss is the mayor."

"So?"

"I don't think you understand the big picture here. At our little church community one-day fair, we're going to be dunking the mayor."

Lynette felt sick, and it wasn't because she was too hungry.

"No. . ." She let her voice trail off. "We can't pull something off on a grand enough scale to include Mayor Klein."

"We're going to have to. He left a message on my voice mail saying he's looking forward to a fun and carefree day as a welcome change to the old grind."

"If the mayor is going to be there, do you think the local newspaper is going to be there too?"

"Yup. This is good public relations for the mayor, so count on it. But just think. We won't have to spend so much on advertising because his own public relations committee will send out a bulletin to the who's whos and community boards telling them about it. So maybe there is good news in this after all."

Lynette didn't think so. She stood and waved her hands in the air at Rick, coming just short of leaning forward over the expanse of the desktop and wrapping her hands around his neck. "Are you crazy? This means we have exactly fifteen days left to organize and prepare an event that's going to draw the mayor and his entourage and the newspaper!"

"Anyone in the paparazzi will tell you there's no such thing as bad advertising. . . ." His voice trailed off.

All Lynette could do was sink back down in the chair and stare at him across the desk in silence, with her mouth gaping open.

Rick stared back, not saying anything either.

The silence dragged on until Rick sighed, leaned back in the chair, and crossed his arms over his chest. "When did I lose control?"

"As soon as you started taking suggestions from the youth group, I think."

Rick narrowed one eye, pressed his lips together with one side crooked slightly downward and nodded without commenting further.

Lynette also leaned back in the chair and crossed her arms. "I know we've discussed this before, but you said you were able to say no to people."

"I think I might have been wrong."

His deadpan expression was her undoing. Lynette couldn't stop her giggle.

The corners of Rick's mouth twitched, and he started to laugh too.

The tension broken, Lynette wiped her eyes. "What are we going to do?"

"I think the only thing we can do is go with it and pray for sunshine. Like you said."

Lynette sighed and slid the list and notes in front of her. "Between the mayor and the goats we should attract a lot of people. What else can we do that will make money? Do you think we can have the worship team playing and put an offering box in front of them? Or is that too much?"

Rick tapped his pen to his cheek. "It's obviously a fundraiser. Whether or not they get any money, it's good exposure to have visitors listen to upbeat Christian music with wholesome and uplifting themes. I'll talk to the team."

"Good idea. If we're going to have lots of people, we're going to need lots of food to sell. Do you know anyone who has one of those popcorn or cotton candy machines?"

"Nope. But I can ask Sarah. For someone who is only seventeen she seems to know a lot of people who have connections."

Lynette made a tick beside that notation. "I'll have to

think of more kids' games. I wonder if we should still have the pie-eating contest?"

Rick leaned forward, and Lynette stopped writing. "I think there's something I forgot to mention."

Lynette buried her face in her hands. "Do I want to know?"

"The mayor asked me to put his name in for the pie-eating contest, which should generate more people entering."

"I wonder how many pies we should make."

"Make as many pies as you have apples. We have to have a pie for anyone who wants to enter, even at the last minute. Besides we can sell any we have left over."

She made a few more notes, sticking her tongue out of the corner of her mouth as she continued to think. "I'll make a few more phone calls for more apple donations. We should plan out everything we're going to do and assign volunteers today."

At his nod they agreed on all the events and booths. The major draw for young children would be a booth where the children threw their fishing line into a make-believe pond. Two volunteers hidden inside the pond would attach a toy fish and a card with Matthew 4:19 where Jesus called everyone to be "fishers of men."

For the older children they planned a paper airplane contest in which they would give away model airplanes as prizes for the different age categories. Since Rick had finally managed to contact his uncle, they had a prize of a getaway weekend to Seattle, including tickets to the Space Needle. They decided to make that a raffle for which the congregation would sell tickets, as well as having them for sale to the community at the fair.

They also planned games that didn't necessarily award prizes, as well as a bake sale and craft table.

Lynette laid her pen on the desk and ran her fingers through her hair. "This has been great. I think we've made a lot of progress. This weekend we can start constructing the booths and games. At first I had my doubts about this, but I think we can pull this off."

"I told you before that we make a great team. We should get together more often."

Lynette jumped to her feet. "Yes. Well. Oh! I think it's way past our bedtime—we both have to get up for work tomorrow. Let's lock up, and we can be on our way."

"Uh. . ." His voice trailed off.

Lynette didn't wait for Rick to continue. She hustled him out of the door and locked up, the whole time yakking and blabbering on and on about anything that entered her head. Anything except getting together with Rick. She didn't want to entertain that thought.

As she slid into her car and closed the door, Rick stood to the side, his arms crossed, watching. His confused expression nearly broke her heart. She knew he liked her. Knowing him as she did and judging from what she'd heard, she sometimes wondered if he fancied himself in love with her.

She knew she wasn't being fair to him. In all the time she tried to discourage him, he never gave up. And now, since they had been seeing each other every day, the situation had become worse instead of better. He left her no alternative but to tell him the reason she couldn't see him outside of church business, no matter how much she liked him.

But not today. Lynette planned to do the cowardly thing and tell him at the end of the fund-raiser when everything was over and she wouldn't have to face him anymore, at least not directly.

Lynette waved in the rearview mirror as she drove off for the safety of her home.

Chapter 5

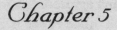

Rick walked into the church building, stepped around the bucket in the lobby, and headed for the pastor's office, where he knew he would find Lynette.

The woman was going to drive him crazy, if she hadn't driven him there already.

Instead of making it better, the past week had made everything worse. He'd wanted the time spent together to confirm or deny everything he felt for her. He could definitely say he loved her more than ever. He now knew for sure that he wanted to spend the rest of his life with her. He also knew she would be happy being a pastor's wife. The problem was, he didn't think she wanted him to be that pastor.

He couldn't count the times in the past week that he'd tried to talk to her, to slip into the conversation that he loved her and had loved her for a long time. And he'd tried to talk about the future they could have together as pastor and wife.

Every time, as she had countless times over the years, the second he began to address the subjects of love and a future together, she'd changed the subject. Twice she mumbled something he couldn't understand and literally ran away.

Rick had always thought of himself as a good, Christian

man, with godly hopes and dreams and a promising future. Obviously Lynette didn't agree.

He stepped into the office to see her comparing figures on a spreadsheet to a calculator tape.

"Hi," she mumbled around the pen in her mouth. "I was adding up how much we have to make. Dad left me all the receipts and estimates. I didn't know we'd have to pay for a disposal bin too. And do you know how expensive it is to advertise?"

Rick pulled a paper out of his back pocket. "Oh. I nearly forgot. Here's the bill for the trophy for the pie-eating contest."

Lynette groaned.

"But I brought a big basket of apples with me."

"Let me guess. From someone Sarah knows."

Rick grinned. "How did you know?"

"Actually, in addition to the four baskets someone brought on Sunday, the Browns dropped off a big bag too. It appears we have plenty of apples."

"How's the entry list coming?"

Lynette laid the pen down and folded her hands on top of the pile of papers. "It's a good thing we have all these apples. It looks as if we've got sixty entries, and we want to have some pies to sell after the contest is over."

Rick rubbed his hands together. "Looking good then. Just like you. You're always looking good."

Lynette's cheeks flushed a deep shade of crimson, giving her more appeal than ever. "Stop that. We have work to do. Sit down."

They set to work finalizing the plans for the last booths and events and decided on who would be best suited to do what needed to be done. Before they went home they divided up the lists so they could each make the appropriate phone calls.

When they were finished, Rick leaned back in the chair and raised his hands, linking his fingers behind his head. "I guess tomorrow we should have the youth group start constructing the props and decorations and things."

"Yes. It'll be a lot of work to build a fake pond, because we'll have to build a frame then somehow cover it. We don't want to run short on time."

Rick studied the calendar on the wall. "Next weekend we'll have to go shopping for all the supplies we need, the table coverings, prizes, groceries, and stuff. Then the weekend after is the big day. We don't have a lot of time, do we?"

"No, we don't. I'd better add the model kits to my list."

Rick sighed. He could see what kind of mood she was in, and today would definitely be strictly business, as would every day this week when they got together with the youth group to begin the building and planning.

But their weekend shopping trip had great possibilities.

"Let's get to it then," he said as he selected a pen out of her father's bin. "We'll have the youth group meet here every night at seven during the week, and I'll pick you up at ten sharp on Saturday morning. The end is near."

For some strange reason he was certain Lynette's face paled.

"Yes," she mumbled and abruptly began making more notes. "The end is near."

Rick was surprised to see Lynette waiting at the curb for him when he arrived at her house for their shopping trip.

"I guess it's silly of me to ask if you've got the list."

She mumbled something under her breath as she fastened her seat belt.

"What's our first stop?"

"First the megastore, then the lumber store; then we have to go to the Chungs' and pick up more apples."

Rick squeezed his eyes shut for a second then shifted into gear. "More apples?" he asked as he pulled into traffic. "You've got to be kidding. How many does that make now?"

Lynette sighed. "I don't have a clue. People have been dropping off bags and boxes of apples at the church all week. I didn't have the heart to tell anyone we had enough."

Rick didn't comment. Right now the apples were the last thing he wanted to think about. Since they would never accomplish all that shopping in two hours, that meant they would be having lunch together. This time he wouldn't be seeing her at her home or at the church. He could take her someplace nice, and most important, they would be on neutral ground.

Finally, they could talk. And it didn't have to be all business.

By the time they finished their first stop it was after one o'clock, and Rick's stomach had begun to make rude noises. Lynette had suggested a fast food restaurant, but he insisted on a little bistro where they could have a more private table in a less hectic atmosphere.

After the waitress seated them and gave them menus, they were finally alone and forced to stay in one place. Lynette had nothing to look at, nothing to fret over, and no place to go.

Or so Rick thought. As soon as he opened his mouth to speak, Lynette picked up the menu, holding it so high he couldn't see her face behind it.

Rick sighed, reached across the table, and pushed it down flat to the table. "Relax, Lynette. Why are you so jumpy? I don't bite. I promise. This is just lunch, nothing more."

"Sorry," she mumbled then tried to pick up the menu again.

Rick kept his hand pressed on it, pinning it to the table. "Why don't you want to look at me? I'd hate myself if I've done something to hurt your feelings and didn't realize it. You must know by now that I like you very much."

Her face paled, and this time it wasn't his imagination. "I know you do. I like you too."

"Ah. Now we're getting somewhere. I don't see that as a problem, but you've been running away from me as if I've done something wrong. Have I?"

She continued to tug at the menu. Rick grabbed it and pulled it away then rested both menus in his lap.

Her face turned three shades of red. He couldn't help but smile, now that she had no choice but to make eye contact.

Lynette cleared her throat. "I know what you are trying to do."

Rick crossed his arms over his chest, still guarding both menus. "Okay, tell me. What am I trying to do?"

"You're trying to get me to go out with you."

"Is that a bad thing?"

Of all the timing the waitress appeared to take their orders. Rather than admit they'd been playing childish games with the menus, they both ordered a hamburger and fries, even though that was exactly what Rick had been trying to avoid by coming to the bistro.

When the waitress left, Lynette folded her hands on the table and looked him straight in the eye. "Did you see that little dog locked in that car in the parking lot at the megastore? That's so dangerous in this kind of weather. It only takes a short amount of time for an animal to be overcome by the heat in a closed vehicle this time of year. I wish I'd written down the license number so I could report it."

"Yes, but you're trying to change the subject. Why is it a bad thing because I want you to go out with me?"

She turned her head down and stared intently at her hands, which were still folded on the tabletop. "Because I won't go out with anyone from my father's congregation."

Suddenly Rick lost his appetite. If it had been something he'd done or something he could change, he could have dealt with it. It was obvious she didn't expect him to leave the church and his ministry with the youth to go out with her. He had a feeling there was more to it that she wasn't saying. "I don't understand."

She raised her head and made direct eye contact. Rick froze.

"You're taking leadership courses at Bible college. You know what they say about spending too much time with someone of the opposite gender. And I'm the pastor's daughter."

Rick shook his head. "But I'm not counseling you, nor are you counseling me. We don't have that kind of mentoring relationship. So what if you're the pastor's daughter? I just want to go out with you."

"That doesn't matter. You'll notice I've never dated anyone from our own church; it's not only you."

"Why doesn't that make me feel any better?"

"Sorry—it isn't the way I wanted it, but that's the way it is."

Rick leaned forward. He wanted to touch her hands, to hold them while sitting across from her; but she must have guessed what he was thinking, because she stiffened and leaned back in her chair.

"Lots of pastors' daughters date men from their father's congregation. I see it all the time." He lowered his voice. "Sometimes they get married too."

"That may be true, but sometimes bad things happen. There can be accusations of favoritism and other improprieties."

Rick blew out a quick breath of air. "Improprieties? Oh, come on."

"It's true. Do you know anything of my family's history, before my father came to be pastor at Good Tidings?"

"No, only that you came from another city in another state. Remember—I was only eighteen then. And you were only sixteen. I'll never forget the first time I met you."

Her face flushed for a second, and she shook her head. "The reason we left the other church was because my mother became involved in a big scandal."

Now he really wasn't hungry anymore. "I didn't know that."

"Yes. She'd been doing some bookkeeping for one of the members of the congregation, helping in the interim while his regular bookkeeper was away for some surgery. I'm not sure of the details; it was so long ago. Suddenly rumors started floating around that more was going on than accounting."

He almost hated himself for asking, but he had to. "Were any of the rumors true?"

"No! My mother was devastated by the accusations, but my father stood by her because he knew the truth. But the other man's wife didn't believe him, about why they spent so much time alone together. Most people in the church took sides, and it ended up dividing the church. It was awful."

"Is that why you didn't want me going to your house? You wanted to do everything at the church."

"Yes."

The waitress chose that moment to deliver their lunches. After a short prayer of thanks for their meal, they began to eat, but Rick only ate it because he had to. Everything tasted like cardboard. Judging from the way Lynette toyed with her meal, she felt the same way he did.

"So what happened? Did it get worked out in the end?"

"No. My mother didn't know until it blew up in her face that they were already having marital problems. His wife ended up leaving him, which made the situation even worse. Rather than live in the midst of the speculation and accusations, which only caused more arguing among the church members, my parents decided to leave that particular church. When my father was offered the position at Good Tidings, he jumped at it with no hesitation. You'll also notice that my mother only participates in ladies-only functions or in a large committee."

"But this is different. Neither of us is married." Although he did want both of them to be married—to each other.

Lynette toyed with her fries then laid the fork down and folded her hands on the table. "Is it different? Improprieties still happen between people who aren't married. And people still talk."

"But we're not kids running on overactive hormones. You're twenty-six, and I'm twenty-eight."

"The rumor mill knows no age limit. Not only was my mother an adult, she was married too. Scandal spreads quickly, and it doesn't have to be based on fact."

"I don't understand how something like that could perpetuate to that degree. I can't help but think that he did something to make it worse. Maybe he had a hidden agenda. What if he was even the one who started the rumor? He could have been using your mother to get his wife to take more notice of him. It wasn't your mother's fault."

"It doesn't matter, Rick. The end result is what counted. The fallout split the church, and my mother was devastated by all that happened. My family ended up having to leave a fellowship they loved, with a lot of hurt feelings. I don't ever want to have to go through that."

His mind raced, but he couldn't think of a thing to say. He wanted to say that their own congregation was above such a thing, but he couldn't. All it took was one person to start a scandal, real or imagined, when someone's feelings were hurt. Rick suspected that the man involved most likely tried to use the situation to his own benefit to salvage or quicken the breakdown of his marriage, but no one would ever know the truth.

He pushed his half-eaten meal to the side. "So where does that leave us?"

"There is no 'us,' Rick. There never has been. But we've always been friends. We can certainly stay friends."

Friends. Rick felt the kiss of death on any relationship he could ever hope to have with Lynette.

"But what about you? Your future?" Rick swallowed hard. The words were almost too hard to say. "If you won't go out with anyone from your own congregation, where are you going to meet people? Do you plan to stay single for your whole entire life?"

"I firmly believe that when the time is right God will place the right man in my path."

According to Rick, the right man was already in her path. She was looking right at him but couldn't see him.

Lynette pushed her plate to the side. "We should get going. We've got a few more stops to make, and I have plans to go out with some friends for dinner."

Rick didn't ask if she was referring to male or female friends. He didn't want to know if they were from another church.

"Okay," he mumbled as he scooped up the bill, and they headed for the cashier to pay. "Let's get the rest of our shopping over with."

Chapter 6

R ick walked past the church office, waved at Lynette's father, and continued into the kitchen. "I'm here. Are we ready?"

"Yes. I'm so glad you could get the day off too. I can't believe how this project has snowballed. I'll never do this by myself."

Rick glanced toward the back wall. He'd never seen so many apples at one time in his life, not even at the grocery store.

Every day they'd met with the youth group at the church to build and plan the booths and displays. Today was Friday, the day before the fair, and everything was ready. Everything except the pies.

"Yeah. I can see why you took the day off." He glanced again at the wall of apples. "How many pies do you think this is going to make? I hope you know I barely cook, and I've never made a pie in my life."

"That's okay. It's my granny's recipe, and it's the easiest apple pie recipe in the world. Besides, I'm not a good cook either. If I can do it, you can do it."

"How many contest entries did we get? We had seventy a few days ago."

"Ninety-something. But we have to remember there are

bound to be some entries from the people who don't come to our church and will come tomorrow. We have to count on that."

Rick rolled up his sleeves. "Tell me what to do."

He watched and listened carefully as Lynette mixed up some vinegar, water, and an egg, combined some flour and stuff with some lard and then dumped the liquid in.

"Watch carefully," she said then reached into the bowl with her hands.

Rick shuddered. "You've got to be kidding. I'm not touching raw eggs."

She grinned, and his stomach did a strange somersault. "Don't be such a wimp."

"Sticks and stones," he grumbled as he drew in a deep breath and slowly stuck his fingers in to start the mixing process.

After considerable poking and prodding, Lynette held up a big ball of pastry dough. "See? When yours looks like this, then you roll it out. Just be careful not to overwork it."

Rick poked the mashy lump in his bowl with one finger. "Overwork it?"

Lynette looked into his bowl. "You mix it until it's like mine; then stop. There, like that. Now it's ready to roll."

He couldn't help but smile as she picked up a rolling pin. "I always thought rolling pins were for chasing errant husbands. Would you like to chase me with that thing someday?"

Her mouth dropped open, and she fumbled with the rolling pin for a few seconds. "Quit it. We have too much to do to be fooling around. This is how it's done."

Rick watched her start from the middle and press it outward, pressing evenly as she worked. She made him help slice up enough apples to fill the crust, and then they sprinkled flour and sugar and cinnamon on top. To finish it off, he watched as

Lynette laid the pastry top on and pressed it down around the edges with a fork.

He grinned. "I can do that."

Without a word Lynette pointed to a box on the counter, where he found another rolling pin. As he began to roll his lump of dough flat, he snickered to himself. "This is so domestic. Wait until the guys hear about this."

Lynette sighed. "Just keep rolling while you're talking. We're going to keep making pies until we run out of apples. You shouldn't be eating the dough—it isn't good for you when it's raw like that. Don't think I didn't see you eating the apples either."

Rick grinned around the chunk of apple in his mouth then picked up the rolling pin and continued to flatten more pastry dough.

At first he thought rolling out pastry and slicing up the apples was fun, but the more he did, the less interesting it became. Since they could only fit three pies in the oven at one time, it didn't take long for the pies to start lining up on the counter. By the time they filled up one side of the counter with pies, Rick no longer thought making pies was a fun way to spend the day.

By noon his back was feeling the effects of lugging around the heavy bags of flour and leaning over the counter while he worked. Lynette didn't complain, but he thought she was definitely slowing down too.

He pressed his floury fists into the small of his back. "I think it's time to quit for awhile."

"We can't. We've got nearly a hundred done, but we've used only half the apples, and we've baked only eighteen. I don't know what we're going to do. We can't put uncooked pies out for the contest, despite the fact that you seem to prefer them raw."

Rick covered his stomach with one hand. At first he thought he was being funny; but he'd eaten a little too much dough, and now his stomach didn't feel so good. Since it was lunchtime, he hoped some real food would cure what ailed him.

Lynette walked to the fridge. "I didn't want to leave because I knew we'd have pies in the oven, so I made sandwiches for lunch."

"Sounds good to me."

He noticed she had made only two sandwiches. With her father in the same building, in the room next to the kitchen, Rick wondered if she'd left her father out of their lunch plans on purpose.

As they always did, they paused for a prayer of thanks and began to eat.

In an odd sort of way he was having a good day. After Lynette had explained what happened with her family, he could understand why she worked so hard to avoid him, even if he didn't agree. Also, now that he knew, a burden seemed to have lifted, and she acted relaxed with him. In his heart he knew it was because she trusted him not to step beyond the guidelines she'd drawn for their relationship, now that everything was out in the open.

If he had to see a bright side, it would be that she trusted him enough to be honest with him, and she trusted him to respect the lines she had drawn.

He knew he would always want more, but if friendship was all he could have, then Rick intended to be the very best friend he could be. Of course, what he really wanted was the best friendship of all, the special friendship of the bond of a man and wife.

For the balance of the afternoon they continued making

more and more pies. He did his best to keep the conversation cheerful, even though both of them were becoming increasingly tired. By the time they were finished it was suppertime. But more than supper Rick wanted a nap. He wondered if it was a sign of old age creeping up on him and then shook the thought from his head.

Since they still had pies in the oven, the second the new batch went in they took off for the drive-thru so they could be back quickly. They talked nonstop the entire drive, neither of them breathing a word about apple pies or anything to do with church business. They simply had fun.

With the arrival of the youth group members, between baking pies, they set everything in order in the lobby, ready to be brought outside first thing Saturday morning.

When all was complete, Rick stood on a chair amidst the mayhem and clutter, stuck two fingers in his mouth and let out a sharp, piercing whistle. The room quieted instantly.

"Attention, everyone! Now for the last job of the day!"

Everyone in the room groaned.

"If anyone here hasn't seen them, Lynette and I made two hundred and seven pies today, and we could bake only fifty-one." He paused while he counted everyone in the room. "There are thirty-two of you here, and I know it's late, but I'm going to give each one of you three pies to take home with a note of how long to cook them. Bring them back, cooked, tomorrow morning at eight o'clock sharp, or earlier if you've been assigned to help with the goats. Class dismissed, and I'll see you all tomorrow."

As everyone left, Lynette counted the remaining pies. "We still have sixty pies to bake. I'm going to be up all night, and I still won't get them all done."

"I'll take half."

She counted on her fingers. "That will still take five hours to bake. The night's too short. We have to sleep."

"Then what about your parents? That's only twenty pies each." Rick paused to calculate three pies per half hour baking time. "No, that's still not good enough. I need a church directory. I'll be right back. You start packing three pies per box. I'm going to be making some deliveries."

Before she could protest that it was too late to be phoning around for favors, Rick took off into her father's office, closed the door, and locked it behind him. In less than twenty minutes he had acquired the help of the eighteen families he needed.

He returned to Lynette in the kitchen. "Let's load up the car. I'm on my way. I'll see you in the morning. And don't forget your three pies."

It took him an hour to deliver all the pies to be baked, which was much better than the original five hours it would have taken if he and Lynette had to bake them all themselves.

As soon as he arrived at home, Rick put his pies in the oven, but they weren't fully cooked by the time he was ready for bed. He waited out the last ten minutes standing near the stove, because he knew if he sat down he would never get up.

He couldn't remember the last time he'd been so tired, but the day's efforts had been worth it in more ways than one. He'd spent the entire day with Lynette, and for the first time in ten years she had made no efforts to get away from him. Not once had she appeared nervous or uncomfortable in his presence. Just as she'd promised, they had spend time together as real friends, sharing and talking about everything with no holds barred. By the end of the day he loved her even more than he did before, if that were possible.

Today a large barrier had crumbled, and with that barrier gone he knew she loved him as much as he loved her. She just didn't know it yet.

Tomorrow, before the fair was over and life returned to normal, he had to do something about it.

The timer for the oven dinged, and Rick removed the pies from the oven.

Tomorrow would be another day.

Chapter 7

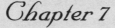

Lynette walked toward the church with all her attention on the clipboard, knowing she had walked this same way so many times that she didn't need to look where she was going. Rick followed directly behind her, carrying the huge box.

"Have you got the trophy?"

"Yup."

"The envelope with the gift certificates?"

"Yup."

"The case of chocolate bars?"

"Yup."

"Fishing rods?"

"Yup."

"Toys?"

"Yup."

"Paper?"

She checked off the colored felt markers without asking. She already knew they were in the Sunday school classroom. Her mom was picking up the hot dog buns and wieners, and her father was picking up the urn for the drinks.

"Plastic forks?"

"Lynette, I had the same list as yours. I have everything in this box except duct tape. Trust me."

She stopped dead in her tracks. Rick bumped into her from behind, not hard enough to knock her down but hard enough to send the clipboard and pen flying to the ground.

She whirled around. "You forgot duct tape? You have to go back."

"You think I should? I was kidding."

She couldn't hold back her giggle. "So was I. Everything will be fine. Look above. Blue sky."

"How can you tell? It's hardly daylight."

Lynette lost her smile. "Quit being so grumpy. Today is going to be great!"

Rick didn't smile. "I haven't had a decent night's sleep in a week, I was up before the crack of dawn, and I didn't have time to make coffee this morning. Don't give me any of that *great day* stuff."

She tipped her head to one side and patted him gently on one shoulder. "Not a morning person, are we?"

He grumbled something she wasn't sure she wanted to hear. Before she had time to respond, a car turned into the parking lot.

"Sarah and her dad are here. The dunk tank won't be far behind. Hurry. Put the box beside the door and go meet them. The animal pen is due to arrive in half an hour." She checked her watch to be sure. "Where are all the boys? They said they'd be here."

Rick also checked his watch. "They're not due for five minutes. They'll be here in ten."

The four of them carried the boxes and paraphernalia out of the building until the first van full of teenagers arrived. Soon they were followed by a pickup truck loaded with the fencing and a few bales of hay.

The youth group members continued to arrive, each bringing the three pies, which Lynette directed to tables set up inside the lobby. The younger boys helped Lynette arrange the tables around the parking lot while the older boys and Rick set up the pen and spread the hay. Those remaining assembled the dunk tank. When everything was together, the boys filled the tank with warm water, and the girls set up the backdrop and erected the fish pond booth, doing their best to make the blue enclosure that would hide the two volunteers inside to resemble a small lake. By eight-thirty the last of the helpers arrived, all the pies were lining the tables in the lobby, and within fifteen minutes all the tables and booths were ready.

"There're the goats!" called out a couple of the girls when the truck and trailer came into view.

Rick checked his watch. "Right on time. This is great."

Lynette wiped her hands on her jeans. "That's what happens when everything is organized efficiently and you have lots of help."

Rick grumbled under his breath again, but this time Lynette didn't have the strength to tease him about his rotten mood. The exhausting pace of the past three weeks had caught up with her; yet she still had many hours of hard work ahead of her. She couldn't afford to slow her pace now. Soon it would be the time they'd advertised they would officially open.

Rick supervised loading the goats into the enclosure, making everything ready. Still, nothing ever went smoothly, despite the most careful preplanning. Even though she felt ready to drop, her insides were still tense, waiting for something to go wrong at the last minute when things seemed perfect.

Once again Lynette tallied up everything around her. The

only person missing was the mayor, who would be arriving at eleven, after the fair was in progress.

Rick appeared at her side. Lynette flinched when he picked up one hand and rubbed it between both of his. "Are you okay?" he asked quietly.

She smiled weakly, grateful for his recovery from the morning grumpies, and shrugged her shoulders. "I guess."

He jerked his head toward the building. "Come into the church with me for a minute."

Not letting go of her hand, Rick started walking, giving Lynette no choice but to follow. He stopped when they were inside the door where they could still hear what was going on outside, but no one could see them.

"Turn around," he murmured as he placed his palms on her shoulders then slowly turned her around so her back was to him.

"What are you doing?" she asked, tilting her head to glance over her shoulder at him.

"Shh. You're so tense." At his words, with his palms still on her shoulders, his thumbs pressed into her shoulder blades then began to move in little circles, loosening up the knots in her muscles. With his touch all the tension of the morning and the past few weeks began to drain out of her.

"I don't know if—"

"Shh, I said. Don't talk. Relax." As his thumbs pressed harder, Lynette struggled not to melt. In only two minutes she couldn't have talked if she wanted to.

"We talked a lot about being friends, and as a friend I've been worried about you," he said without easing up on the pressure. "I can't help but wonder why you took on a project like this. Before we got involved in this whole thing, you seemed ready to drop. I even thought you were starting to pull away from the church. The grapevine told me you've dropped out of every committee. I'm glad you're finally learning how to say no to people before you reach your breaking point. It isn't selfish—it's critical to know your limits so you can have an effective ministry. As for this fair, even though it's been hard on both of us, I'm grateful for this time we've been able to spend together. It's meant a lot to me. I hope that when it's over we can stay friends. Or more."

His touch slowed and stopped. Slowly she felt herself being turned around to face him. "More?"

He replaced his hands on her shoulders and raised his thumbs to brush her cheeks. "Special friends, Lynette. I want to be special friends. Forever."

Lynette's heart went into overdrive. For eight years she'd been distancing herself from him, and now she knew he'd loved her all that time. Now that he agreed to be friends she could finally admit to herself that she had loved him for a long time too, but she'd been too frightened to explore a relationship. After their discussions on what happened with her mother, she had done nothing but think about how she'd let it affect her life and mostly her relationship, or lack thereof, with Rick.

The more she thought about what happened to her mother, the more she suspected Rick was right. The man involved must have perpetuated the rumors for some reason, even if no one would ever know or understand why, or the situation would never have gone so out of control for so long.

Rick had no hidden agenda. For as long as she had known him he'd been open and honest with her in both thought and deed. Lynette had been the one to put up all the roadblocks. She needed to talk to him about what could lie ahead for them, while she still had the courage to do so.

Lynette raised her hands to touch the sides of his waist. "We don't have a lot of time, so—"

She couldn't finish her sentence. Before she could think his mouth was on hers. This was not a sweet, gentle kiss. He kissed her as if he meant it, from the bottom of his heart.

So Lynette kissed him back the same way because she meant it from the bottom of her heart too. She no longer wanted to keep hidden away from him as she'd done for so many years. She had wasted too much time, and she wasn't going to waste any more. She wanted to have that special relationship with him, as he said.

She slipped her hands around his back and held him tighter. His hands slipped to her back, and he pressed her against him. He lifted his mouth away only long enough to whisper her name, tilt his head a little more, and kiss her again.

A sharp whistle cut the air. All talking and banging outside stopped.

Rick and Lynette broke apart and stepped back from each other. As her brain slowly started to clear, Lynette thought she saw Rick shake his head to do the same. Without a word between them, they hurried outside.

Her father stood in the center of everything with his hands raised over his head.

"Attention, everyone! We're ready to start, in plenty of time before the first people get here. While it's still quiet and it's just us, I want to take this time to pray for God's blessing on this day."

Lynette almost smiled to herself at her father's "just us" comment. The "just" consisted of about one hundred and fifty church members.

They all bowed their heads. Lynette struggled to push

aside thoughts of what had just happened and concentrate on her father's words as he prayed, which was extremely difficult with Rick at her side.

After a slight pause her father thanked God for the joined effort of the entire congregation. He then praised the Lord for the blessings of everything from the small donations to the large specialty items that would make the day a special attraction for the community. He prayed for God to be glorified in everything they did and to bless their time with the people of the community. Last of all he prayed for the proceeds to be enough to fix the church roof.

The group called out a boisterous "amen," and everyone proceeded to their stations.

Fortunately for Lynette, one of the teens pulled Rick away toward the goat pen, giving her a chance not to be distracted by his presence. She needed time to think.

Chapter 8

I t's okay." Rick pressed the two pieces of wood together then stood back. "It's still connected, but I think I'll get some twine and reinforce it to be sure. Thanks for bringing this to my attention."

"Glad it's nothing," Andrew said as he ran his fingers over the joint in the portable fence. "I'll go back in with the goats now. I didn't know if they could knock this down."

As soon as Andrew walked away, Rick let himself sag. He couldn't believe what had happened with Lynette. He certainly hadn't planned on kissing her; he'd only wanted to talk about seeing each other after the fund-raiser was over. But when she put her hands on his waist it was too close to a hug, and he lost it.

Then she hadn't pushed him away, nor had she hesitated. She'd kissed him back. Not a light little friendship kiss either. She had kissed him for real. It was there, the connection he'd hoped and prayed for. He'd thought about it and dreamed about it for so long that over the past few days, when she had begun to respond to him, he didn't know if her reaction was real or in his over-optimistic imagination.

But today, ten minutes ago, he certainly hadn't imagined the way she'd kissed him.

He continued to fiddle with the fence, even though it was fine, because he knew he couldn't wipe the sappy grin off his face quite yet. He was a man in love, and she loved him back. He knew it now without a shadow of a doubt.

Today, after everything was over, he could do something about it. Already, fifteen minutes before their advertised opening time, guests started to arrive, which was a good indication for the rest of the day. Soon a steady stream of people flowed in.

By the time the mayor arrived, the place was bustling. Most of the crowd hovered around the dunk tank as Mayor Klein climbed onto the collapsing platform. The newspaper camera caught him giving Pastor Chris a wink and a thumbs-up as he settled into the seat. They also took a picture of Pastor Chris buying the first ticket for a chance to dunk the mayor. The crowd hushed as he aimed the ball for the target, wound up— and missed.

Rick smiled, almost sure the pastor had missed on purpose.

Many people bought a chance to dunk the mayor, who was attracting quite a crowd. A man Rick didn't recognize finally hit the target, and the mayor slipped down into the warm water as the people cheered and applauded. As Mayor Klein came out of the tank, he made a show of pretending the water was cold, toweled off his face, and returned to the seat, which a couple of the church deacons had put back into position.

After a few dunkings the crowd began to disperse. Pastor Chris remained beside the mayor, encouraging everyone to buy a ball and dunk their fine mayor again. Of course, having a photographer from the local newspaper presenting a potential chance for everyone to be in the paper greatly encouraged people to try their aim.

Since the mayor was in questionably good hands, Rick left

on his quest to find Lynette. He made a big circle of all the booths, checking the goat pen, the bake and craft tables. Not finding her there, he moved on to the children's games and contest tables. After he'd checked every booth without success, Rick stood beside the fishing pool and crossed his arms. The only place he hadn't checked was the church building, where all the pies were stored.

"Rick?"

He turned his head without moving. "Yes, Sarah?"

"I have to, uh, go, uh—can you do the fish thing for me?"

Rick nodded. "Sure, Sarah."

As Sarah took off at a run toward the building, Rick walked behind the backdrop, dropped to his hands and knees, and lifted the blanket to crawl into the make-believe lake where he could attach prizes for the children when they threw in their line. A familiar voice came from within.

"Hi, Rick."

He grinned as he crawled inside and let the blanket drop, hiding them from everyone. "Hi, Lynette. I was wondering where you went."

She smiled, and his heart went wild. "I'm down here, a little fish in a big pond. Keep your head up. Those little balls aren't heavy when they hit you in the head, but they can get tangled in your hair. I've recently found that out the hard way."

He ran his fingers through the top of his hair as he parked himself on the padded surface beside her. "I don't think that's possible with me. But I appreciate the warning."

A little ball with a fishing line attached sailed through the air and landed between them.

Lynette giggled. "You can do this one."

Rick quickly clipped on a toy fish with the Bible verse

attached and tugged gently on the line.

"Mommy! Mommy! I caught a fish!" a child squealed from the other side of the backdrop.

The line tightened, but Rick didn't let go. He tugged again.

"Mommy! It's a big one!"

Lynette covered her mouth with her hand and giggled again. "I hope the fight is worth it."

Rick released the line, allowing the toy fish to be reeled in.

"I caught one, Mommy! It's so pretty!"

Rick and Lynette smiled at each other.

"I like kids," he said, his voice coming out strangely husky.

She ran her fingers across his chin. "I know."

The tap of footsteps on the cement of the parking lot surrounded them, and voices echoed all around. Yet, bchind the backdrop and surrounded by the cloth-covered wire circle, the enclosure felt strangely private.

His throat clogged, but he cleared it. "We have to talk."

"I know."

"About the future."

"I know."

His heart pounded in his chest. It may not have been the ideal place to propose, but if he didn't he thought his heart might burst. "Lynette—"

The blanket lifted, and Sarah crawled in to join them. In the cramped quarters Rick shuffled to the side.

"I'm back. Thanks. Ryan is looking for you. They want to put more warm water in the dunk tank, because Mayor Klein is starting to shiver for real."

Rick gritted his teeth, crawled out from beneath the blanket, and made his way to the dunk tank to do his duty. He hadn't said what he wanted to say to Lynette, but on the bright side at least now he knew where she was.

He made pleasant conversation with the mayor and the pastor while he added more warm water to the tub. As soon as the temperature was pleasantly warm again, Rick made his way to the barbecue, where he found Lynette's mother.

Ever since Lynette had told him what had happened in their other church, he found he respected Mrs. Charleston even more than before. She had handled the situation with class and dignity, and above all she had trusted the Lord with her heart and soul in times of trouble. In retrospect it was only because of the unpleasant incident Lynette had told him about that they'd moved on to Good Tidings, where they were truly happy and the people of Good Tidings were equally happy with them.

Rick reached into his back pocket and pulled out his wallet. "Two hot dogs, please. Loaded with onions."

"Onions? Are you sure? Are these for you and Lynette?"

He nodded.

Lynette's mother shrugged her shoulders and loaded two hot dogs each with huge piles of extra fried onions.

Rick grinned. If they both had onions, they would be safe with each other, but not anyone else.

As he approached the fish pond booth, he watched as Lynette crawled out through the blanket. She stood, glanced over her shoulder, and rubbed her bottom with her hands.

"Hi," he said as he neared her.

Her face flamed, which he thought cute.

"Sitting for so long on the cement like that is hard, even with that padded blanket."

He nodded and handed her one of the hot dogs. "I know. Who's in there now with Sarah? I hope it's not Brad."

"Don't worry—I know better than that. Melissa is with her.

I'm not going far so I can see if Brad comes around."

"You're good in church leadership roles, you know."

She took a big bite of the hot dog, closing her eyes to savor the rich onions. "So are you."

"Do you think you could do this kind of thing on a regular basis?"

"Not run community fairs, but, yes, I like being in leadership roles. As long as I remember to take a break every once in awhile. I learned that the hard way, I think."

Rick's heart pounded at the possibilities. He was a volunteer youth leader now, but with a couple of more years of Bible college at night school, he could one day fulfill his dream of pastoring a church of his own.

"I was wondering, one day, do you think—"

"Lynette! I've been looking all over for you!" a voice called out from the masses. Mrs. McGrath pushed her way through the crowd and joined them. "We're almost ready for the pie-eating contest. I noticed that Mayor Klein is signed up too."

Rick stuffed the rest of his hot dog into his mouth in one bite. "How many entries do we have?" he asked around the food in his mouth.

Mrs. McGrath beamed. "We have over a hundred and fifty."

He nearly choked. Lynette patted him on the back with her free hand.

Mrs. McGrath raised her eyebrows and pressed her wrinkled hands to her cheeks. "Gracious! I just thought of something! Do we have enough pies?"

Lynette nodded and spoke first because Rick still couldn't talk. "Yes. We made somewhere around two hundred pies. But where are all those people going to sit? I planned on bringing out about eight tables and putting them in the middle of the parking lot. We'd better get more out, real fast."

Rick pressed one fist into the center of his chest. "I'll get the boys to start bringing them out, along with more chairs. I'm going to need a calculator to figure out how many tables we'll need to seat that many people."

Lynette turned to him and folded her arms across her chest. "This isn't a difficult question, Rick. One table fits four people on each side and one at each end. That's ten people per table."

He felt his cheeks heating up. "I knew that," he mumbled.

Lynette took one step with Mrs. McGrath and then suddenly stopped and turned back to him. "Do we have enough plastic forks?"

Rick shook his head. "No. Maybe you'd better run off to the store while I get the boys to help me with the tables and chairs."

"But what about Sarah in the fish pond?"

"Don't worry. I'll have Brad with me."

Rick took off in one direction, while Lynette took off in another. While he scrambled to find all the available teen boys from the youth group, he heard the announcement for the last call for the apple-pie-eating contest.

He had finished setting up the last table when Lynette returned with a grocery bag full of plastic forks.

"Are you ready?" she asked.

"Yes. Do you have any idea how much money we've made, just with the pies?"

"Yes." Lynette broke out into a huge smile. "So many people are here. Wouldn't it be wonderful if we made enough money to fix the roof and not have to ask the congregation for any?"

While that would have been wonderful, one thing on his mind would have been more wonderful, if only he could get the chance to talk to her.

"Yes. Now get up to the podium. They're signaling for you."

Chapter 9

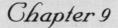

Lynette faced the crowd. She estimated that twice as many people surrounded her in the parking lot as on a busy Sunday morning service, which would bring the number to about a thousand people. Her head reeled to think how much their church had been blessed today. And such a gathering usually drew more families to their humble church family.

She cleared her throat and tapped the microphone with her index finger. "Is this thing on?"

Feedback screeched through the speaker system.

Lynette felt her face grow warm. "Oops. Sorry. First of all, I'd like to say thank you to everyone for participating. I think I can say we're all having fun, right?"

A round of applause and cheers was the reply.

She smiled, doing her best to hold back her tears. "Before we get to the crowning event of the day, our apple-pie-eating contest, I'd like to award the prizes for the raffle and the children's contests."

She called out the name of the person who had won the weekend in Seattle and the trip to the Space Needle, but they had apparently already left. Lynette tucked the envelope into her back pocket for safe keeping then gave out the awards to the children. She was pleased to see the prizes equally divided between church members and people from the community.

"Now for the moment we've all been waiting for. Before we start, I'd like to say that for those of you who have entered and don't finish your pie, we have plastic wrap over there." She pointed to four ladies at a faraway table, who waved at the crowd.

"For those of you who didn't enter but still would like a pie, we'll be selling the remaining pies after the contest for ten dollars each. If all the contestants will now proceed to the tables corresponding to your entry number, we'll hand out the pies. Take a seat at one of those tables over there and wait for the signal to begin. The winner will be awarded with this trophy." She held up the huge loving cup for all to see. "Also, since this is a church, the winner will get this lovely leather-bound, gold-embossed, brand-new Bible." She held up the Bible as well.

Considering that the four ladies had to hand out one hundred and sixty-two pies, the process went surprisingly well. Soon everyone who entered was seated and ready for the signal.

Rick appeared at her side. She covered the microphone with her hand. "Rick? What are you doing here? Why didn't you enter the contest?"

He covered his stomach with his hand. "After yesterday I can't even look at an apple pie, never mind eat one. I don't see you in the contest entrants either."

Lynette stiffened. "I have to be the emcee. I can't."

At her reply Rick made a strange snorting sound. She elbowed him in the ribs and uncovered the microphone. "Is everybody ready? Forks down, hands in your laps. The first person to finish, stand and raise both hands in the air, and call out that you're done." She scanned the seventeen tables of entrants, sucked in a deep breath and yelled, "Go!"

Most people in the crowd cheered on someone they knew as men, women, teens, and children alike did their best to gobble down their pies as quickly as they could. Each entrant had been supplied with one glass of water to help wash it down, and one volunteer stood at each table to refill the cups, if necessary.

Lynette could see three men in particular, only one of whom she recognized, down to the last sliced piece of pie.

A forty-five-ish man she didn't know with a bald head and green T-shirt jumped to his feet. "Done!" he yelled at the same time as one of the boys from the youth group started to stand.

"We have a winner!"

The crowd cheered and applauded.

Lynette walked up to him, announced his name to the crowd as best she could, and presented him with the Bible and trophy.

"Thanks," he said as he failed to hold back a small burp.

The crowd around him laughed, and his ears reddened. "I think you might be seeing me and my family here one Sunday soon."

"That is great. It has been wonderful to have you, and congratulations."

With the fair officially over, the crowd dispersed slowly, and volunteers began to pack up their tables. They decided for safety's sake to leave the goats and their pen for when the last volunteers remained so as not to disturb the animals, although Lynette couldn't believe how tame and friendly they were. When the guests had gone and only the church volunteers remained, Rick drained the dunk tank. Lynette and her parents walked around to collect the money that hadn't yet been put away and thank the volunteers for their help and contributions.

As she walked, Lynette's father followed, punching up

figures on a calculator.

"Daddy!" Lynette whispered behind him as he added the numbers from the fishing pond into his total. "Why are you doing that now?"

"I couldn't help it," he whispered back. "I can't believe how much money we raised. I think we're going to make everything we need in one day!"

Lynette's breath caught in her throat. "Are you serious?"

He nodded and kept punching in figures.

He followed her to the last table, which was the pie table. One sad, lonely pie remained. "I guess no one wanted to buy the last one," her father mumbled while he waited for her mother to count the money.

He punched in the amount. "I can't believe this. According to my calculations we're only a hundred and fifty dollars short of our total goal. That covers everything, even the cost of the advertising and paying for the gas to get the goats and the pen here."

Lynette's mother sighed and looked at the last pie. "That's too bad. We came so close. If only we could find a way to make a hundred and fifty dollars on this one pie."

Suddenly Brad raised one finger in the air. Lynette hadn't noticed him beside her. But of course since Sarah had been trailing behind her after the fish pond was taken down, she should have known Brad wouldn't be far behind.

"I have an idea that will get you a hundred and fifty for that pie. Maybe more."

Lynette's heart raced. "Really? That would be wonderful! What are you going to do, auction it?" She couldn't see anyone paying a hundred and fifty dollars for a simple apple pie, especially since so many had already been purchased.

"Something close. I'll be right back."

Chapter 10

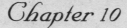

Rick stacked another piece of the dunk tank into the back of the pickup truck then stopped to wipe the sweat off his brow with the sleeve of his shirt. He gritted his teeth at the action behind him.

Rick turned around to the crowd of teen boys. "Brad, quit talking and get back to work. I'm tired and want to go home, and I'm sure everyone else here does too."

He saw something being passed to Brad, and Brad took off. He opened his mouth to call after him, but the rest of the boys got back to work, saying nothing about Brad's not helping.

Rick sighed. He was too tired to care. If the boys were okay with Brad's goofing off, then he would deal with him later. Rick wanted only to go home and lie down.

He knew he wouldn't get any sleep. As tired as he was, he would think only of Lynette.

All day long he'd been hoping and praying for a miracle, but with all the distractions and interruptions it didn't happen. He wanted to talk to Lynette while she could remember everything that passed between them when he kissed her. He needed to assure her that whatever passed between them was mutual, and it was real.

He watched while the man who owned the goats herded them into their trailer. Lynette's father handed the man some money to pay for the gas, and the goats were on their way.

Since the goat pen was the last thing left to be cleaned up, a number of the teen girls joined in to help. Some of their parents got involved, and then more people did too.

It made Rick wonder why they suddenly had too many people volunteering to do the work.

Someone behind him cleared their throat.

Rick froze, with his hands full of hay. He stiffened and turned around.

Lynette stood in front of him with an apple pie in her hands.

"What are you doing here?" he asked.

"This is for you. It's the last pie."

"No, thanks," he mumbled. The last thing he felt like was pie. He'd eaten too many raw apple pieces and far too much raw pastry to be interested in it, no matter how good everyone said the pies were. Besides that, his hands were covered with dirty straw, and he was coated in dust and sweat from head to toe. "You can have it."

As he began to turn around, he couldn't help but notice that everyone seemed to be watching him, as they had slowed down their clean-up efforts.

"Rick?"

He turned back to Lynette. "Yes?"

"All day long I've had something I wanted to say to you, and I never got the chance. I want to say it before I give you the pie."

His heart stopped then started again in double time. Despite the heat and the hard work Rick broke out into a cold sweat.

Lynette's voice dropped to a whisper so low he barely

heard what she said. "I love you, Rick."

His stomach flipped over a dozen times. This wasn't the ideal moment for such a discussion, especially in the middle of a crowd and with him covered in hay and who knew what else. But he'd learned the hard way that often the right moments had to be made, rather than waiting for them to happen.

"I love you too," he ground out. "I've loved you for years."

She cleared her throat again. "Close your eyes."

Rick also cleared his throat, which had gone very dry, and closed his eyes obediently. His voice came out in a hoarse croak. "Lynette, I know this isn't the most romantic setting, but will you marry me?"

He squeezed his eyes tighter and waited. He didn't think it in her character to kiss him in front of a crowd; but then again he wouldn't think she'd ever been proposed to before, so he didn't know what she would do. She had already surprised him by kissing him so profusely in the church, where anyone could have walked in on them.

Instead of a tender kiss to his lips, a slight scratchy substance pressed into his entire face. The scratchy sensation instantly broke up, changing to something slimy pushing against his skin. At the impact he jumped backward. The pressure disappeared. Something clanked to the ground.

Slimy lumps slithered down his face, along with the drier, crusty lumps, which landed with a plop at his feet. Something stuck in his hair and didn't fall down. His eyes remained clamped shut while all the people around him cheered, applauded, whistled, and laughed. Putting two and two together, he remembered Brad walking around to all the church members, teens and adults alike, instead of helping clean up the mess. Now he knew what Brad had been up to. That everyone had teamed up against him to have a pie thrown in his face didn't surprise him. What did surprise him was that Lynette had been the one to do the dirty work.

He pressed the lengths of his fingers to his eyebrows akin to windshield wipers. With a downward motion he swiped down his face to push away what he could of the remnants of the apple pie.

Lynette stood in front of him, her eyes wide and both hands covering her mouth. She was the only one not laughing or smiling.

He cleared his throat again and forced himself to smile, even though he knew it was weak. "I hope that was a yes."

Her eyes widened even more, if it were possible. "Are you mad at me?" she asked through her fingers. "We made it. With that last pie we made all the money to pay for the roof."

Rick smiled and stepped closer to Lynette. He paused to look at his fingers, wiped them off on his jeans as best he could, and reached up to run his fingers through the hair at Lynette's temple.

"Of course I'm not mad, but I must admit I am surprised. I do believe I asked you a question, though, and the question still stands."

Slowly she raised her right hand and touched his cheek. He could feel her fingers trembling, so he reached up and covered her hand with his, pressing her palm to his face, trying his best to ignore the slight slime still coating his skin.

"Yes, that was a yes," she whispered.

Rick thought his heart would burst. He wanted to kiss her well and good, but between the crowd surrounding them and the pie covering his face he couldn't. Instead he leaned forward to brush an appley kiss across her tender lips. Despite the public atmosphere he didn't move and remained standing toe to toe, gazing into the eyes of the woman he loved.

"That's it!" Pastor Chris called out from somewhere behind him. "Let's all get back to work. We need somewhere to park our cars tomorrow morning."

Around them the sound of movement returned.

Rick couldn't make himself move. One day in the near future he was going to marry the sweetest, most wonderful woman in the world.

A quick smile flittered across her face then dropped. "I guess we should get back to work."

One corner of his mouth quirked up. "I think we've done enough work. Let's take off."

Her eyes widened, and she broke out into a full grin and covered his hands with hers. Her eyes absolutely sparkled. "You're right. We've done most of the work so far, and now it's time for us both to learn to say no once in awhile. Let's let everyone else finish, while we go somewhere and talk. I've wasted too much precious time. I don't want a long engagement—how about you?"

Rick thought he must be dreaming. He would have pinched himself to make sure he was awake, but Lynette was holding his hands steady. Instead he rubbed two fingers together. Since he could still feel some apple-pie slime residue between them, he knew this was really happening. "That sounds like a great idea. I need to clean up first, though. Where would you like to go?"

Lynette gave his hands a gentle squeeze. "Let's go to the coffee shop on the corner. But if they offer me apple pie for dessert, I'm going to say—"

Rick waited for her reply

Lynette grinned. "Yes!"

Dear Readers,

Few things are as comforting and traditional as a good old-fashioned apple pie. The best recipes in the world are those passed down through the generations. In the story this is the apple pie recipe passed down to Lynette from her grandmother. In reality it's the recipe passed down to me from my own mother-in-law. Of course the best part of an apple pie is sharing it with someone you love.

Lynette's Granny's Apple Pie

PASTRY (makes 3 pies)

5 ½ cups flour
2 tsps salt
2 tsps baking powder
1 pound lard
1 egg

2 tsps vinegar
enough cold water to
  make 1 cup with the
  egg and vinegar

Mix the dry ingredients with your hands. Cut in lard with a pastry cutter. Make a well and pour in the liquid—mix with your hands—do not overmix. Roll out on a lightly floured surface.

FILLING

Slice 4-5 apples thin and put in the crust.

Combine 2 tablespoons flour and ¾ cup sugar and sprinkle over top of the apples.

Sprinkle cinnamon on top to taste—about 1 tablespoon.

Top with pastry; press edges with a fork; make slits to vent.

Bake for 10 minutes at 400°; reduce to 350° and continue baking for 25–30 minutes or until golden.

GAIL SATTLER

Despite the overabundance of rain, Gail Sattler enjoys living on the West Coast with her husband, three sons, two dogs, three lizards, and countless fish, many of which have names. Gail Sattler loves to write tales of romance that can be complete only with God in their center. She's had many books out with **Heartsong Presents** and Barbour Publishing. In 2001 and 2000, Gail was voted as the Favorite Heartsong Author. Visit Gail's webpage at http://www.gailsattler.com

A Letter to Our Readers

Dear Readers:

In order that we might better contribute to your reading enjoyment, we would appreciate you taking a few minutes to respond to the following questions. When completed, please return to the following: Fiction Editor, Barbour Publishing, Inc., P.O. Box 719, Uhrichsville, OH 44683.

1. Did you enjoy reading *As American as Apple Pie?*
   - ❑ Very much. I would like to see more books like this.
   - ❑ Moderately—I would have enjoyed it more if _____
   _____
   _____

2. What influenced your decision to purchase this book? (Check those that apply.)
   - ❑ Cover
   - ❑ Back cover copy
   - ❑ Title
   - ❑ Price
   - ❑ Friends
   - ❑ Publicity
   - ❑ Other

3. Which story was your favorite?
   - ❑ *An Apple a Day*
   - ❑ *Apple Annie*
   - ❑ *Sweet as Apple Pie*
   - ❑ *Apple Pie in Your Eye*

4. Please check your age range:
   - ❑ Under 18
   - ❑ 18–24
   - ❑ 25–34
   - ❑ 35–45
   - ❑ 46–55
   - ❑ Over 55

5. How many hours per week do you read? _____

Name _____

Occupation _____

Address _____

City _____ State _____ Zip _____